Praise for *OutWrite*

"Oh, please, please, powers that be, have the smarts and curiosity to bring OutWrite back into our lives. This collection reveals the dialogic community in negotiation/inspiration from all its corners: where the most rewarded meet the most marginalized, the grass roots meets the corporate, the dying meet the future—and they all sit on the same panels; eat and drink together; make friends and lovers, business deals and friendships; share aesthetics, politics; and argue and thereby influence the creation of literature."

—Sarah Schulman, author of *Let the Record Show:*
A Political History of ACT UP New York, 1987–1993

"The OutWrite conferences of the 1990s marked a critical turning point in the history of LGBTQ literary life and culture. This collection restores to historical memory the anger, the militancy, and the vibrant cultural voices that confronted directly the pain of the AIDS epidemic as well as the racial and gender divisions within the community. The editors have given us a wonderfully moving and inspiring gift by bringing into print these powerfully insightful speeches from the past."

—John D'Emilio, author of *Queer Legacies:*
Stories from Chicago's LGBTQ Archives

"*OutWrite: The Speeches That Shaped LGBTQ Literary Culture* is an incredible collection that taps into the heart of the queer literary community in the 1990s—the struggles, the successes, the visions, and the revisions. Reading it, I was struck by our loss of an entire parallel culture of LGBTQ businesses, conferences, and infrastructure that existed before the wide spread of the internet—but I was also struck by the continuity of hope, the clarity with which these authors fought for a freer future against incredible odds. *OutWrite* is a history that feels searingly present."

—Hugh Ryan, author of *When Brooklyn Was Queer*

T0246210

"The incredible importance of queer culture to American culture is usually ignored by heterosexuals and often underestimated by LGBTQ people. *OutWrite: The Speeches That Shaped LGBTQ Literary Culture*, edited by Julie R. Enszer and Elena Gross, is a magnificent testimony—and, until now, undocumented archive—of the expanse and the depth of LGBTQ literary and political culture that was the legacy of decades of struggle. Every piece here brilliantly embodies the insights, intellectual bravery, political acumen, and sheer courage that went into building a fiercely independent literary and political culture that redefined American culture and still illuminates how we live today. This is an invaluable contribution to LGBTQ literature, queer studies, and the everyday reader of queer literature."

—Michael Bronski, professor of the practice in activism and media studies of women, gender, and sexuality at Harvard University

"What a fabulous and fascinating collection of speeches from leading figures in queer arts and letters in the 1990s! For everyone who wishes that they had attended the OutWrite conferences, for those who will enjoy reexperiencing them, and for all who are interested in cultural activism, this valuable anthology will inspire with words, wit, and wisdom."

—Marc Stein, author of *The Stonewall Riots: A Documentary History* and *Queer Public History: Essays on Scholarly Activism*

"The vital, urgent need to tell our stories, to share, to write within and for a community is an inspiring part of any gathering of writers and publishers, but it's especially evident in the speeches collected in *OutWrite: The Speeches That Shaped LGBTQ Literary Culture*. This anthology documents the pivotal role the OutWrite conferences played in shaping and inspiring a generation of LGBTQ writers. The diversity of speakers gathered here and the explicit links they make among silenced and marginalized sexual communities and other oppressed communities amid the devastation wrought by the AIDS epidemic and the 1990s culture wars are especially valuable. This collection honors the memory of our forebearers—many of whom fired my own passion for critical queer writing—and is sure to bolster today's artists and activists working against a global pandemic, climate crises, and the continued ascendency of white supremacy and conservative politics."

—Dwight A. McBride, PhD, president and university professor at the New School

OutWrite

OutWrite

The Specches That Shaped LGBTQ Literary Culture

Edited by
Julie R. Enszer and
Elena Gross

RUTGERS UNIVERSITY PRESS
NEW BRUNSWICK, CAMDEN, AND NEWARK,
NEW JERSEY, AND LONDON

Library of Congress Cataloging-in-Publication Data

Names: OutWrite (Conference) | Enszer, Julie R., 1970– editor. |
Gross, Elena, editor.
Title: Outwrite : the speeches that shaped LGBTQ literary culture /
edited by Julie R. Enszer and Elena Gross.
Description: New Brunswick : Rutgers University Press, [2022] |
Includes bibliographical references.
Identifiers: LCCN 2021025110 | ISBN 9781978828032 (paperback) |
ISBN 9781978828049 (hardcover) | ISBN 9781978828056 (epub) |
ISBN 9781978828063 (mobi) | ISBN 9781978828070 (pdf)
Subjects: LCSH: Speeches, addresses, etc., American—Congresses. |
Sexual minorities' writings, American—Congresses.
Classification: LCC PN6122 .O98 2022 | DDC 815/.540992066—
dc23/eng/20211129
LC record available at https://lccn.loc.gov/2021025110

A British Cataloging-in-Publication record for this
book is available from the British Library.

References to internet websites (URLs) were accurate
at the time of writing. Neither the author nor Rutgers University Press
is responsible for URLs that may have expired or changed
since the manuscript was prepared.

♾ The paper used in this publication meets the requirements of the American
National Standard for Information Sciences—Permanence of Paper for Printed
Library Materials, ANSI Z39.48-1992.

www.rutgersuniversitypress.org

Manufactured in the United States of America

To everyone who worked on OutWrite conferences as volunteers and paid organizers, named and unnamed in the archives, and everyone who attended the OutWrite conferences between 1990 and 1999, with hope for continued passion, vision, and dancing in our literary and political lives

Contents

OutWrite

Introduction

Between 1990 and 1999, eight national OutWrite conferences convened, first in San Francisco, then in Boston. Initially, *OUT/LOOK*, the glossy, national gay and lesbian magazine that published from 1988 until 1992, organized these gatherings of lesbian, gay, bisexual, transgender, and queer writers, editors, readers, and activists; then when *OUT/LOOK* ceased, activists from the Bromfield Street Educational Foundation, better known for its leftist journal *Gay Community News* (*GCN*), organized OutWrite. OutWrite played a crucial role in defining, expanding, and amplifying LGBTQ literary culture by bringing together many important LGBTQ writers of the 1990s in raucous events highlighted by keynote addresses, plenary sessions, and workshops coupled with late nights of drinking, dancing, hookups, and other forms of literary revelry. The OutWrite conferences helped define a new, queer literary canon and a movement of queer literary production. The speeches, arguments, and ideas from these conferences shaped and continue to shape indelibly the work of LGBTQ writers, and this history provides a touchstone for contemporary LGBTQ writers and activists imagining what the future might hold for our creative, literary, and artistic work.

The first OutWrite conference was at San Francisco's Cathedral Hill Hotel on March 3 and 4, 1990, less than five months after the 1989 earthquake. Originally, OutWrite was a project of *OUT/LOOK* magazine. Founded by Jeffrey Escoffier, Kim Klausner, Peter Babcock, Michael Sexton, and Debra Chasnoff, *OUT/LOOK* was a co-gender publishing project with a commitment to racial diversity; *OUT/LOOK* editors and activists wanted to bring ideas about LGBTQ life into broader public discussions. The *OUT/LOOK* editorial board members quickly realized that to fulfill their vision, they needed to meet more writers; Escoffier advocated the idea of a writers' conference to achieve that goal.[1] A San Francisco–based planning committee with over twenty participants organized the first event. Organizers included Escoffier; writer, editor, and book reviewer Richard Labonté; publishing professional Amy Scholder; and authors both emerging and established, such as Dorothy Allison, Roberto Bedoya, Matias Viegener, Nisa Donnelly, and Alex Chee. Lisa Kahaleole Hall, then a graduate student at the University of California–Berkeley, worked as the conference coordinator. In the program, the planning committee captured the excitement of the moment, noting that "the number of books, newspapers and magazines published by and for lesbians and gay men is growing at a furious rate."[2] Emerging threats tempered optimism, including an increase of "attacks on the basis of sexuality, race, and gender."[3] Judy Grahn and Allen Ginsberg both addressed these challenges in their plenary speeches. Grahn opened with the provocation "If there is a gay or lesbian writer who has never done any organizing, that person is taking a free ride," demanding that gay and lesbian writers organize around issues essential to their lives. From the stage during his address, thirty-five years after the publication of *Howl*, Ginsberg recited addresses for people to call and object to a proposed Federal Communications Commission regulation

---

1. OUT/LOOK and the Birth of the Queer, a public history and activism project, provides more information on *OUT/LOOK*, including an interview of Jeffrey Escoffier by Gerard Koskovich; see OUT/LOOK and the Birth of the Queer (website), accessed September 27, 2021, http://www.queeroutlook .org/. The complete run of *OUT/LOOK* is available digitally at "Electronic Archive of Out/Look," Lesbian Poetry Archive, accessed September 27, 2021, http://www.lesbianpoetryarchive.org/outlook.

2. OutWrite 90 program book, author collection, p. 1.

3. OutWrite 90 program book, p. 1.

limiting speech on the radio based on concerns that children might be listening. At the beginning of a decade that ushered in broad transformations in the United States for gay, lesbian, bisexual, and transgender people, OutWrite gathered queer creatives for thinking, strategizing, and celebrating.

The 1990s offered significant challenges and threats to LGBTQ people in the United States. Increases in HIV infections and AIDS deaths at the beginning of the decade continued to devastate a community already awash with grief. As of the end of 1989, 69,233 people had died from AIDS, and there were 117,781 reported cases, according to the CDC; over 70,000 of these cases were gay and bisexual men.[4] Vibrant actions by ACT UP and the Treatment Action Group advocated for effective treatments, reliable vaccines, and optimistically, a cure, but treatments offered only brief glimmers of hope.[5] As weeks and months wore on, debilitating illnesses continued, and death, with its attendant rituals, engulfed urban queer communities. In addition to the crisis of AIDS, attacks on LGBTQ communities from conservative leaders like U.S. senator Jesse Helms, who also viciously opposed abortion and civil rights, presented dangers to the "lesbian and gay community's freedom of expression," as the 1990 OutWrite program book noted. Existential threats to the community loomed, such as the Supreme Court's 1986 *Bowers v. Hardwick* decision that affirmed state

---

4. *HIV/AIDS Surveillance Year-End Edition; U.S. AIDS Cases Reported through December 1989* (Washington, DC: U.S. Department of Health and Human Services, 1990), https://www.cdc.gov/hiv/pdf/library/reports/surveillance/cdc-hiv-surveillance-report-1989-vol-2.pdf.

5. Excellent books explore this activism, including Randy Shilts's *And the Band Played On* (New York: St. Martin's, 1987); Deborah Gould's *Moving Politics: Emotion and ACT UP's Fight against AIDS* (Chicago: University of Chicago Press, 2009); David France's *How to Survive a Plague* (New York: Knopf, 2016); and Sarah Schulman's *Let the Record Show: A Political History of ACT UP New York 1987–1993* (New York: Farrar, Straus & Giroux, 2021).

criminalization of sodomy, including oral and anal sex, between consenting adults in private.[6]

Facing these challenges, gay and lesbian activists increased their visibility, clout, and organizing canny. The 1987 March on Washington proved a galvanizing moment, prompting the creation of an array of new community-based projects, organizing initiatives, and actions: gay and lesbian community centers, state-wide political organizations, and community newspapers and magazines, but this work initially yielded few political successes or meaningful allies.[7] In 1990, the futures and outcomes for the gay and lesbian movement were, at best, uncertain. Even as the decade unfolded, advances like presidential candidate Bill Clinton's recognition of gay and lesbian people were offset by challenges and compromises like the Don't Ask, Don't Tell, Don't Pursue military policy and the sense of betrayal from the Defense of Marriage Act.

In this environment, the first OutWrite conference was an extraordinary success, attracting, according to the *New York Native*, over 1,200 participants.[8] In addition to the two keynote addresses, OutWrite 90 featured two plenary sessions, one titled "AIDS & the Responsibility of the Writer," moderated by Roberto Bedoya with Essex Hemphill, Pat Califia, Susan Griffin, John Preston, and Sarah Schulman, and the other "Lesbian & Gay Literature in the Marketplace," moderated by Amy Scholder and featuring Sasha Alyson, Samuel R. Delany, Barbara Grier, Barbara Wilson, SDiane Bogus, and Michael Denneny. Workshops were packed and included topics such as uncovering histories, science fiction, censorship, magazine publishing, scholarly work, book reviewing,

---

6. The Supreme Court reversed the Bowers decision seventeen years later in *Lawrence v. Texas.*

7. Amin Ghaziani, *The Dividends of Dissent: How Conflict and Culture Work in Lesbian and Gay Marches on Washington* (Chicago: University of Chicago Press, 2008).

8. "The Largest Gay Writers Conference Ever," *New York Native*, March 10, 1990, no. 361, p. 29.

and curating writing groups and classes. During the three days leading up to the conference, Small Press Traffic, A Different Light bookstore, and the Poetry Center of San Francisco organized readings.

Bolstered by the success of the first conference, organizers booked San Francisco's Cathedral Hill Hotel again for a second conference in 1991, the weekend of March 1–3. Participation jumped to more than 1,900 "gay and lesbian writers, editors, publishers, and their readers," according to the *Advocate*.[9] Conference attendees had more panels to attend; organizers reported in the program that the sessions "almost doubled to fifty-five panels with two hundred and sixty-three panelists," and they highlighted the "cultural and racial diversity of the authors and topics represented," including panels on "Chicano/a, Native American, Mexican, Jewish and Latin American writing, as well as writing by sexual minorities and bisexuals."[10] In addition to the Persian Gulf War, censorship again was an important theme, particularly reactions to the National Endowment for the Arts restrictions in the wake of the defunding of grants to four performance artists, all with queer content in the work, in June 1990.[11]

During and after the conference, outrage brewed over one keynote speech. Friday night welcomed conference attendees with four keynote addresses by Edward Albee, Kate Millett, John Rechy, and Paula Gunn Allen. With nearly two thousand attendees, the excitement in the grand ballroom must have been brimming: people abuzz with seeing old friends and whispering with excitement at sightings of queer community celebrities. Unfortunately, we were unable to find audiotapes of this event; these speeches live only in our imaginations and the memories of participants. Reports of

---

9. "Stonewall Pride '91: The Year in Pictures," *Advocate*, July 2, 1991, no. 580, p. 52.

10. OutWrite 91 program book, author collection, p. 1.

11. The NEA Four are Karen Finley, John Fleck, Tim Miller, and Holly Hughes.

Albee's speech, however, abound. In it, Albee parses the difference between being "a writer who is gay and a gay writer," opting for himself to "not limit what I write to gay themes." Eschewing the label "gay writer" upset many in the audience; Albee's suggestions that "white people are a minority" and that his identities as a man and as an "Anglo-Saxon Protestant" also mark him as a minority enraged even more.[12] According to the *Advocate*, this speech "only added luster to an event that symbolizes the rapid growth and increasing excellence of gay and lesbian literature."[13] *OUT/LOOK* 14 featured reflections on the event and its controversy by conference coordinator Lisa Kahaleole Hall and *OUT/LOOK* publisher Jeffrey Escoffier.[14]

In 1992, the conference moved from the West Coast to the East Coast and was a shared production between *OUT/LOOK* and *GCN*. This partnership increased the volunteer infrastructure, with planning committees in both Boston and San Francisco; Sue Hyde was the program coordinator in 1992. The success of the previous two conferences helped OutWrite grow. The Boston planning committee framed the conference with the 1992 observance of "500 Years of Indigenous Resistance" and focused on creating time and space for writers of color.[15] Mariana Romo-Carmona and Dorothy Allison opened the third OutWrite conference with speeches on Friday night, March 20; Melvin Dixon and Allan Gurganus closed the conference on Sunday, March 22. Organizers also noted in the conference program the continued devastation of

12. Edward Albee, "One 'Minority' Speaks to Another," an excerpt from Albee's speech, is in *OUT/LOOK*, Fall 1991, no. 14, p. 18.

13. "Stonewall Pride '91," 52.

14. Lisa Kahaleole Hall, "Chock Full of Irony," *OUT/LOOK*, Fall 1991, no. 14, pp. 17, 24–27; Jeffrey Escoffier, "Arguing in Public," *OUT/LOOK*, Fall 1991, no. 14, pp. 17, 28–29. Also of interest is Andrea Lewis's essay "Who's Afraid of Edward Albee?," *OUT/LOOK*, Fall 1991, no. 14, pp. 16, 19–23.

15. OutWrite 92 program book, Bromfield Street Educational Foundation records at the Northeastern University Library's Archives and Special Collections, box 10, Program Book 1992, p. 2.

AIDS: "By the time our brochures were printed, two writers we had hoped to invite had died of AIDS, and others were too ill to plan a trip to Boston."[16] In 1992, the organizing committee initiated two new elements of the conference. Book publicist Michele Karlsberg organized the OUTSPOKEN Literary Series, reading sessions by writers, that happened throughout the weekend. This OUTSPOKEN Literary Series continued through the end of the decade. The organizing committee also added "public conversations" to the program, where "two noted authors will spend 90 minutes talking with each other."[17] Public conversations held throughout the conference in 1992 included Melvin Dixon and John Preston, Richard Howard and Michael Cunningham, Kate Clinton and Jewelle Gomez, and Larry Kramer and Sarah Schulman. Over the next five years, these conversations became both cherished spaces at the conferences and some of their most memorable moments.

While it appears that there was an exhibit hall at the second conference in San Francisco, attention to the exhibit hall at the third conference grew, signaling both the increase in the size of the conference and also the increase in marketing to gay and lesbian readers.[18] In 1992, the exhibit hall at the host hotel, the Park Plaza in Boston, featured a number of gay and lesbian organizations, including the International Lesbian and Gay Human Rights Commission, National Gay and Lesbian Task Force, and National Writers Union, Boston Local, Gay/Lesbian Caucus; publications like *RFD*, *Sojourner: The Women's Forum*, and the *Women's Review of Books*; and a handful of mainstream presses, including Penguin USA, Temple University Press, and Routledge, Chapman & Hall. In an article for the *Nation*, Jan Clausen and Andrea Freud Loewenstein provide a rich portrait of OutWrite 92,

---

16. OutWrite 92 program book.

17. OutWrite 92 program book.

18. The OutWrite 91 program book names Dee Jones as the exhibitor coordinator, but the program book does not list exhibitors.

including its significance to contemporary writers. A series of snapshots from the conference, printed in italics, capture Melvin Dixon's keynote speech, a panel on humor, and the roll call of names of people who had died from AIDS, among other poignant moments. Clausen and Loewenstein note that for the gay and lesbian community, knowledge of the "facts of historical erasure and all-too-current censorship battles" is palpable and leaves writers knowing that "the integrity of words on the page must be backed by heroic efforts to insure their place in the world." For conference attendees, OutWrite was a space "about the survival of the institutions that support writers and writing."[19]

OutWrite 92 was not without controversy. Activists objected to an award named after the iconic Black gay writer Joseph Beam, who died in 1988 from complications of AIDS. Writing for the Black gay journal *BLK*, L. Lloyd Jordan explains that Sasha Alyson's idea was to give an award for the "book of 1991 which most successfully broke new ground or reflected a fresh approach to lesbian or gay subject matter. The objective was to encourage new talent or to prod old talent into new daring, even at the risk of being too raw to secure more conventional awards for aesthetic excellence."[20] The award was for $1,000, funded by Alyson, then the owner of one of the largest gay and lesbian book publishers. Alyson approached Beam's mother for permission to name the award after him, but she denied the request—partly, according to Kevin Mumford, "because of strained relations with the press."[21] Alyson then asked the *OUT/LOOK* Foundation to administer the award, which it did, and the award proceeded using Beam's name. A committee, including one African American judge, selected

19. Jan Clausen and Andrea Freud Loewenstein, "OutWrite '92," *Nation*, May 18, 1992, 673.

20. L. Lloyd Jordan, "OutWrite," *BLK* 4, no. 2 (May 1992): 18–21.

21. Kevin J. Mumford, *Not Straight, Not White: Black Gay Men from the March on Washington to the AIDS Crisis* (Chapel Hill: University of North Carolina Press, 2016), 197.

Jacquie Bishop and Essex Hemphill at OutWrite 92 (*Photo credit: Courtesy of the Bromfield Street Educational Foundation records at the Northeastern University Library's Archives and Special Collections.*)

finalists for the award on a short timeline in advance of OutWrite. Ultimately, when the finalists were announced, none were African American; one was Chicana. With the leadership of Jacquie Bishop of Mama Doesn't Know Productions and poet Essex Hemphill, Black writers and their allies met during the conference to discuss concerns about the award.[22] Clausen and Loewenstein report, "It quickly became clear that the awards ceremony would not take place, and the course shifted from what Bishop characterized as a too-familiar if inevitable 'reactive mode' to energetic plans for a new award under black community control."[23] Ultimately, over 250 Black lesbian and gay writers and activists signed a statement

22. Mumford provides a clear-eyed account of this situation in his book *Not Straight, Not White*. He particularly considers Beam in relation to African American feminists; see chapter 6 and the epilogue of his book.
23. Clausen and Loewenstein, "OutWrite '92," 674.

objecting to the award, according to Thom Bean in the magazine *NYQ*.[24] Assotto Saint summarizes the incident succinctly: "Sasha Alyson and *OUT/LOOK* are free to do whatever they wish with their money. Except when it comes to misappropriating a Black gay icon to establish an award under the guise of pretending to do multicultural work."[25]

Clausen and Loewenstein also describe "a quieter controversy" about "the absence of panels dealing with specifically Jewish concerns, the lack of identified Jewish presence in 'multicultural' panels and the omission of anti-Semitism as part of the antiracist commitment." They conclude, reflecting on these controversies and Albee's 1991 speech in concert with the continuing deaths from AIDS, that "we are writing with urgency, in whatever time is left to us" and that gay and lesbian writers "finally understand the stakes, we are writing as though it matters."[26] Twenty-five years later, this assessment resonates.

Gay critics from the Right also took aim at OutWrite. In *Christopher Street*, Bob Satuloff, who did not attend the conference himself, criticized OutWrite as "the furthest outpost of self-righteous political correctness in the socio-political-semiotic wilderness that is present-day gay publishing," a jab that must have delighted the organizers at *GCN*.[27]

In 1993, OutWrite moved from the spring to the fall and was held on October 8–10, again at the Park Plaza Hotel in Boston. The previous year, 1992, was a hard one for gay and lesbian publications and for the community more broadly despite the growing clout of organized, vocal, and increasingly political gay and lesbian activists and the ultimate win of presidential candidate Bill Clinton in November 1992, who, though he did not embrace

24. Thom Bean, "Blackout at OutWrite," *NYQ*, April 19, 1992, 28.
25. Bean, 28.
26. Clausen and Loewenstein, "OutWrite '92," 674.
27. Bob Satuloff, "Is P.C. Going Down on Itself?," *Christopher Street* 180, vol. 14, no. 20 (1992): 2.

the queer community, acknowledged it with more compassion and humanity than the community had witnessed in the past twelve years of Republican rule. Increasing conservatism throughout the United States, the continued devastation of the HIV/AIDS epidemic, and a growing neoliberal economic order in the United States and around the world created a challenging environment for gay and lesbian publications. *GCN* suspended weekly publication in June 1992; it returned with a special edition for the National March on Washington in June 1993 and planned to use OutWrite and a new issue celebrating the conference to jump-start its regular monthly publication in January 1994. *OUT/LOOK* ceased publishing in September 1992; thus the Bromfield Street Educational Foundation became the exclusive organizer of OutWrite 93. Community commitment to both publishing and activism, combined with additional financial support from individuals and a growing gay and lesbian philanthropic community, kept the Bromfield Street Educational Foundation solvent through the 1990s.

OutWrite 93 saw additional growth in the size and scope of the conference. The letter from the organizing committee in the program book notes the "gay book boom";[28] during 1993 and 1994, mainstream publishing houses released a number of influential gay and lesbian books. Writers and queer activists greeted attention to queer writing from mainstream institutions with both appreciation and skepticism. The organizers of OutWrite ask in the program book, "Is this the beginning of a new trend, or a bleep in marketing strategy?"[29] They also note a gender disparity: many of the independent feminist presses were still operating, but independent gay male presses were not, though there was "an emergence of a small and self-published press movement led by African-American

28. OutWrite 93 program book, Bromfield Street Educational Foundation records at the Northeastern University Library's Archives and Special Collections, box 10, Program Book 1993.
29. OutWrite 93 program book.

men, such as Other Countries and Galiens Press."[30] The organizers
end their note by asking, "Why is this happening now, and what
does it mean for lesbian and gay culture?"[31] With an eye toward
cultural organizing, Michael Bronski, program coordinator, and
the planning committee for OutWrite instituted a new event, the
Audre Lorde Memorial Lecture. Lorde died on November 17,
1992. This new lecture, delivered for the first time by Kate Rushin
and funded by the Legacy Fund for Lesbian Enrichment, allowed
the community to honor Lorde's work and legacy. As the conference continued to grow and thrive, with new exhibitors and a
vibrant array of offerings, the organizers addressed questions of
access for the first time in 1993. They designated seating in the
plenary sessions and workshops for people with disabilities,
announced the availability of interpreting services, and created a
"Chill Out Room" for people who needed a quiet space. At the
next conference, in 1995, they provided childcare for participants
free of charge.

No conference was held in 1994. Instead, the fifth OutWrite
conference happened the weekend of March 3, 1995, at the Park
Plaza Hotel, Boston, returning the conference to a spring cycle.
Michael Bronski and Judith Katz were programmers for the event.
Keynote speeches by Linda Villarosa and Tony Kushner greeted
participants of OutWrite 95, as did public conversations between
Scott O'Hara and Susie Bright, Dorothy Allison and Bertha Harris, Norman Wong and Kitty Tsui, and Alison Bechdel and Howard Cruse. OutWrite 95 was a vibrant gathering with new program
developments, including a special track of programs for young
people and a more robust sponsorship program. The magazine
wilde, edited by John Fall, from PDA Press, celebrated its debut by
cosponsoring OutWrite 95, and demonstrating gay and lesbian
print culture's commitment to activism, Fall invited conference
participants to sign a postcard to the Queen of England to be

30. OutWrite 93 program book.
31. OutWrite 93 program book.

delivered as a part of *wilde*'s campaign to pardon Oscar Wilde. OutWrite 95 also featured the first poetry slam, underwritten by a new bookstore in Boston, We Think the World of You. Having bookstores and new queer-focused magazines to underwrite elements of the conference was an exciting development. While activists decried the increasing commercialization of queer life, with good reason, businesses seeking gay and lesbian consumers made events like OutWrite possible.[32] OutWrite 95 also included a preview of the exhibit *Love Makes a Family: Living in Lesbian and Gay Families* by writers Peggy Gillespie and Pam Brown and photographer Gigi Kaeser. The exhibit opened in Boston in June 1995 and then toured nationwide; in 1999, the University of Massachusetts Press published a book by the same name. Panels, readings, and workshops continued to proliferate at the conference. The exhibit room bustled with activity. The only glitch was the cancellation of Cherríe Moraga due to illness; she was scheduled to give the Audre Lorde Memorial Lecture. The time slot was filled with a showing of Ada Gay Griffin and Michelle Parkerson's film *A Litany for Survival: The Life and Work of Audre Lorde*. This film coupled well with the special showing of Marlon Riggs's final film, *Black Is . . . Black Ain't*, as a part of the conference program. OutWrite 95 concluded with a performance by artist Luis Alfaro.[33]

OutWrite 96, the sixth national conference, convened on February 23–25 again at the Park Plaza Hotel in Boston. Michael Bronski and Kanani Kauka were the programmers. The planning committee described OutWrite as fulfilling four functions: first, as "a community-based conference with a strong commitment to a

---

32. For critiques of commercialization of the queer movement, see Alexandra Chasin's *Selling Out* (London: Palgrave Macmillan, 2000); and Sarah Schulman's *Ties That Bind* (New York: New Press, 2012).

33. OutWrite 95 program book, Bromfield Street Educational Foundation records at the Northeastern University Library's Archives and Special Collections, box 11, Program Book 1995.

progressive, grass-roots political vision"; second, as "a vital site for queers in the publishing industry to meet, deal, network and do business"; third, as an event that creates space "where established authors are celebrated and where new authors are discovered"; and finally, as "a forum for political discussion and a venue for the mainstream publishing marketplace."[34] Featuring keynote addresses by Minnie Bruce Pratt and Edmund White, an Audre Lorde Memorial Lecture by Cheryl Clarke, and a closing performance by Craig Hickman, OutWrite 96 continued with the same energy and verve as in previous years. Public conversations in this conference included Michelangelo Signorile and Gabriel Rotello; Christopher Bram and Randall Kenan; Mark Doty and Sarah Van Arsdale; Craig Lucas, Holly Hughes, and Jon Robin Baitz; and Robyn Ochs and Marjorie Garber. An array of readings, panels, and film screenings happened at the conference. PlanetQ, a new online business that was "helping to create a new queer cyber-community," sponsored the technology sessions of the conference.[35] OutWrite 96 also featured an exhibition—the archival project *Public Faces / Private Lives*, a project of the Our Boston Heritage Educational Foundation, displayed artifacts from the history of Boston's lesbian and gay community.[36] This exhibition also became a book, *Improper Bostonians*, published by Beacon Press in 1998. The concatenation of a community-based history project with the OutWrite conference and book

34. OutWrite 96 program book, Bromfield Street Educational Foundation records at the Northeastern University Library's Archives and Special Collections, box 11, Program Book 1996.

35. OutWrite 96 program book, p. 5.

36. This exhibition was a preview of the formal opening of the full exhibition at the Boston Public Library in May and drew over fifty-five thousand visitors. Our Boston Heritage Educational Foundation, which was founded in 1980, changed its name to the History Project: Documenting Boston's LGBT History in 1997. For more information, see the History Project (website), accessed October 4, 2021, https://historyproject.org/.

Reading at OutWrite 98 (*Photo credit: Courtesy of the Bromfield Street Educational Foundation records at the Northeastern University Library's Archives and Special Collections.*)

publishing opens one window into the many ways OutWrite cultivated and honored LGBTQ history.

In 1997, energies and finances at the Bromfield Street Educational Foundation waned. Limited resources and an absence of volunteers made a 1997 conference impossible, but a daylong conference, dubbed OutWrite Lite 97, filled the space. Billed as a day "of writing, exploring and challenging our ideas of literature, queerness, and artistry," the conference was held on September 13, 1997, at the Massachusetts Institute of Technology. The conference included nine panels and six workshops and a performance by John Kuntz from his play *Freaks*. OutWrite Lite announced the next OutWrite conference for February 1998.[37]

---

37. Flyer for OutWrite Lite, Bromfield Street Educational Foundation records at the Northeastern University Library's Archives and Special Collections, box 11, OutWrite Lite.

Audience members at OutWrite 98 (*Photo credit: Courtesy of the Bromfield Street Educational Foundation records at the Northeastern University Library's Archives and Special Collections.*)

As announced, OutWrite 98 convened at the Boston Sheraton at Copley Place on February 20–22, 1998, with the theme of "writing that expresses the full dimension of our experiences." Keynote addresses were scheduled to be given by Pratibha Parmar and Craig Lucas; Parmar could not attend, so conference programmers Lawrence Schimel and Cecilia Tan tapped Nancy Bereano to speak in her place. Jewelle Gomez delivered the Audre Lorde Memorial Lecture, and Peggy Shaw provided the final performance. The usual panoply of workshops, film screenings, and a large dance party filled the weekend schedule.[38] The 1998 program reserved rooms for Jewish writers, transgender writers, sex panic, media queers (TV, film, and radio), the queer Left, librarians, writers of

---

38. OutWrite 98 program book, Bromfield Street Educational Foundation records at the Northeastern University Library's Archives and Special Collections, box 11, Program Book 1998.

color, queer writers under thirty, women and smut, and Massachusetts Orgasmic Bitches.

Recognizing the significance of OutWrite, the *Lambda Book Report* published a lively debate after the 1998 conference between Phil Willkie, the publisher of the *James White Review*, and Michael Bronski, a key OutWrite organizer. Willkie decried the Bromfield Street Educational Foundation for using OutWrite to "prop up their long-deceased *Gay Community News*" and described the conference instead as "community property," calling for the conference to move out of Boston to find "new blood and a new location, both of which will revive us." Bronski disagreed with Willkie, noting that many community institutions are privately owned, including bars, newspapers, and magazines; he argued for a more nuanced understanding of the relationship between community and institutions, including exploring the idea of community responsibility, and concluded with a request for people to send praise and criticism to the planning committee via email, a means of communication that had barely existed eight years before.[39] Unbeknown to Willkie and Bronski at the time, the next OutWrite conference in 1999 would be the last.

OutWrite 99 kicked off with a Friday luncheon titled "Voices and Visions" hosted by Sarah Schulman and featuring Pratibha Parmar, Michael Bronski, Minnie Bruce Pratt, Paul Bonin-Rodriguez, Patricia Powell, and Mark Doty. Parmar and Doty provided the Friday night keynote addresses. Barbara Smith delivered the Audre Lorde Memorial Lecture on Saturday; Michele Karlsberg curated the OUTSPOKEN Literary Series, and an array of workshops filled the days. A full film series happened at the conference, and the closing plenary was a performance by Paul Bonin-Rodriguez, a playwright from San Antonio, perhaps best known for *The Texas Trinity*. Co-programmers G. Winston James, a Jamaican American man based in New York City, and Kris Kleindienst, a

---

39. Phil Willkie and Michael Bronski, "Behind-the-Scenes / Community Property: The OutWrite Debate," *Lambda Book Report*, May 1998, 11–12.

white woman based in the Midwest, were hired by Karen Bullock Jordan, the conference director. The selection of programmers for the conference, consonant with past conferences, demonstrated a commitment to co-gendered, multicultural leadership. In the program book, the co-programming chairs hint at the fragility of the conference and anxiety about its future; they write about the return to the Boston Park Plaza Hotel as a homecoming that occurred with "some soul searching and evaluation of its history and future direction." Yet they declare an intention to be a national conference for the "professional development and empowerment of LGBT writers" and note, "We have been continually amazed at how various and vast is the LGBT literary contribution to late 20th century life." James and Kleindienst reflect on their desires to increase participation, particularly of folks coming from the Midwest and West Coast, as well as to create a space that would "feel relevant to people of color," but they wonder, "Could we get writers to OutWrite whose marginalized position in this country, either by sex, race or class would make a trip to Boston for any reason inconceivable?" and then, "Could we do this with the postage stamp budget afforded to LGBT cultural efforts?"[40] Although it seems that there are no audio recordings of this conference, by all accounts, it was a success for attendees, panelists, and presenters.

The final page of the program book for OutWrite 99 announced the intention to have OutWrite in 2000, but it never materialized. *Lambda Book Report* noted in April 2000, "Sadly, the news you've been hearing about OutWrite is true. This eight-year-old annual conference, which has been so effective and important in bringing together hundreds of gay and lesbian writers across a broad spectrum of genres and specialties, will not be held this year. According to past organizers, there is a search on for a new organizing

---

40. OutWrite 99 program book, Bromfield Street Educational Foundation records at the Northeastern University Library's Archives and Special Collections, box 11, Program Book 1999.

committee to run the annual conference, but until that resource is found, OutWrite is suspended."[41] Other gatherings of people in queer literature and publishing happened that year, however. *Lambda Book Report* noted a Gay and Lesbian Press Summit in conjunction with the Millennium March on Washington and Lambda Literary Foundation's own Behind Our Masks conference, but the energy and inspiration of OutWrite ended.

OutWrite represented a vibrant expression of the importance of literature, language, books, and writing in the 1990s to gay, lesbian, bisexual, and transgender communities growing in their power while suffering legislative and electoral defeats and grappling with the devastating effects of AIDS. *OutWrite: The Speeches That Shaped LGBTQ Literary Culture* is only a beginning for historians, literary scholars, and LGBTQ writers who want to engage with OutWrite. These keynote addresses, plenary speeches, and Audre Lorde Memorial Lectures provide a way for contemporary readers to revisit this vibrant time in queer history. An array of speeches exists from OutWrite; some speeches were published after conferences (Grahn's speech was in *OUT/LOOK*, for instance, and Kushner's speech is included in a volume of his writing), and other speeches survive in draft form in author archives or the archives of OutWrite at Northeastern University. Many of the conferences were recorded by a commercial company, and recordings were available for many speeches. However, some of the material from the conferences was inaccessible. While researching this book, we especially missed not being able to listen to the voices of those who opened the conference in 1991: Kate Millett, John Rechy, Paula Gunn Allen, and Edward Albee. Likewise, the conference in 1999 appears to have not been recorded—perhaps because by 1999, cassette tapes were becoming outmoded. While working on the project, we yearned to hear the opening plenary by Pratibha Parmar and Mark Doty, the Audre Lorde Memorial Lecture

---

41. Jay Quinn, "Inside Out Publishing," *Lambda Book Report*, April 2000, 14.

by Barbara Smith, and the closing plenary performance by Paul Bonin-Rodriguez.

A few selections in *OutWrite: The Speeches That Shaped LGBTQ Literary Culture* are not keynote speeches. The panel discussion with Sarah Schulman, Essex Hemphill, Susan Griffin, Pat (now Patrick) Califia, and John Preston is included in the collection as a way to enter into the thinking and period in which OutWrite came into being—and because we found these speeches to be extraordinarily moving and to address contemporary issues, even as some are now more than thirty years old. A protest statement from Lesbians and Gay Men of African Descent that circulated at OutWrite 91 offers insight into the controversy surrounding Albee's keynote as well as other race concerns within the conference community from the perspective of people of color. We also include a speech by Janice Gould for the lyricism of her work—and to ensure the presence in the volume of a second Indigenous woman, taking seriously the words of Chrystos in her 1993 conversation with Cheryl Clarke at OutWrite to be wary of situations where women of color are tokenized and her powerful statement in the conversation that she would not agree to participate in endeavors where she is the only woman of color. Some speeches, like Tony Kushner's magnificent "On Pretentiousness," were edited for length. Participants of the conference will remember his wonderful conversation about lasagna and not find it in the book; we encourage people intrigued to consult his collection for the full text of the speech. Some authors edited other speeches lightly for inclusion in this book. Performances were a memorable part of the later conferences; we include only small selections here from a few of the closing performance plenaries that happened at OutWrite.

We hope that *OutWrite: The Speeches That Shaped LGBTQ Literary Culture* will engage more curiosity about the decade of the 1990s and the role of writers, artists, and creatives in agitating for social change. Archives from the conferences are held at the GLBT Historical Society in San Francisco, which also holds the papers for *OUT/LOOK* magazine, and at Northeastern University, which holds the papers of the Bromfield Street Educational Foundation. While OutWrite is no longer, there are other vibrant gay and lesbian community literary conferences, including Saints and Sinners in New Orleans, the Rainbow Book Fair in New York City, and a different OutWrite sponsored by the DC Center for the LGBT Community in Washington, DC. We encourage readers inspired by this book to support these existing conferences and imagine what other opportunities they might create. Ultimately, throughout our research into OutWrite and by listening to the tapes from the conferences, we found a treasure trove of conversations, performances, humor, and insights into lesbian and gay life. Our greatest hope is that *OutWrite: The Speeches That Shaped LGBTQ Literary Culture* will spark renewed interest in this conference from the 1990s as a source for powerful engagement in our queer literary legacies and as an inspiration to fuel new spaces for our individual and collective literary futures.

Your First Audience Is Your People

KEYNOTE ADDRESS

MARCH 3, 1990

WE DID IT! The lesbian and gay movements have created overtly lesbian and gay writing (for the most part), and this writing, in turn, has created and sustained and furthered the movements—they are phases of the same moon.

If there is a gay or lesbian writer who has never done any organizing, that person is taking a free ride. The rest of us have had to devote some amount of time, some of us many years of our lives, to developing an audience. Meaning: to give our people something tangible to hope for, to help them identify as gay enough to want to read about themselves. Hope is what entices people to read, to see themselves reflected accurately and respectfully, to imagine participating in the world of culture and activity that reflects them as they actually are—that tells their story in the stream of all story.

By "develop an audience," I mean develop some aspects of the political and cultural movements as physical entities and events. Sometimes that means going into the streets and public halls in action, shouting, risk-taking, demonstrating at top volume. Sometimes it means staying in airless rooms for hours and hours every day and every week and every month holding and attending endless dull meetings, or voter registering, or paper pushing of one kind or another. Sometimes it means taking years of effort and sweat and money starting and running and promoting gay and lesbian businesses, especially those based in the media—spreading

Judy Grahn. (*Photo credit: © Lynda Koolish.*)

ideas and images through independent presses and papers, magazines, bookstores, and distributorships.

Sometimes it means taking time to help the "audience," one's people, with healing, keeping them from suiciding or OD'ing or dying of poverty and despair and neglect—or if not keeping them from it, at least noticing and witnessing that they are doing these things. Sometimes it means helping them wend their way through the endless health and welfare mazes. Sometimes it means helping them die as dignified gay people, holding their funerals, and writing their funerals for them to use.

No one ever said all this was part of what we take on with the otherwise privileged and exotic-sounding job title "gay or lesbian writer"—but it is. This is anything but an alienated occupation. This is a difficult, holistic occupation that involves remaking the world even as you observe it, absorb it, experience it, and write about it for the consumption of others. Your first audience is your people, and by reflecting them to themselves and to the public at large, you help in very large measure create them and sustain them as an existent entity.

How appropriate it is that two poets are leading off this historic and important conference, this gathering of an explosive people. Poetry is the mapmaking of our movement; in fact, it's the orientation of civilization. Prose and fiction come later, to fill in the details, flesh out the muscle and bone of the structures that poetry lays down first. Poetry predicts us, tells us where we are going next. This is because, more than most other writing, poetry requires listening to spirits, to the largest voices of the cosmos. Poetry sets the rhythm for what we are doing as a group.

I hope those of you who are primarily prose writers can pay attention to the teaching in poetry and don't listen to stupid advice about not writing poetry because "there is no money in it." There is no money in anything holy. There is probably no money in love, beauty, or wisdom. Everybody throws money at pain and trouble and sudden sensation, emotion, and anesthesia. But poetry is a way of channeling divinity from the core of the earth herself, and poets are mapmakers who follow those key lines.

Standing as we are at the edge of a rapidly dying world, and with, we hope, another one trying to be born, we begin to articulate new understandings of the nature of death, transformation, life, sex, love, and what humans are. These articulations alter the world.

We didn't necessarily choose this cauldron, but it is the one we are in. I've always thought that if you become gay, you are choosing one cauldron or another. And if you decide to be a writer, you are choosing to cook something up in your cauldron, something that the population at large, sooner or later, is going to eat. This food is called literature, and it leads nations, it establishes the imagery of entire populations, and it manifests reality based in its own strength, imagery, and rhythm.

Speaking as a poet, I can say that if you breathe out bitterness, your audience will breathe bitterness back to you; if you breathe out sarcasm, your audience will breathe sarcasm; if you breathe out humor, humor; if anger, anger; and if you breathe out love, your audience will breathe back to you love.

What movement, what culture, what civilization is it that gay people are leading? I ask this not as a rhetorical question but as a reminder to us of who we are. I know that we are not in the habit—except for the queens, the queens who Larry Mitchell says wipe their asses with the priceless papers of our civilization—we are not in the habit of thinking of ourselves as leading our civilization, and yet we do.[1]

This power to influence is the major reason for our suppression. We are the measure of suppression. And we constitute here, in this gathering, a marvelous and, I know, quite anarchistic propaganda tool for ourselves, our gay culture and experience, our place in modern history. A chance, now, to expand into some new tribal names for who we are—cultural definitions of ourselves that go beyond lesbian and gay, that acknowledge and maintain same-sex gay bonding, leadership, and culture while spinning out to include bisexual relationships, celibacy, flaming queenship, whoredom, cross-cultural traditional marriage, and the multitude of alternative family systems needed to meet the needs of actual people in a shifting environment, when animal and plant environments themselves are shifting, when the earth is shifting.

This is why California is so at the heart of it, because the earth shifts so obviously here. This is why we call everything that we do here in California a "movement." I am glad so many gay people have gotten into the recovery movement, because to a large extent, it seems to me, the recovery movement advocates the telling of secrets. In a world that is dying and being born, there is not much

---

1. Larry Mitchell (1939–2012) was the founder of Calamus Books and the author of *The Faggots and Their Friends between Revolutions* (New York: Calamus Books, 1977; New York: Nightboat, 2019).

use in keeping secrets—we may as well tell everything we think and everything we know.

As a feminist, I am not so much interested in taking back the night as I am in taking back the world. And this world keeps coming back to us itself as we recover our history and our gods and goddesses.

It is to a large degree through poetry that we can trace the antiquity of our existence:

- In the oldest mythologies in the Mideast of five thousand years ago, life and death danced in the underworld in the forms of two female figures named Inanna and Ereshkigal.[2]
- In the same area, there is the story of Gilgamesh (where we can find the roots of materialism as a philosophy), in which two male friends are kissing and loving each other, loving to touch each other . . .
- Seventeen hundred years before Sappho, the first signed poetry by an individual was written by a woman named Enheduanna, who in all probability—guess what—was a lesbian, was a priestess of the goddess of life and beauty.
- Inanna's poetry contains a description of a gay ceremony in which the goddess takes two people, a man and a woman, and performs a ceremony called head overturning, in which she changes their gender. They are then given a special title and called pili-pili. After the ceremony of head overturning, each takes on the tools of the opposite gender and then takes on a special gay office described as ecstasy and trance, expression and lamentation. Does this sound familiar?

---

2. Grahn's most recent book *Eruptions of Inanna: Justice, Gender, and Erotic Power* (New York: Nightboat, 2021) examines the stories of Inanna, Ereshkigal, Enheduanna, and other female figures.

There was a public gay presence, and it was happening on the eve of the establishment of the first cities. Such a public gay presence seems associated with those centuries of gigantic transition, of the passage of huge sectors from rural to urban bases, of the inclusion of matrilineal goddesses into the newer patriarchal religions, of the taking of women's technology and passing it into male hands, sometimes very traumatically—as with the witch burnings (from which we have not yet begun to recover and the memory of which is carried in patterns of family violence) and what appears today to be a flowering of worldwide male technology that's badly out of balance and in need of female input.

Male and *female* are images, metaphors, as I have just used them, referring as much to lobes of the brain as to people. Gender-bending is one of the tasks of gay artists. Here we are again, in the current age, with a mass public gay presence. We are an indication of huge changes taking place everywhere. To tell you the truth, I actually thought you might all run out when the going got a little tough, but no, here you are, ready to take on the world in all its agony and glory.

I'm excited for all of you, and for your writing careers, and I'm proud and honored to be here with the kickoff talk, and I'm relieved that I can turn the artistic and political burden over to you all. This is what it feels like to me: sharing this great and good and terrible load and sharing it publicly. For the first time in my life, I feel proud of myself.

The remarkable thing about this conference is the mixture of men and women and the representation of people of color—still not enough but a beginning. This mixture is also presented and reflected in the Larkin/Morse anthology *Gay and Lesbian Poetry in Our Time*.[3]

Twenty years ago, I attended another gay conference, and at that conference, I think there were ten women, probably three hundred men; there was one person of color, a very outspoken

---

3. Carl Morse and Joan Larkin, *Gay and Lesbian Poetry in Our Time* (New York: St. Martin's, 1988).

Black woman named Ama. I read a paper there saying that men and women should work together. . . . I've never been all that timely with my predictions!

We got so frustrated at that conference that we women gathered together and formed lesbian separatism. This mixture that we have at this conference is formed by separatism, which was already being practiced by people like Barbara Grier and by One, Inc., an organization of gay men in Los Angeles.[4] The Black Power movement, led by Malcolm X, taught us how to use separatism as a tool, how to recover a base for who you are. And when it's used in that fashion, as a tool, it gives rise to what's here today. You can credit it exactly for this because it allowed us women, for instance, to develop our own agendas, networks, confidence, media, and presses, and it left men free to do the same thing without having to take responsibility for us. For a decade or so, this happened.

So now we can come together from bases of power. The same thing happens with every kind of group—you see it in things like Kitchen Table: Women of Color Press and anthologies such as *Nice Jewish Girls*[5] and *This Bridge Called My Back*,[6] bases of power that enable us to come together as equals and share actual power.[7]

This conference, then, took at least twenty years to develop. And we earned every word of it, every interaction, every disagreement, every common recognition. Guard them and grow them carefully.[8]

---

4. Barbara Grier was involved with the Daughters of Bilitis, including running their newsletter, and founded Naiad Press, a publishing house dedicated to lesbian literature, with her longtime partner Donna McBride.

5. Evelyn Torton Beck, ed., *Nice Jewish Girls*, rev. and updated ed. (Watertown, MA: Persephone, 1982; Boston: Beacon, 1989).

6. Cherríe Moraga and Gloria Anzaldúa, *This Bridge Called My Back: Writings by Radical Women of Color* (Watertown, MA: Persephone, 1981; New York: Kitchen Table: Women of Color Press, 1982).

7. The State University of New York Press published a new edition of *This Bridge Called My Back* in 2015.

8. This speech was published in *OUT/LOOK*, Summer 1990, no. 9, pp. 38–41, with the title "'Gay or Lesbian Writer': Hardly an Alienated Occupation."

American Glasnost and Reconstruction

KEYNOTE ADDRESS

MARCH 3, 1990

Welcome to American glasnost and Reconstruction.[1] As you've noticed, as eastern Europe and the repressive police state, authoritarian, Jehovaic governments of the East have been losing their grasp on people's genitals, hearts, and brains, we in the United States have efficiently entered an age of repression, counter-glasnost with a phony war on drugs, war on the underclass, war on nature itself. The ecological devastation wrought by hyper-, hyperrationality and hypertechnology attempt to outdo the vastness of the universe in an organized fashion and with very specific concerns for ourselves: censorship and homophobia. I would like to give a little bit of historical background to that recent history, which many of you know and I hope will be taken up in the panels when we get our heads together to talk.

To begin with, you know of the Heritage Foundation; among other foundations, it is funded by alcohol. I said "phony" war on drugs because statistics are maybe twenty to thirty thousand people a year die of illicit drugs, illicit substances as the Orwellian language goes. One hundred thousand (people) a year in America die of alcohol, and 385,000 (people) a year die of tobacco, heart

---

1. Ginsberg opened his speech reading the poem "Old Love Story," published in Allen Ginsberg, *White Shroud: Poems 1980–1985* (New York: Harper Perennial, 1987), and reprinted in Allen Ginsberg, *Collected Poems 1947–1997* (New York: Harper Perennial, 2007).

attack, cancer, high blood pressure. Funded by alcohol money, Joseph Coors, the "Coors beer" Heritage Foundation began planning a counterattack on the American glasnost that had begun in the 1960s and that inspired the east European glasnost. Following that, there was a formulated effort by Heritage Foundation think tank heads, pinheads, eggheads—following the Meese Commission—with a number of pieces of legislation slowly introduced into the body politic, many of them by Senator Jesse Helms.[2] And we have to consider Helms himself. Well, who is he? What does he represent? First of all, we must understand his obsession with homophobia. His homophobic obsession indicates obviously some sort of sexual disturbance on his own part. There could not be such a preoccupation without an unbalanced and oddly focused attention span to the subject. Beyond that, there is something else that he is covering up with his loud mouth and his aggressive activity, which is the fact that he is the tobacco cult senator who is not above spending taxpayers' money without asking them for the subsidization of North Carolina tobacco agriculture and not above throwing his weight around in the Senate Foreign Relations Committee, threatening Malaysia, the Malay people, with economic retribution from America if they don't accept American tobacco advertising and American tobacco sales, American cigarettes. So that might give you some hint as to his Achilles' heel—that he's the cancer peddler. He's the tobacco lobby senator. He's the legal dope pusher. He has no place assuming the insolence of declaring himself the moral arbiter of this nation. And we should all be on the very clear about that in discussing Helms's legislation. Following the Meese Commission and Heritage Foundation formulations, we know much about the

2. The Meese Commission was an investigation into pornography ignited by President Reagan; the final report of the Attorney General's Commission on Pornography (popularly known as the Meese commission) was released in July 1986. Republican senator Jesse Helms represented North Carolina from 1973 until 2003.

attack on the National Endowment for the Arts and the great
Mapplethorpe scandal that Helms cooked up with others.[3] There
are other areas, of phone sex, there is an attempt to stop all phone
sex, and there are child porn laws that were circulated around
the nation, which in an Orwellian fashion redefined the word *child*
from someone who has not yet been bar mitzvahed to include the
ages thirteen to eighteen. So those of you who are a little worried
about NAMBLA (North American Man/Boy Love Association)
might consider that NAMBLA is one of the organizations that is
having to deal with this Orwellian imposition of a new definition of
what a child is.[4] For instance, in Colorado, if you take a photograph

---

3. In June 1989, three months after the artist's death from AIDS-related
complications, *The Perfect Moment*, a show of photographs by Robert Mapplethorpe, was due to open at the Corcoran Gallery of Art in Washington,
DC. The exhibition, which was funded in part by a National Endowment
for the Arts (NEA) grant, had drawn the ire of Congress and right-wing
conservatives who were critical of the NEA's awarding government funds
to projects deemed explicit, blasphemous, or inappropriate, following the
controversy around Andres Serrano's *Piss Christ*. Seven photographs from
the show were cited as examples of such indecency. Faced with this insti-
tutional pressure, the Corcoran canceled the show, leading supporters of
Mapplethorpe's work to claim accusations of censorship and to protest. The
largest protest was led by the Washington Project for the Arts, which projected the censored photographs against the external facade of the Corcoran's
building in defiance. For a thirty-year retrospective on the controversy, see
Travis M. Andrews, "Behind the Right's Loathing of the NEA," *Washington
Post*, May 20, 2017, https://www.washingtonpost.com/news/morning-mix/
wp/2017/03/20/behind-the-loathing-of-the-national-endowment-for-the-arts
-a-pair-of-despicable-exhibits-almost-30-years-ago/. A variety of discussions
of Mapplethorpe's work are available, including analyses of race in his work,
which Essex Hemphill's speech in this volume mentions.

4. Readers interested in learning more about NAMBLA controversies may
consult Charles Shively's entry on the organization and its bibliography
in "NAMBLA," in *The Encyclopedia of Lesbian, Gay, Bisexual, and Transgender History in America*, ed. Mark Stein (Detroit: Thomson Gale, 2004),
2:349–350.

of a young man at the age of seventeen, he's considered a child, and you've committed a felony. And if you have three copies of that photograph, as I might have as a photographer who shows his photography, three copies in Colorado are now prima facie evidence of commercial porn. And any photographer here knows you make three or four test copies if you're at all making art photos. So there are the child porn laws, and above that, beyond that, and perhaps one of the most important intrusions into the marketplace of ideas is the central market, which is the media.

There is now a new doublethink law on the Federal Communications Commission (FCC): a slow-growing attempt to ban "indecent" language from broadcast on the air. Now the history of that I'll run through very briefly 'cause you may not know it all. There was the Carlin decision.[5] Pacifica lost seven dirty words. George Carlin discussed on the air the etymology and the legal implications of it, and the Supreme Court said he had no right to at two in the afternoon because they had to channel indecent language away from the mouths of children and the ears of children. This was fought in several cases by Pacifica; then the FCC extended the ban and said no indecency may be pronounced on the air between 6 a.m. and 10 p.m. And the FCC extended that further in 1987 to 6 a.m. to midnight. Then a coalition of Pacifica and other people, including myself as the friend of the court, sued the FCC in the appeals court in the District of Columbia in mid-1988—the decision saying that yes, the FCC might have the right to channel indecency away from children's ears during certain hours, but they had to figure out scientifically which hours.[6] You could not reduce

---

5. The decision by the U.S. Supreme Court in 1978 in the case *Federal Communications Commission v. Pacifica Foundation*, 438 U.S. 726 (1978), took up questions about a radio broadcast by George Carlin on a Pacifica Foundation radio station in New York. The decision banned the use of seven words on the radio and defined the powers of the FCC.

6. Ginsberg refers here to the 1988 appellate case in the DC appeals court *Action for Children's Television v. F.C.C*, 852 F.2d 1332 (D.C. Cir. 1988). The DC

the entire adult population of America to the level of minors between 6 a.m. and midnight, when most people are listening. So that put up a dilemma.

Then in retaliation, the Heritage Foundation prepared a position paper and legislative language and packet—which Senator Helms introduced in October 1988 through Congress, signed by Reagan—directing the FCC to ban all indecency twenty-four hours a day, which put all of us out of business if we were going to depend on the vocalization and oral tradition as well as the written tradition for our work on radio and listener-supported radio, university broadcasts, or even mainstream radio and television.[7] So as of last week, the twentieth of February (1990), there were hearings at the FCC, paper hearings in which Pacifica, the listener-supported stations, and the PEN Club (poets, essayists, novelists) and a number of other organizations that were involved with literature and broadcasting submitted their appeals and pleas to the FCC. And the decision will be made sometime this year.

But you still, you still have time to submit your opinions and your objections to the applications to this law till the twentieth of this month (March). So in terms of getting organized, I would suggest you do something like that. What you would do is write it, say it briefly, but check with me later during the day. You can send

---

appeals court asks the FCC to review the time regulations and the intent to "assist parents" rather than act as a censor. The DC appeals court case is available at "Action for Children's Television v. F.C.C," Casetext, accessed April 21, 2021, https://casetext.com/case/action-for-childrens-television-v-fcc-7.

7. Senator Helms's rider on an appropriations bill triggered this twenty-four-hour-a-day ban. Dennis McDougal reported on the planned protests: "Broadcasters May Protest New Indecency Ban," *L.A. Times*, October 7, 1988, https://www.latimes.com/archives/la-xpm-1988-10-07-ca-3616-story .html. The ban was challenged and modified over the next decade. Lili Levy's report—"The Regulation of Indecency," First Amendment Center, April 2008—provides an excellent overview and is available here: https:// www.freedomforuminstitute.org/wp-content/uploads/2016/10/FirstReport .Indecency.Levi_.final_.pdf.

either to the PEN Club, your statement and a sample of work of yours that would be banned from the air, which they can turn over to the lawyers preparing material on behalf of the PEN Club, Freedom to Write committee.[8] And I'll be around all day to repeat this (the mailing address). And it's in matter of enforcement of decency regulations—FCC docket, MM 494, to be very precise—but we'll be around for that. I'll be around for that all day. The FCC doublethink is basically parallel to the old Nazi book burning of degenerate works, the Chinese antispiritual pollution campaigns, or the old Stalinist campaigns against bourgeois individualists and ruthless cosmopolitans. In that case, William Blake has the last word about the so-called neoconservative anti-red fag beaters: they became what they beheld.[9] In the campaign against communism, they have taken the instruments and language and attitudes of repression of the totalitarian states. So what is our job now? Certainly organize and take practical, clear action, remembering that any action taken in anxiety creates more anxiety. Any action taken in anger creates more anger. Any action taken in equanimity, accuracy, and compassion creates equanimity, accuracy, and compassion.

Walt Whitman in the last century pronounced the orders for ourselves, the poets, and the orders to come. He said that our work should be marked by candor, spontaneousness, and inadvertent frankness. Candor ends paranoia—the candor of truth, not merely the candor of being gay. From the candor of frankness, truth, just being human is our agenda. Basically, we are gay, not such a special case, but as human beings, we're interested in accuracy and truth. As William Carlos Williams said, the government is of words. As Plato said, "When the walls, when the mode of the

---

8. Ginsberg gave the full mailing address for the PEN Club to audience members.

9. This paraphrase is from William Blake's *Jerusalem: The Emanation of the Giant Albion*. It is found in chapter 2, plate 32, line 14; the full line is "The Seven Nations fled before him they became what they beheld."

music changes, the walls of the city shake."[10] If we base our art, writing, on the accuracy of our perceptions, we don't have to worry whether we're gay, straight, bi, or anything. All we have to do is represent ourselves with exquisite accuracy and clarity. And we have a place to stand on earth that's ours, our own space, which nobody finally can put down. We might be temporarily discouraged, but truth and accuracy are cheerful matters to work on.[11]

---

10. Ginsberg's iconic paraphrase of Plato comes from book 4 of *The Republic*. One translation is "For the modes of music are never disturbed without unsettling of the most fundamental political and social conventions"— available online at Plato, *Republic* (Cambridge, MA: Harvard University Press, 1969; Perseus Digital Library, n.d.), http://www.perseus.tufts.edu/hopper/text?doc=Perseus%3atext%3a1999.01.0168.

11. Ginsberg ended by reading two poems: "Grandma Earth's Song," in *Cosmopolitan Greetings: Poems 1986–1992* (New York: Harper Perennial, 1994), 973–974; and "Written in My Dream by W. C. Williams," in Ginsberg, *White Shroud*. Both poems are reprinted in Ginsberg, *Collected Poems 1947–1997*.

AIDS and the
Responsibility of the Writer

PANEL: AIDS AND THE RESPONSIBILITY OF THE WRITER

MARCH 3, 1990

First, I want to talk about writing, and then I want to talk about responsibility. I've just published a novel, *People in Trouble*, about the AIDS crisis.[1] I spent three years working on it and in the process confronted a lot of questions relevant to AIDS fiction. When I began working, there were very few books about AIDS. They were mostly about facing one's own illness or the death of a lover. I knew that I was not writing from either of these perspectives and so identified for myself the category of "witness fiction" so that I could understand the position of my words in this event.

To be writing about something of this enormity when it surrounds you leaves those of us who write about AIDS no possibility of objectivity. Nor can there be any conclusiveness, since the crisis and our responses to it change radically and daily. So I knew that I was committing to ideas and impressions that would already be history by the time the book actually reached readers.

In *People in Trouble*, I imagined a small demonstration by AIDS activists outside Saint Patrick's Cathedral in New York City. Two and a half years ago, I imagined forty nervous men cautiously

---

1. Dutton published *People in Trouble* on January 31, 1990; the novel was reissued as part of the Vintage Stonewall series in 2019. Schulman writes more about this novel and its publication in *Stage Struck: Theater, AIDS, and the Marketing of Gay America* (Durham, NC: Duke University Press, 1998).

standing up to disrupt a religious service. By the time the book was published, there had been a real-life demonstration of seven thousand angry men and women confronting the cathedral.[2] In this case, the community I was writing for and about made the boundaries of my imagination obsolete.

There is no existing vocabulary for discussing AIDS. To expect one would be unreasonable, since this is an event that we will be spending generations trying to understand and define. In order to discuss it in novel form, I needed to identify a series of words that were generally resonant. This is a challenging task in a culture that does not acknowledge truth and a community that is emotionally overwhelmed. I started out by making lists of hundreds of details pertaining to the crisis. Rock Hudson at the airport being whisked off to Paris.[3] Watch alarms going off in public places reminding their bearers to take their AZT. Men with teddy bears. Friends spreading AL721 on their toast in the morning. People spending their life savings on Ampligen or Dextran Sulfate.[4] Finding out later that those drugs were worthless. Then I chose fifty that I felt would be meaningful symbols to large groups of people, symbols that might have lasting resonance. It was an attempt to identify a vocabulary while understanding that to establish this group of words is perhaps all that the first generation of AIDS writers can do in the hope that future writers can use this foundation to develop a comprehensive and challenging literature. I also had to reject words. Words that were being used to distort. Words that were lies. Words like *innocent victim*. Words like *general population*.

---

2. On December 10, 1989, ACT UP interrupted mass at Saint Patrick's Cathedral.

3. Rock Hudson, a well-known actor, was the first celebrity to acknowledge having AIDS; he died from AIDS-related complications on October 2, 1985.

4. AZT, AL721, Ampligen, and Dextran Sulfate were all drugs in clinical trials to counter HIV infections at the time Schulman presented.

I also made a decision for myself personally that I was not writing a novel documenting the life and death of a single individual. Instead, I wanted to use the examples of people's lives to express a precise political idea—namely, how personal homophobia becomes societal neglect: that there is a direct relationship between the two and that this nation needs to confront this configuration in order to adequately address this crisis.

In the past, I've written novels about the interior lives of people in marginal communities, and this enabled me to have some approval from the straight press because my work could be read voyeuristically. This time, I knew I wanted to accuse straight people—to bring them into the literature in a manner equal to the role they play in this crisis: one of apathy, neglect, and denial. For that reason, I had to write a primary character who was a straight man. That's when I discovered that just as literature has distorted women into the virgin/whore dichotomy, straight men have been distorted into the hero/villain dichotomy—neither of which I find generally appropriate. So when I committed to violating these conventions by describing someone unaware of how other people are living and unaware of how much power he wields, I found myself vulnerable to being dismissed with "Oh, she's a lesbian; she hates men." There does not yet exist a way for lesbian and gay male writers to address the straight male character and his societal power without being subjected to this dismissal. The fact remains that marginal people know how they live, and they know how the dominant culture lives. Dominant culture people only know how *they* live. And so the people with the most power have the least information. And to state this is still considered didactic or extreme.

I had more surprises when I began touring with the book. Since, except in New York and San Francisco, men do not generally come to my readings, or those of lesbian writers in general, my audiences were mostly women. In cities where AIDS is not as much in people's daily lives as it is for us in San Francisco and New York, I found that people no longer wanted to talk about writing or books. They wanted to talk about AIDS. They asked me various questions about transmission in addition to expressing levels of discomfort with the politics of AIDS activism. One question that came up over and over again was, "If the shoe were on the other foot and this were happening to lesbians, don't you think the guys wouldn't help *us*?" And of course, I had to answer *yes* but, at the same time, not give in to the homophobic stereotype that gay men hate women and assert, instead, that this lack of reciprocity exists between all men and all women. Straight men are noticeably absent from the battle to win full abortion rights for straight women—and they're *married* to them. It's more about being raised male in this culture, which insists that the male experience is the objective, neutral experience from which all other experiences can be generalized. This is why we see so little awareness or advocacy by gay men on women's behalf—not only with regard to AIDS but also with regard to sexual assault, economic oppression, cancer, and abortion. However, I know at the same time that gay men have been allowed to die because they are *gay*, not because they are men. And I also know, from two years of involvement with ACT UP New York, that there is a general understanding in that organization that sexism is not only wrong—it is politically inefficient.[5]

On a human level, the fact of the gay community going coed is something that has certainly enriched my life personally and intellectually, although it has been a strange experience, in a country where women earn half of what men earn, to go from a movement

---

5. Schulman's history of ACT UP is *Let the Record Show: A Political History of ACT UP New York 1987–1993* (New York: Farrar, Straus & Giroux, 2021). Other excellent resources on the topic are Deborah Gould's *Moving Politics: Emotion and ACT UP's Fight against AIDS* (Chicago: University of Chicago Press, 2009); Benita Roth's *The Life and Death of ACT UP / LA: Anti-AIDS Activism in Los Angeles from the 1980s to the 2000s* (Cambridge: Cambridge University Press, 2017); and Jennifer Brier's *Infectious Ideas: U.S. Political Responses to the AIDS Crisis* (Chapel Hill: University of North Carolina Press, 2011).

of all women to a movement of men. I guess it is something akin to experiencing heterosexual privilege for the first time because we now have access to money, power, visibility, and resources that men move with in this culture, and I hope we can use these resources to benefit all of us.

I'd like to say one more thing about responsibility. There are people in this room, many people, who would not be alive today if it weren't for ACT UP. There is no book that got any drug released, any drug trial opened, or any service provided. Reading a book may help someone decide to take action, but it is not the same thing as taking action. The responsibility of every writer is to take their place in the vibrant activist movements along with everybody else. The image created by the male intellectual model of an enlightened elite who claims that its artwork *is* its political work is parasitic and useless for us. At the same time, I don't think that any writer must write about any specific topic or in any specific way—writers have to be free of formal and political constraints in their work so that the community can grow in many directions. But when they're finished with their work, they need to be at demonstrations, licking envelopes and putting their bodies on the line with everybody else. We live in the United States of Denial, a country where there is no justice. The way we get justice is by confronting structures that oppress us in the manner that is most threatening to those structures. That means in person as well as in print.[6]

6. Sarah Schulman published this chapter in her collection *My American History: Lesbian and Gay Life during the Reagan and Bush Years* (New York: Routledge, 1994), 194–197.

Does Your Mama Know about Me?

PANEL: AIDS AND THE RESPONSIBILITY OF THE WRITER

MARCH 3, 1990

Throughout the 1980s, many of us grieved the loss of friends, lovers, and relatives who were one moment strong, healthy, and able-bodied but then in an instant became thin framed and emaciated, with hacking and wheezing, their bodies wracked with horrible pain. Sometimes brave souls would return to the family roost to disclose their sexuality and ask permission to die in familiar surroundings. Too often, families were discovering for the first time that the dear brother, the favorite uncle, the secretive son was a homosexual, a Black gay man, and the unfortunate victim of the killer virus, AIDS. Some parents had always known, and some had never suspected that their son was a Black gay man, a sissy, a queer, a faggot. For some families, this shocking discovery (and grief) expressed itself as shame and anger; it compelled them to disown their flesh and blood, denying dying men the love and support that friends often provided as extended family. In other instances, families were very understanding and bravely stood by their brethren through their final days.

Joseph Beam, in his powerful essay "Brother to Brother: Words from the Heart," defined *home* as being larger, more complex and encompassing than one's living room:[1] "When I speak of home, I

---

1. Joseph Beam (1954–1988) was an activist, writer, and editor based in Philadelphia, Pennsylvania, who worked nationally on gay liberation, particularly Black gay liberation. His papers are available at the Schomburg Center for

mean not only the familial constellation from which I grew, but the entire Black community: the Black press, the Black church, Black academicians, the Black literati, and the Black left. Where is my reflection? I am most often rendered invisible, perceived as a threat to the family, or I am tolerated if I am silent and inconspicuous. I cannot go home as who I am and that hurts me deeply."[2]

Beam articulated one of the primary issues Black gay men are faced with when our relationships with our families and communities are examined. We cannot afford to be disconnected from these institutions, yet it would seem that we are willing to create and accept dysfunctional roles in them, roles of caricature, silence, and illusion. In truth, we are often forced into these roles to survive. This critical dilemma causes some of us to engage in dishonest relationships with our kin. It can foster apathy between us and the communities of home that we need and that need our presence. The contradictions of "home" are amplified and become more complex when Black gay men's relationships with the white gay community are also examined.

The post-Stonewall white gay community of the 1980s was not seriously concerned with the existence of Black gay men except as sexual objects. In media and art, the Black male was given little representation except as a big Black dick. This aspect of the white gay sensibility is strikingly revealed in the photographs of Black males by the late Robert Mapplethorpe. Though his images may be technically and aesthetically well composed, his work *artistically* perpetuates racial stereotypes constructed around sexuality and desire. In many of his images, Black males are only shown as parts of the anatomy—genitals, chests, buttocks—close-up and close-cropped to elicit desire. Mapplethorpe's eye pays special attention to the penis at the expense of showing us the subject's

Research in Black Culture, Manuscripts, Archives and Rare Books Division, the New York Public Library.

2. Joseph Beam, "Brother to Brother: Words from the Heart," in *In the Life: A Black Gay Anthology*, ed. Joseph Beam (Boston: Alyson, 1986), 231.

face and thus a whole person. The penis becomes *the* identity of the Black male, which is the classic racist stereotype recreated and presented as "art" in the context of a gay vision.

Mapplethorpe's *Man in a Polyester Suit*, for example, presents a Black man without a head, wearing a business suit, his trousers unzipped, and his fat, long penis dangling down, a penis that is not erect. It can be assumed that many viewers who appreciate Mapplethorpe's work, and who construct sexual fantasies from it, probably wondered *first* how much larger the penis would become during erection as opposed to wondering *who* the man in the photo is or *why* his head is missing. What is insulting and endangering to Black men is Mapplethorpe's *conscious* determination that the faces, the heads, and by extension, the minds and experiences of some of his Black subjects are not as important as close-up shots of their cocks.

It is virtually impossible while viewing Mapplethorpe's photos of Black males to avoid confronting issues of objectification.[3] Additionally, Black gay men are not immune to the desire elicited by his photos. We are drawn to the inherent eroticism. In "True Confessions: A Discourse on Images of Black Male Sexuality," Isaac Julien and Kobena Mercer accurately identify this dichotomy when they observe that Mapplethorpe's images of Black males reiterate "the terms of colonial fantasy" and "service the expectations of white desire." They then ask the most critical question of all: "What do

---

3. For additional consideration of my charge that Mapplethorpe's images of Black males are primarily images of objectification, see the images on the following pages in his catalog *Black Males* (Amsterdam: Galerie Jurka, 1980): 9, 15, 18, 19, 37, 39, 45, 47, 48, and 49. The images cited all depict headless men presented as sexual objects. Further justification for my charge can also be found in Mapplethorpe's *The Black Book* (New York: St. Martin's, 1986). *Man in a Polyester Suit* is specifically cited because that image of a Black male is one of his most well known. It might have been more appropriate to title it *Black Dick in a Polyester Suit*, since the emphasis is hardly on the suit or the man.

[Mapplethorpe's images] say to our wants and desires as black gay men?"[4]

It has not fully dawned on white gay men that racist conditioning rendered many of them no different from their heterosexual brothers in the eyes of Black gays and lesbians. Coming out of the closet to confront sexual oppression has not necessarily given white males the motivation or insight to transcend their racist conditioning. This failure (or reluctance) is costing the gay and lesbian community the opportunity to become a powerful force for creating *real* social changes that reach beyond issues of sexuality. It has fostered much of the distrust that permeates the relations between the Black and white communities. And finally, it erodes the possibility of forming meaningful, powerful coalitions.

When Black gay men approached the gay community to participate in the struggle for acceptance and to forge bonds of brotherhood, bonds so loftily proclaimed as *the vision* of the best gay minds of my generation, we discovered that the beautiful rhetoric was empty. The disparity between words and actions was as wide as the Atlantic Ocean and deeper than Dante's hell. There was no gay community for Black men to come home to in the 1980s. The community we found was as mythical and distant from the realities of Black men as was Oz from Kansas.

At the baths, at certain bars, in bookstores and cruising zones, Black men were welcome because these constructions of pleasure allowed the races to mutually explore sexual fantasies, and after all, the Black man engaging in such a construction only needed to whip out a penis of almost any size to obtain the rapt attention withheld from him in other social and political structures of the gay community. These sites of pleasure were more tolerant of Black men because they enhanced the sexual ambience, but that same tolerance did not always continue once the sun began to rise.

---

4. Isaac Julien and Kobena Mercer, "True Confessions: A Discourse on Images of Black Male Sexuality," *Ten-8*, no. 22 (1986): 6.

Open fraternizing at a level suggesting companionship or love between the races was not tolerated in the light of day. Terms such as *dinge queen*, for white men who prefer Black men, and *snow queen*, for Black men who prefer white men, were created by a gay community that obviously could not be trusted to believe its own rhetoric concerning brotherhood, fellowship, and dignity. Only an *entire* community's silence was capable of reinforcing these conditions.

Some of the best minds of my generation would have us believe that AIDS has brought the gay and lesbian community closer and infused it with a more democratic mandate. That is only a partial truth that further underscores the fact that the gay community still operates from a one-eyed, one-gender, one-color perception of "community" that is most likely to recognize blond before Black but seldom the two together.

Some of the best minds of my generation believe AIDS has made the gay community a more responsible social construction, but what AIDS really manages to do is clearly point out how significant are the cultural and economic differences between us— differences so extreme that Black men suffer a disproportionate number of AIDS deaths in communities with very sophisticated gay health-care services.

The best gay minds of my generation believe that we speak as one voice and dream one dream, but we are not monolithic. We are not even respectful of each other's differences. We are a long way from that, Dorothy. I tell you, Kansas is closer.

We are communities engaged in a fragile coexistence, if we are anything at all. Our most significant coalitions have been created in the realm of sex. What is most clear for Black gay men is this: we have to do for ourselves *now*, and for each other *now*, what no one has ever done for us. We have to be there for one another and trust less the adhesions of kisses and semen to bind us. Our only sure guarantee of survival is that which we create from our own self-determination. White gay men may only be able to understand and respond to oppression as it relates to their ability to obtain orgasm without intrusion from the church or state. White gay men are only "other" in this society when they choose to come out of the closet. But all Black men are treated as "other" regardless of whether we sleep with men or women—our Black skin automatically marks us as "other."

Look around, brothers. There is rampant killing in *our* communities. Drug addiction and drug trafficking overwhelm us. The blood of young Black men runs curbside in a steady flow. The bodies of Black infants crave crack, not the warmth of a mother's love. The nation's prisons are reservations and shelters for Black men. An entire generation of Black youths is being destroyed before our eyes. We cannot witness this in silence and apathy and claim our hands are bloodless. We are a wandering tribe that needs to go home before home is gone. We should not continue standing in line to be admitted into spaces that don't want us there. We cannot continue to exist without clinics, political organizations, human services, and cultural institutions that *we* create to support, sustain, and affirm us.

Our mothers and fathers are waiting for us. Our sisters and brothers are waiting. Our communities are waiting for us to come home. They need our love, our talents and skills, and we need theirs. They may not understand everything about us, but they will remain ignorant, misinformed, and lonely for us, and we for them, for as long as we stay away hiding in communities that have never really welcomed us or the gifts we bring.

I ask you, brother, Does your mama *really* know about you? Does she *really* know what I am? Does she know I want to love her son, care for him, nurture and celebrate him? Do you think she'll understand? I hope so because *I am* coming home. There is no place else to go that will be worth so much effort and love.[5]

5. Hemphill published this speech as part of the introduction to *Brother to Brother: New Writings by Black Gay Men* (Boston: Alyson, 1991; Washington, DC: Redbone, 2007) under the title "II. Does Your Mama Know about Me? Does She Know Just What I Am?," xvii–xx.

The Effects of Ecological Disaster

Panel: AIDS and the Responsibility of the Writer

March 3, 1990

For much of my writing life, I've been very concerned and focused about the way in which in this culture we tend to deny the fact that we are mortal and that we are part of the life cycle of nature. I've also been very concerned with the relationship between social justice and ecology—that is, the way that we treat each other as human beings and the way we are treating nature. It has come to be obvious to me in the last years that there is a very deep connection between the issue of compassion and the issue of our connection to nature. As we sever our connection to nature, we also sever our compassion toward each other.

I want to talk to you a little bit about my process of discovery. I've been working on a book on nuclear war for the past six years—I'm in my seventh year working on it now—and I became very moved and very riveted by the issue of people who have been exposed to local radiation.[1] I started to attend meetings of the National Association of Radiation Survivors and hear their stories, and obviously, moved by this phrase *witness fiction* that Sarah Schulman used, it seemed to me very important to bear witness. Another area that's denied severely in this culture is that people are suffering terribly who have been exposed to radiation, and what is also denied, what I came to understand myself

1. Griffin published *A Chorus of Stones* in 1992; it was a finalist for the Pulitzer Prize.

Susan Griffin. (*Photo credit: © Lynda Koolish.*)

personally after a few years working with this, is that we're all exposed to local radiation. I have, and there are very many of us who are becoming ill from it. I have an illness that is called chronic fatigue immune dysfunction syndrome (CFIDS, now called myalgic encephalomyelitis). It's now one of the illnesses that is included in ACT UP's program, along with HIV. It's an immunological disorder. It has been characterized in the press as a yuppie disease, and it's been falsely connected to depression. Laboratory work shows damage to the T cells, natural killer cells, and it is a very severely disabling disease that can even at times cause death.

I came to understand that in fact radiation affects the immune system directly. The way that we're usually introduced to radiation is through the indication of cancer. But in fact, what radiation does is it affects the immune system. Any disease that is related to the immune system—which includes cancer, anything you can name, lupus, arthritis—all of these diseases increase when the immune system is affected by radiation.

Rosalie Bertell and Alice Stewart, two scientists who run very extensive epidemiological studies on the low-level effects of radiation, show a higher incidence of these diseases during periods where there's been more atmospheric testing in the area, where there is radiation.[2] I think that one of the effects of looking at AIDS as a gay disease and looking at CFIDS as a women's disease, and then playing the two of them with the scapegoating that we as gay people and that we as women experience, is that it separates the disease process away from the rest of the population. People can say, "Well, this is not going to happen to me, this is not happening to me, and I'm safe from this." And in fact, the result of this is that, at this point, we are not seeing a very clear path. We're blind to what's actually going on.

We're in a very profound level of denial about the fact that the human immune system is being affected (by radiation), and what is one of the extremely important elements of the disease process, of both AIDS and CFIDS and a number of other immunological disorders that have either newly arisen or risen in their incidence, is the environment, radiation, and radiation combined with ecological contaminants.

We're living in an atmosphere that has never existed before on the face of the earth, that has been profoundly altered. The human organism took billions of years to grow and has not changed in relation to the way that we've changed the environment. It's not only trees that are suffering, but we as human beings are beginning to show the effects of ecological disaster. There's not a single major government-funded study that's looking at the relationship between ecological contamination and AIDS, or CFIDS,

2. For more, see Rosalie Bertell, *No Immediate Danger: Prognosis for a Radioactive Earth* (Toronto: Women's Press, 1985); and Gayle Greene, *The Woman Who Knew Too Much: Alice Stewart and the Secrets of Radiation* (Ann Arbor: University of Michigan Press, 1999).

or any of the immunological disorders. And by the way, there are also serious immunological disorders showing up in animals— whales in the Saint Lawrence Seaway; I don't know if you've read about the seals. I had a major attack of CFIDS when I was in Germany, and there were headlines all over about the seals in the North Sea and this immunological disease.

Albert Camus begins *The Plague* with a description, and I want to read it to you. It's a description of Oran, and it's a town that was suddenly beset by the plague. He opens the novel by describing the town: "The town itself, let us admit, is ugly. It has a smug, placid air."[3] He speaks of the life in this town as being devoid of any life except work life and the energy and the effort of earning money. And he says about this town—and it's a very, very bad place to die because no one's very interested when you're dying, and no one is present to the actual experience of dying. It's a very isolated, atomized community. The town is also upset by racism. There's a pervasive pattern of prejudice toward the Arabs in the town. All of these attitudes, all of these issues come together to make the town unable to deal in an effective way with the plague when it comes to the town. In fact, the plague spreads much more rapidly because people are dying, because the town is ill already. It has a very profound illness (characterized by) this lack of compassion and lack of connectedness. And I think that that's what we're dealing with in this culture today. The cruelty that is implicit in an attitude that conflates disease with the behavior of the person who is ill is something that I really think we need to get inside and understand. It's quite something to be on the other end of that kind of attitude. I'm speaking, for instance, of the idea that AIDS is caused by sexual practice or the idea that CFIDS is caused by depression, in which women and depression are linked somehow to women working too hard. I think that you know where such cruelty exists, it really comes back to injure the society itself.

---

3. Albert Camus, *The Plague*, trans. Stuart Gilbert (New York: Vintage International, 1991), 3.

Very crucially, those of us who are ill are the canaries in the mine. If you don't know what that metaphor means, there was a practice in the earlier days of mining in which they took the canaries in a cage down into the mines, and if the canaries died, they knew that the mines were not safe for the miners because there were noxious fumes. But those of us who are ill are the ones who are first to signal the effects of the planet, which is ill, and the society, which is ill.

As writers, it is extremely important to attend to this experience directly in all its shapes and forms, to be able to listen to and give voice to this rich physical experience, the emotional experience; it's a profound experience to experience illness, to experience losing someone you love, the experience of death. And along with all of our other protests, it is very important for us to cherish and to hold on to the significance and the meaning in those actual experiences and not let them be stolen from us or redefined or disconnected from us.

I want to end this speech with this play that I wrote, called *Thicket*, about the sudden death of a close friend:

One, two, three, four. One, two, three, four. I'm counting the loose threads. Four means everything is all right, three, one, two, three, four, one, two, three, four, three means bad luck, one, two, three, three, four, one, two, three, three four, things don't always come out the way you want, one two, three four, one two, three four, going down underneath into the midst of it, I didn't turn back, I fell into that place myself, one two, one two, three four, three four, I recovered, fell ill again, recovered again, fell ill again, recovered, fell, recovered, fell, one, two, three, four, fell, fell, fell, it's me now at the edge, one two three, one two three, one two three. Isn't it the way it's supposed to be, one two three. When I stand, I don't know how strong my legs will be. One two three, get across, I don't know if I can get across, one two three, beginning a sentence, beginning, beginning a sentence I don't know, I do not know what the words will be.

More Fuel to Run On

PANEL: AIDS AND THE RESPONSIBILITY OF THE WRITER

MARCH 3, 1990

I can't separate very easily the impact that AIDS has had on me personally or the impact that it has had on me as a writer. Like most people in this room, I think I have lost more friends than I can count or sometimes even remember, which is really scary. But I want to just take a little time today to just talk about some of the losses that I felt most deeply. Among the people who are no longer here for me are Fred Heramb, who was a man who owned a fist-fucking club called the Catacombs; Geoff Mains, who was a leatherman and the author of *Urban Aboriginals*; Robert McQueen, a former editor of the *Advocate*, who used to call himself in his rowdier moments Rim McQueen; and Cynthia Slater, who is an ex-lover of mine, who was one of the founders of the Bay Area's S/M community and, in some ways, a leatherman in her own right.

None of these people were sexual moderates. And sometimes they were real jerks about it, y'know? They were capable of being cruel, selfish, and stupid about their quest for pleasure. But they were also intelligent and kind and willing to go into shadowy places to seek intense and very intimate experiences, even if those experiences were with strangers. What they gave me was a real treasury of goodness and honor for the human body and the ability to be honest about all of my desires, even if I think it's not wise to act on all of my desires. And none of them were writers. None of them were writers, and the world that they lived in, a world in which they were sexual outlaws, is gone. So if it's going to survive, it survives in me, and people like me, and our work.

I publish both fiction and nonfiction, and a lot of the fiction that I write and most of what I publish is pornography. Now, maybe because in terms of my life, I can't tell a reader who I'm having breakfast with every day without telling them stuff that they don't want to hear because of the nature of these relationships. To survive, my strategy has been that if people are going to tell me my life is unspeakable, I will speak about it. If they tell me that it's horrible, I will frighten them. And if they tell me that I am garbage, I will make them eat every bite of it. The fact that I am, as Dorothy Allison has coined the phrase, "a queer sort of queer" means that I am isolated not only by virtue of my homosexuality but also within the gay community. Now, that doesn't mean I feel sorry for myself. I like my life; I like being this bad girl. But it does mean that in these times, which are getting progressively more conservative, when there's more censorship from the state, I am growing evermore concerned about censorship within our own community. Because the bookstores that won't carry my work for damn sure are not going to help the benefit to contribute to my defense fund.

In addition to writing fiction, I also do a lot of sex education, mostly in the *Advocate* advice column, where I am in the odd position of being a dyke who is telling faggots how to have sex.[1] Gender dysphoria has its advantages! What I can tell you about that is that, outside of the big city, safe sex education is not working. It's not happening. And even inside major cities where we have done intense grassroots education about how to have safer sex, people are looking for any excuse not to do it. You will not believe the letters I get. Well, some of you will because some of you wrote them.

---

1. Califia published an advice column in the *Advocate* titled Adviser from 1981 until 1992. Initially, the column ran with the pullout classified ads; later, it was in the magazine. In 1991, Alyson Books published *The Advocate Adviser*, which collected these columns.

Now, y'know, some of these complaints are valid. "Condoms don't fit me," men write in to say. And that's true. People are afraid of them breaking, so they don't use them. The most common strategy people employ is to find a lover, they both get tested, they're both HIV negative, and so they figure they can do anything with each other. Should we ask for a show of hands? We know that does not work all the time. I even get letters from men who say, "I gave up sex until I can find somebody who really turns me on because I'm afraid of AIDS and my ideal partner is a four-foot-tall purple man from Venus who has three penises." That won't be a short period of celibacy. People are actually willing sometimes to give up sex rather than change their sexual practice.

Logically, doesn't AIDS mean that what we should do is just get rid of all the porn that shows people exchanging body fluids—blood, semen, vaginal secretions, all that stuff? I mean, wouldn't that help? And shouldn't we even ban the personal ads of people who are soliciting all of those activities? There are some gay papers that have done that, with the best of intentions. Much evil has been done in history with the best of intentions. After all, many of us logically supported closing the bathhouses. Now I think that is an act that history will teach us to be ashamed of, but who am I to argue with all of the experts?

The problem with censorship is that it does not work any better than celibacy. It leaves a gap in the discourse, and it makes people feel that the thing that is most important in their lives, maybe the only thing that gives them pleasure, is forbidden, and it's hateful. And when people have a decrease in self-esteem, a decrease in that sense of camaraderie, when they feel more isolated, they become even less able to change their sexuality and even less likely to get the information about what changes they should make if they want to stay healthy.

I don't think educators have acknowledged just how hard it is to change those patterns. Most of us have one, maybe two ways that we know we can get off. And if you change that, what you're risking is that you won't come. The most frequent letters I get are from people who are saying, "I can't meet anybody. I can't find partners. I can't connect." In a world where we still have that much trouble connecting with each other, when you ask people to risk getting off, you're asking them to take a big gamble. And for a lot of gay people who don't have access to organizations, activities, a community, gay sex is their gay identity.

And if you think it's hard to get gay men to use condoms, you should try to get dykes to use dental dams. A glove is not such a big deal because it's not like my hand is going to lose its hard-on if I put it on. But you just try to get someone to give up the way sex tastes. It's a big loss.

I do think it would be really nice if porn magazines would take some of the obscene profits that they make and, instead of diverting them to the Mafia, use them to pay health educators to put in more nonfiction information about safe sex. I think that you need nonfiction information because when people ask questions, they need detailed information. They need more detailed information than those goddamn little boxes of "Safe," "Possibly Safe," and "Unsafe" activities. I also think that it's a really good thing that more and more gay erotic writers are writing safer sex porn. I've written some myself, sometimes under duress because my editor says, "We're not publishing anything that has filth and slime going back and forth from orifice to orifice." Or a little more refined version of that.

I reminded myself that this is not the first generation of writers who have had to deal with the fact that sex sometimes has fatal consequences. Boccaccio's *The Decameron* was set in the context of the plague. And in fact, it's used as the reason all of these ladies are sitting around telling these ribald stories, because who cares? It's the end of the world. They have nothing to lose; they might as well make fun of the church and tell hot stories about adultery. In Victorian porn, you see writers employ a lot of devices to help readers suspend their anxiety about venereal disease. Today, they look silly because we know these techniques are not effective. So women douching after sex for birth control and coitus interruptus, otherwise known as sticky cement, just make us laugh. We have people ingesting mysterious herbs and wine that are supposed to keep them invulnerable from harm. Pregnant women just taking trips to Paris, where everything is fixed. Abortions and even occasional condoms, or as they call them, French letters.

I do a lot of similar things. I employ all kinds of strategies in my writing to help me continue to do creative work and still cope with the fact that we have an epidemic—or actually an endemic, a disease that kills people. I write future sex; I try to imagine what the impact of AIDS is going to be five hundred years from now. I imagine worlds where it doesn't exist.

But I still write porn about unsafe sex. And I also write porn and other fiction that include drugs. I want to talk about that a little bit. I'm a lesbian, and in the lesbian community, IV drug use is still the major vector for transmission of AIDS. And we never talk about it. We never, never talk about it. Again, a lot of us are shooting up to get high. And we continue to kill ourselves, and we continue to kill our partners because there's a secret, and it's stigmatized, and we don't talk about it. Now, I support twelve-step programs; I support getting clean and sober, but just saying "Everybody should go get clean and sober" is like Nancy Reagan saying "Just say no." It doesn't work. It doesn't stop people from getting high. Even if you don't believe there is such a thing as recreational drug use, you still have to be prepared to tell people how to get high without getting sick because a dead junkie never got into treatment. And I have as much trouble getting gay men and lesbians to deal with IV drug use in our community as any of us have had getting straight doctors and straight politicians to deal with this disease. We have our own epidemic of ignorance and shame about this that we have got to cope with. Most of the people I know who got sick from AIDS during the glory days of the 1970s and 1980s can't honestly tell me if they got sick from sex or from shooting up.

Like most writers, I'm usually in an adversarial relationship with publishers. So as much as it hurts me, I have to say that they have rights too. They have a right to refuse to publish material that they think won't sell or that they find morally offensive. But I do want to encourage publishers and editors to keep an open mind about graphic sexual material that does not consist solely of frottage, mutual J.O., and the mandatory donning of rubber underwear. Writing is what I do to stay alive. I don't want someone else messing with the really delicate balance that I have to maintain in order to be able to do my work. When I write about unsafe sex, what I'm trying to do is salvage the love and the veneration I have for the human body. This is an attitude that was really hard-won. I mean, I don't know if you remember the very first time you put your nose down there, but it was scary. No one had ever told you that you could, or should, or ought to do that. Nobody. You are alone before you take that dive. When you do it, and you discover that there's something there that welcomes you, I think that you never feel quite as alone in your life. To say that I would have to stop writing about every aspect of sexuality that I find fascinating would be like saying, "You have to stop writing about men. You have to stop writing about characters who are people of color. You have to stop writing about sex. Period." Writing is really hard work, and in order to put up with the frustration, I need to be able to feel passionate about my topics, and I also need to pick my own subjects. I think that what writers do to continue to write about safe and unsafe sex is that they give us all a little bit of encouragement and a little bit more fuel to run on while we're trying to live in really difficult times.

JOHN PRESTON

AIDS Writing

PANEL: AIDS AND THE RESPONSIBILITY OF THE WRITER

MARCH 3, 1990

John Updike has complained that today's writers are losing relevance: "The modern writer, perceiving that his reach is not wide, hopes that it is high. Priestly longings cling to writer-consciousness—pre-Vatican II priests, who kept their backs to the congregation while chanting in Latin."[1] According to Updike, the writer is no longer connected with real life; the writer is indulging in his or her own world, incapable or even disdainful of reaching out to connect with what is happening in the reader's reality.

Nowhere is that disconnection more obvious than in the stories of AIDS. As I approach what's going on in my world, I find that the doctrines of contemporary literature and the taste of the current publishing scene simply cannot tolerate AIDS writing that's meaningful.

One of the volunteers who works with the writer-in-residence program at the AIDS Project in my hometown of Portland, Maine, tells about his work with one of our clients, a man in the terminal stages of the disease. The client wanted to leave behind a series of letters for his son. He asked the volunteer to take his dictation; he was too ill to do the writing himself. The letters were to be left behind to be opened at certain significant moments of the son's life. There was a letter for the day of his First Communion, another for his entrance into high school, one for graduation. The list went

---

1. John Updike, *Odd Jobs: Essays and Criticism* (New York: Knopf, 1991), 791.

58

on. The purpose, so simply stated, was to give the son actual proof of how much his father loved him. The father was beset with grief that he would not witness these markers of his son's progression into adulthood. He wanted the boy to pass those markers with evidence that the man who had been his father cared for him and, even from the grave, was with him at those moments.

The story is the kind of anecdote I tell groups when I want to describe the utter humanity of people who are living with HIV infections and who face death. It always works—how could it not? But there's a kicker to the story. Just as everyone in the audience has taken it in and tried to reconcile its emotion, perhaps dismissing it to bathos, I add another fact: the father was nineteen years old at the time.

That's the problem with writing about AIDS. The emotions are too raw. And the scale is too great. Modern writing tends to want controlled feeling that has a narrow scope. Tom Wolfe has written in *Harper's* that the American novel has lost touch with the story of American life. To Wolfe, the contemporary writer is willing to settle for too small a stage; today's novelist ignores the epics of our daily life and retreats inward, avoiding the sweeping narratives moving all around.[2]

The story of the young father proves Wolfe's point. It is only one of many examples of life in the time of AIDS that would be easily and contemptuously dismissed by critics and publishers alike. The narrator's appeal to what would be called the reader's most base sentiments would keep such a story from ever being accepted by our critical establishment. The argument that it is true would have no standing.

But the true stories of AIDS in our world, in our country, in my home state of Maine, are too large to stand the confinement of the current critical canon. This is another story about AIDS in Maine:

2. Tom Wolfe, "Stalking the Billion-Footed Beast: A Literary Manifesto for the New Social Novel," *Harper's*, November 1989, 45–56, https://harpers.org/archive/1989/11/stalking-the-billion-footed-beast/.

One of the first people I knew with AIDS was a man who bred dogs. His constant companion was Martha, the bitch who gave birth to all the others and who had been with him for years. The man, originally from Georgia, still had a southern drawl. He and I used to stand in bars and watch televised college football games together. He followed his University of Georgia Bulldogs with a passion matched only by his love for Martha.

None of us was used to AIDS when he became sick. We hadn't yet learned how to cope with young men dying, handsome men becoming ugly with damage, their muscular bodies whittled down to stick figures by the wasting of the disease. We did not ignore him. We took him to the hospital. We made sure he kept his doctors' appointments. We visited him. But we didn't know how to talk to him about this strange and frightening illness. We didn't know how to discuss his coming death, even among ourselves. We joined him in a process of communal denial. He wasn't really in danger, we agreed with him. This was just a passing discomfort, we said. There was really nothing to worry about. We kept up that pretense even through the last time he was able to come home from the hospital. When we helped our friend into his house, Martha heard the doors opening and closing and the sounds of our voices. She ran from the back of the house, running to greet her master as she had done countless times in the years before. She cavorted toward us and we all laughed, waiting for her to jump up on us. But she stopped in mid run, in the middle of the living room floor. She froze. Then she fell back on her stomach, cramping her legs beneath her. She began to move backward, away from us and her master. A loud, mournful, keening cry came from deep inside her. She had seen death in the lesions that covered his now emaciated body.

And so the defenses of a whole group of adult men were destroyed by a dog's honesty. We all wept then. The forced laughter was gone, shown to be the lie we had all known it to be. We sat down and we held our friend while he cried, finally able to confront what was going on.

Use that in a novel and see what an editor says. Put that in a short story and watch your work dismissed as overly emotional. What's more, take a dozen of these stories—and every gay man has them, many other people are going to have them in the future—and you will be dismissed as an hysteric.

That a contemporary person could witness dozens of deaths in a single year and do it in the face of ignorance and bigotry, and also be forced to cope with the possibility that his own death will become one of the statistics, is a story of such breadth that modern writing cannot contain it. This story has to be dismissed because horror at these narratives isn't something that the dogma of contemporary writing can accommodate.

Do you think this is all too much? That I'm still only pulling strings? I have known, literally, hundreds of men who have been infected with HIV; I have known, literally, dozens who are dead. I am forty-five. I am also the oldest of us all. I live in a time that offends nature, a time when the old are burying the young. How can that be written about in any way that doesn't sound like a bizarre comic book contrivance? How does this become part of our story?

What does it mean to our writing? Now, to me, it means that the purpose of AIDS writing has to be found outside of any conventions that contemporary criticism and publishing might try to impose. The canons are proven ineffective, inappropriate. What is "literature" becomes a meaningless academic question when what is defined can't accommodate what is happening in our lives. What is happening to us because of AIDS is too great for modern writing to measure. That's not the fault of AIDS; that's the limitation of modern writing.

Those of us who are writing about AIDS can't worry about these definitions anymore. We can't be concerned with careerism, with academic acceptance, or with having the fashions of the day dictate how we write. We must not be worried about the styles and trends of a real or perceived literary establishment. We can't use AIDS to enter doors of a house that can't or won't entertain our issues.

The purpose of AIDS writing now is to get it all down. Andrew Holleran says the purpose of the writer in the time of AIDS is to bear witness.[3] Sarah Schulman makes the case that we cannot allow ourselves to be separated from what's happening by being seduced into an observer status. To live in a time of AIDS and to understand what is going on is to know that writing must be accompanied by action. Writing is not what our teachers told us, something that stands alone.

To be a writer in the time of AIDS is to be a truth teller. The truth is more horrible than anything people want to hear. The truth is that millions of people in the world are dying of a disease that could be controlled. The truth is that care is not reaching people who need it. The truth is not the comfortable television movie of the family reconciled with the victim. The truth is homeless young people wandering our cities without a national health-care program. The truth is hundreds of thousands of women in Africa dying because they've never been educated about risk reduction and because they live in a society that makes women chattel, torsos to be used by men without concern. The truth is devastating. The truth can't be contained in a pleasantly structured short story that will satisfy the readers of a literary magazine.

We have to *get it all down*. All we can expect of our writing that does get published is that it creates the historic documents that might make sense to people in the future. That's all published AIDS writing can hope to be today.

In our writer-in-residence program, I've learned another important function of the writer in this time of AIDS. I had thought we'd find art in our work, helping our clients become like Updike's priests. Isn't there the romantic notion that literature comes from suffering? How much more suffering can there be than that experienced by people with AIDS?

---

3. Preston likely references Andrew Holleran's book *Ground Zero* (New York: William Morrow, 1988), a collection of essays original published in *Christopher Street* as the AIDS epidemic unfolded in New York.

But there was no art, not in that sense. There was need. I have ended up transcribing thoughts and emotions. I began with the story of the father who wanted to leave letters for his son. That kind of work is the unexpected major function of my project. I take dictation from clients who are furious with the media and politicians. We help our clients write letters to family members, forgiving them for never having come to the soon-to-be-dead person's hospital bed. "My mother will feel so bad when it finally hits her," one man told me. I write letters of thanks for people who want their loved ones to know their help and patience were needed, welcomed, adored by those who received them.

So far away from being a modern-day priest who tries to reach high, I find myself brought back down to earth. I am instead a scribe in the marketplace of a society where literacy is so rare it has become a profession. I have become not the author of the story but the means for telling the story, the tool used by people to let the world, their families, their friends understand what is going on.

This is the best writing I can do in a time of AIDS.[4]

---

4. Preston's speech at this panel is available on YouTube: "Outwrite 1990," ACT UP Oral History, September 21, 2015, YouTube video, 1:15:51, https://www.youtube.com/watch?v=ufkZuZWUgYg. It is also reprinted in his collection *Winter's Light: Reflections of a Yankee Queer*, ed. Michael Lowenthal (Hanover: University Press of New England, 1995).

Lesbians and Gays of
African Descent Take Issue

STATEMENT TO THE MEMBERS OF THE PLANNING
COMMITTEE OF THE NATIONAL OUTWRITE 91

Edward Albee, noted writer, claimed at OutWrite 91, the national lesbian and gay writers' conference, that being a "quadruple minority" (white, Protestant, gay, male) has not hindered him.[1] This statement is a response to the OutWrite 91 planning committee, which chose Albee as the conference's keynote speaker.

The members of the ad hoc caucus of Lesbian and Gays of African Descent met in response to Albee's keynote address on Friday, March 1, 1991. Many of us took serious objection to points that he made in his speech. However, in discussing the points of Albee's address, we discovered larger issues that may undermine the conference's purpose, organization, and ambience. Here we would like to introduce our concerns.

The first concern that arose in the keynote address is to Albee's characterization of himself as a minority. It is true that in a world where People of Color are in the majority, and in which women outnumber and outlive men, Albee is indeed a minority. But what he failed to acknowledge, and what we recognize, is that he occupies a position of privilege. It is not Albee whom we wish to target here, for we recognize his contribution to gay letters. In fact, we are grateful that his remarks generated a discussion between

---

1. This statement was published in its entirety in *Aché* 3, no. 2 (April–May 1991): 10–11.

People of Color who otherwise might not have come together at this conference.[2]

Below are our concerns about the conference as a whole that took place during a dialogue within our caucus.

Objections

We do not wish to censor or deny any speaker her or his right to speak, but rather we insist there be an open forum in which people may take constructive issue with the same for the good of the order.

We appreciate the listing of celebrated gay male authors for their contributions to our movement and literature, but we object to the citing of examples from one culture or from one segment of our community without giving recognition to others or indicating that others are known to exist.

We recognize that positions of privilege and power among us have been hard-won, but it is inappropriate for white gay male authors, editors, and publishers to fail to acknowledge the multicultural, multiethnic tenor of these times.

We recognize, too, that the conference organizers must recruit volunteers and work against the constraints of other peoples' schedules and commitments in their daily lives, and they will not always be able to find competent and unencumbered assistants from the many ethnicities that exist, but the task of including a representative sample of our diverse gay cultures (i.e., African American, Native American, Asian, Pacific Islander, Semitic people [Arab and Jewish People of Color], Chicano, and Latino, as well as bisexuals and people with disabilities) on the planning committee must become an absolute prerequisite.

We understand the constraints of finding representative People of Color for every panel and every topic, but if the conference

---

2. The term *People of Color* refers to people of African, Asian, Latino/Latina, Chicano/Chicana, and Indigenous peoples of the Americas and Caribbean heritage.

is to represent our truly diverse community, there must be a commitment to an ambience of natural inclusion. It is no longer acceptable to us to have you say, "We can't find qualified people from various communities to fill panel positions or to deliver keynote addresses," because we have visible organizations with whom you can network.

We understand that scholarships were available to attend this conference, but scholarship criteria were not publicized adequately, and it was not clear how these funds were to be allocated. There was inadequate information about whom to contact for scholarships; the information was difficult to access, even upon request, which made it appear that there was an "inside" and biased distribution of funds. By the same token, accommodations for panelists appeared to be arbitrary as well.

We assert that, as participants at this conference, we are a literate and intellectual asset to the gay and lesbian literary community, but we sense the naive and distasteful assumption that minorities are not intellectuals.

Recommendations

We recommend that keynote speakers better reflect the multiculturalism of the community.

We recommend that persons of color be included on every panel and that persons of color serve as moderators.

We recommend that the organizers affirm the use of inclusive language.

We recommend that People of Color be included in committees selecting speakers and developing panels. However, the responsibility of including People of Color in this conference should not be left with one or two people from that group. We further recommend that organizers publicize the conference in national and local lesbian and gay People of Color publications in the form of paid advertising.

We recommend that moderators be trained to have a broad enough understanding of their topics so that they can facilitate a discussion that integrates diverse perspectives and that multicultural training be a part of the planning process.

We recommend that conference organizers improve information and clarify criteria for available scholarships and develop a clear policy for determination of recipients.

We recommend also that the goals of the conference be clearly stated with regard to issues of inclusivity. Such a statement ought to prevent some of the problems that have plagued this conference.

Lastly, we insist upon publication of this letter in *OUT/LOOK* magazine.[3]

Pledges

We pledge to provide assistance in providing possible panelists and moderators.

We pledge to provide a bibliography that includes the works of People of Color so that moderators will be more capable of including our voices.

We pledge to remain in dialogue with you so that the conference fully serves all of its attendees.

Final Remarks

Last year, SDiane Bogus[4] and Essex Hemphill[5] made significant contributions to the spirit of the conference. This year, many of us

---

3. A portion of this statement appears in *OUT/LOOK*, Fall 1991, no. 14, p. 19.

4. SDiane Bogus, who also uses the names SDiane Adamz-Bogus and Shari-ananda Adamz, ran Woman in the Moon, a feminist publishing house, for two decades. Her papers are available at the New York Public Library: "SDiane Adamz-Bogus Papers," New York Public Library, accessed September 29, 2021, http://archives.nypl.org/scm/20915.

5. Bogus and Hemphill were each on plenary panels at OutWrite 90. Hemphill was on the panel "AIDS and the Responsibility of the Writer," included in this volume. Bogus was on the panel "Lesbian and Gay Literature in the Marketplace" addressing the questions, "Will the lesbian and gay publishing boom last or will it prove illusory? How can the trade and small presses best

felt a diminished presence of figures of their stature in the primary forums. We are committed to having a more visible and effective presence at future OutWrite conferences. This letter is an effort toward achieving that goal.

The African American caucus would like to recognize the conference organizers' willingness to provide a space for the caucus to meet.

The caucus also acknowledges and appreciates the many hours of hard work it obviously took to make this conference possible.

The caucus wishes to state that this statement has the support of the People of Color who were in attendance at this conference.

Submitted by Natalie Devora, member of the ad hoc
caucus of Lesbians and Gays of African Descent[6]

---

serve the diverse needs of writers and readers?" Other panelists were Sasha Alyson, Samuel R. Delany, Barbara Grier, Barbara Wilson, and Michael Denneny, with Amy Scholder as the moderator.

6. Natalie Devora continues to be active in the San Francisco Bay area community. In 2018, BookBaby published her memoir *Black Girl White Skin: A Life in Stories*.

The Color of My Narrative

(This is 1992, and for people in the United States, a world ravaged by famine and war is made smaller. A free trade agreement with Mexico is marketed as a remedy for this country's ailing industrial economy, as if Mexico and the United States did not inhabit the same soil, as if ships would sail off the edge into an abyss upon reaching the U.S. border. This is not merely an election year. Every day we witness attempts to misappropriate the significance of this date. Take, for example, the U.S.-appointed commission for the official celebration of the quincentennial, which, together with the government of Spain and underwritten by a large grant from Texaco, has built replicas of the three ships that sailed with Columbus. These ships are intended to tour not only some of the sites that Columbus first encountered but also ports such as Boston and New York to attract a great flood of tourism. Staging this bizarre event will highlight the sense of this as a celebration of the encounter of two worlds, viewing the whole thing as a benign, glorious, heroic deed that saved the Americas from barbarism and ignorance. The media, meanwhile, jumps in and glorifies any event that presents the quincentennial as an excuse to justify and rationalize genocide and exploitations as necessary evil. Two major studios will release movies this year that will bring the experience of the discovery to your neighborhood in surround sound. Any detractors of this official party are seen as wet blankets, complainers, malcontents, fringe agitators. Meanwhile,

Mariana Romo-Carmona. (*Photo credit: Photo by Robert Giard, copyright Estate of Robert Giard.*)

there is little, if any, objective coverage of the Native American and Indigenous communities throughout the world who have united to observe and commemorate resistance and survival. There is no coverage of the Indigenous Alliance of the Americas, which, in 1991, held the First Continental Conference on 500 Years of Indian Resistance in Quito, Ecuador, whose mandate declares the inviolability of their ancestral territories and demands respect for their sovereignty and self-determination. It also demands the release of political prisoners and rejects militarism and denounces the International Monetary Fund for crimes attempted against the physical and cultural integrity of Indigenous people on this continent.

We have to fight for our awareness. This is a call to educate ourselves.)

This is 1992.[1] The year to tell the truth. This is not a time of forgiveness or a time to assuage guilt. This is a time not to make things

---

1. Romo-Carmona published this keynote speech in *Radical America* 24, no. 4 (1992): 79–85.

easier but to stir things up. But also, this should not be a threat to anyone unless they cling to the established order of Western civilization, and then it's very definitely a challenge. This is a moment to be alert, to raise our collective consciousness, to be fully aware that as we approach the end of the millennium, we cannot allow the same lies to be perpetuated. As storytellers of many cultures, every lesbian and gay male writer is faced with a choice. We cannot pretend that we did not hear the truth or that we don't have a responsibility to tell it. . . . History is never as important as when we don't have access to it. This is something of great value that we have learned as gay men and lesbians who carefully comb archives for evidence that we have existed, who write books and anthologies so that our lives will not be lost again.

I came to the United States when I was fourteen, from a South American country to a North American country, during a time when it was considered kind to refer to nations like Chile as "countries in development" instead of simply as "underdeveloped" or "banana republics." During my sojourn as an immigrant from a Third World country, I learned not only about the painful historical omissions practiced in this country's history classes but also about the historical racism practiced in my country of origin. I recall that in school I was taught superficially about the cultures that inhabited Abya-yala, the American continent, before the arrival of Europeans. We learned a great deal about colonial times and the formation of Latin American republics based on European forms of government. We even memorized speeches that our creole heroes were supposed to have delivered in the heat of battle. We learned their words, their names, the origins of our Spanish names while knowing next to nothing about the Araucanos, Mapuche, Quechua, Inca, Aymará, Guaraní, Quiché, Maya, Aztec, Toltec, and all the northern nations, like the Cree, Mohawk, Sioux, Cherokee, Anasazi, Pueblo, Navajo, Zuni, Hopi, Lakota, and so many more, and with this ignorance, we were taught to believe that some lives are important and others aren't.

I believe I had to come here, to be faced violently with racism and discrimination in my own skin, before I could really appreciate the effects of a Eurocentric education upon entire nations. I was confronted with all the stereotypes about Latinos that defined me and my culture before I even spoke. They were written by someone else, to serve someone else's ends. As a writer, I struggle to break away from the negative images written about me as a Latin American, but I must also unlearn the internalized lies about our origin as mestizos, people of "mixed blood," on which all those stereotypes are based. Voltaire wrote that Latin Americans were lazy and stupid; we were not human, according to Francis Bacon and Baron de Montesquieu, Joseph de Maistre, David Hume, and Jean Bodin, while Georg Wilhelm Friedrich Hegel viewed the continent as physically and spiritually impotent. Gonzalo Fernández de Oviedo, a sixteenth-century historian, explained that the native people of Haiti poisoned themselves and their children or strangled themselves with their own hands, not to avoid torture and mutilation while panning for gold, but to avoid work. Is the pervasive effect of centuries of lies an exaggeration? René Dumont wrote in his 1970 book about socialism in Cuba: "The Indians were not totally exterminated. Their genes subsist in Cuban chromosomes. They felt such an aversion for the tension which continuous work demands that some killed themselves rather than accept forced labor."[2] So this is 1992, and we are in the New World. As a Latina lesbian, the significance of this date rarely leaves my consciousness. I want to examine what is our collective responsibility. No, I don't claim to represent all of us, but then very few ever admitted not representing me. I want to speak to all of us but particularly to Latinas and Latinos. We don't often have the opportunity to address each other, pulled as we are in several directions, caught in the middle of our allegiances to varied heritage and history.

---

2. René Dumont, *Cuba: Socialism and Development*, trans. Helen R. Lane (New York: Grove, 1970).

As part of the lesbian and gay community in the United States, we attempt to participate in its life, become part of its institutions, contribute to the development of its theory, literature, and politics. But very often, we are rudely awakened to the fact that we are merely part of an endless panel exploring the wonderful diversity of our population. We find that our point of view is only accepted parenthetically, to make note of how different our cultures are, yet we still managed to crawl out of el barrio to find the university "Gay and Lesbian Community Center." We are seen as newcomers, recently washed up on the gay and lesbian shore, not as a people whose history is intrinsically part of the land we inhabit, but as a decoration, a piñata, or a little merengue.

Not long ago in New York City, I was invited to speak on a panel about the diversity of the lesbian community and to read some of my work. When questions were opened to the audience, I was asked if I could elaborate on the differences between coming out as a Latina lesbian and a normal lesbian. After my heated reply and the amens! of a few outraged sisters, the discussion resumed its course, this time dealing with subjects that directly addressed lesbian issues.

In order to explain why this arrogant perspective still permeates our dealings with each other, we have to start at the beginning. In our communities, the histories of people of color, the struggles of women against sexist systems, the identification of economic oppression—these subjects are not popular. When we talk about the importance of getting back to our communities and doing work that makes sense culturally, the attention span is remarkably brief. For those of us who are writers, we cannot accept to be separated from our origins in order to be palatable to a universal lesbian or gay audience. We cannot tolerate to be written about by sprinkling a little chili pepper across white pages, nor can we allow ourselves to fall in the habit of appropriating the spice of other cultures that we don't experience, sincerely and honestly. Who among us feels flattered to make a salacious appearance in the pages of a Norman Mailer product or a brutal killer cameo in *Basic Instinct*? Then as readers, too, we must refuse to be condescended to with writing that is less than the vibrant representation of our world.

But this is precisely the problem, to take the time to learn about this world, to know who we really are.

Imagine the year is 1540. In the forty-four years since the discovery of the New World, very important events have taken place. Gold—in incredible quantities, of the purest grade—has reached the coffers of Spain. The Aztec Empire has been brought to its knees. Elsewhere along the Antillean seas, once peaceful islands are engorged with the blood of several million Indigenous peoples. In 1534, the port of Seville received the ransom for the Inca emperor Atahualpa, whose life Francisco Pizarro promised he would spare. Atahualpa filled a room with gold and two with silver, but Pizarro strangled Atahualpa and then decapitated him. Chocolate has reached Europe. For the first time, perhaps, European nobility has experienced true sensual pleasure. Tomatoes have reached Europe, and the world has witnessed the birth of cacciatore. Corn and potatoes have reached Europe, and thousands have been saved from famine.

In Quauhtlemallan, now Guatemala, the Quiche Empire has also been attacked by moving hordes of the Spanish crown's emissaries. Led by Pedro de Alvarado, they bring civilization, the word of God, empty galleons waiting to be filled with gold and silver, and smallpox, tetanus, typhus, leprosy, trachoma, yellow fever, tooth decay, syphilis, and various other venereal, intestinal, and lung diseases—as well as horses and gunpowder.

The great city of the Quiché, Utatlán, is burned down, and in front of the most important buildings, the Quiché kings and queens are immolated as a sign of complete defeat. Imagine being a survivor. Your entire world is destroyed; your universe of knowledge is gone in flames with the leaders of your people. The libraries are burned. The history of your world is in those books, your knowledge of the stars, of agriculture, of medicine, of mathematics, of architecture. They are burned along with your temples and your goddesses, your artwork and your sculptures. You are raped repeatedly by many foul-smelling men. Your children are taken from you and sent far away as gifts to a pale queen. The new priests, who come in ships across the waters and on horseback through the continent, tell you that they are burning your gods so that you may have a new god, a life in the hereafter. And they teach you a new way to speak. They give you a new name. This is not unusual. From Tenochtitlán to Utatlán, as far south as Machu Picchu and Araucanía, all temples and sculptures are burned; objects sacred and artistic, particularly those revealing a many-faceted sexual nature, are melted down into gold bars. There is no sign left of Viracocha, the bisexual god of the Incas, or of Alom, the mother goddess of the Quichés. Very commonly, an edict is issued by the arriving conqueror to assassinate not only the chiefs of a nation but their descendants for four generations.

For several years, you and your children still carry the old stories with you; deep in your memory, you preserve bits and pieces of yourselves. The scribes among you begin a new task in secret. Using the new alphabet the invaders have brought, you attempt to rewrite the history of your world. When you are gone, you want your children and their children to know what has been passed on to you. You reconstruct history out of the ashes, the tale of the beginning of the world, with all the teachings you can remember, with all the goddesses and gods whose names you still remember. The Popol Vuh. It is a sacred book. You hid it. You revere it and preserve it. When you are gone, your children continue to hide it, and their children's children, for nearly 150 years.

But time is relentless. There is disease among your people, and your lives are short. The work in the gold mines is hard, and you are whipped into oblivion; many die quickly. Building churches, roads, palaces for the new lords takes years and all your strength. Yet some of the new priests are kind. They want to save your soul and sometimes your body. They intercede on your behalf to stop the whippings, the rapes, and the dismembering routinely used as punishment. Can you trust them? Is there another choice? So you bring the Popol Vuh to a priest and hand him your world. The last piece of your world.

By 1650, the Taino and Arawak were close to extinction; the continent of Abya-yala's 70 million people was reduced to 3.5 million. It is said that by 1600, the abuse and murder of Indigenous peoples had been outlawed thanks to the efforts of notable men of the cloth such as Bartolomé de las Casas. But in fact, it was sanctioned before each attack on the population. A wordy sentence was read, without translation but in the presence of a notary public, stating that untold violence was about to befall them if they did not at once yield to the church and the crown or if they maliciously delayed in doing so. By the end of the century, the entire wealth reaped from the invasion mismanaged and scattered, the regime of the Habsburgs was bankrupt, but the European economy had been lifted out of the Dark Ages. As the Native populations dwindled, the exploitation of resources did not end. Most European nations were involved in the occupation, and the world, both Old and New, was a tapestry bearing the flags of the Spaniards, Portuguese, Dutch, British, French. To replace the dead, African people were sequestered or brought and enslaved to work in the plantations and the mines in the Caribbean and North America and as far south as Brazil, Perú, and Chile. Workers from Asia, India, and the Pacific Islands were lured, indentured, or otherwise coerced to leave family and home forever and resettle in the Caribbean and throughout the continent.

In 1688, the Dominican friar Francisco Ximénez was sent from Spain to Guatemala, to the city now known as Chichicastenango. Being quite familiar with the language of the Quiché people, he was trusted to receive the Popol Vuh, the ancient book of the Quiché. Father Ximénez understood the value of the book he had been given. He transcribed the book using two columns, one to reproduce the text in the original Quiché and one for his translations into Castilian. There is no indication as to who wrote the book, or who preserved it or how, or the names of the families who kept it. In 1722, Father Ximénez wrote another version of the book, which is considered to be more readable than the original translation. He then wrote two other volumes on the languages of the Kaqchikel (formerly spelled Cacchiquel), Quiché, and Tzutuhil, the first containing a vocabulary and the second a complete grammar of the three languages.

Many translations and other celebrated books have been written based on the Popol Vuh and the work of Father Ximénez, such as the Quiché grammar published in Paris by Charles Étienne Brasseur de Bourbourg and a history published in 1854 by the Austrian Carl Scherzer. Other works on this American mythology were published by such authors as George Bancroft, Daniel Garrison Brinton, Hyacinthe de Charencey, Richard Sharpe Shaver, Max Müller, Edouard Seler, Georges Raynaud, Lewis Spence, and so on. In 1925, Georges Raynaud published another translation, which was finally translated into modern Spanish. In 1927, the book was published in Guatemala for the first time by Antonio Villacorta and Flavio Rodas. Today, the original translations can be found not in Guatemala but in the Newberry Library in Chicago.

Recovering the other heritage, the one that has been denied, means that we are willing to balance our skewed view of the world, and this takes effort. This is a time when the truth will be told with or without us, and we have to be committed to take part in the struggle. Civilizations have risen and fallen, and the world is still reluctant to respect basic human rights, even something so basic to human nature as sexual orientation. If we understand the importance of telling our history as lesbians and gay men, if what we are talking about here today is survival, then it has to be the survival of all of us.

For the past five hundred years, the Old World has been reproducing itself in the New. Exploiting the resources of the New World to maintain the values of the Old. Enslaving people to build reconstructed images of the old European civilizations. Supplanting Native cultures to breed its own. Brilliantly exemplifying its inability to coexist peacefully with the environment, with the variety of people who form our world. This is imperialism. And it is a lesson that we can refuse to learn. . . .

Inclusiveness does not mean taking the SNAP! out of Black gay male culture and leaving the Black queen behind. To use Audre Lorde's name but not the wisdom of her words. To share that dish of spicy pad nam and feel exotic under the Thai moonlight but ignore the plight of mail-order brides. To learn the salsa and swoon to the lambada but forget the real name of that adopted light-skin baby from Perú. To wear that fantastic turquoise but shut out the U.S. government breaking treaties and stealing land. To maintain a collective structure and make decisions by consensus but forget to call anybody until the last minute when it's already decided what the agenda is. Inclusiveness does not mean setting up an award with the name of a deceased African American but then forgetting that there are countless African Americans writing, who are very much alive, who should have some say in the nomination process.[3] We can't be who we are, none of us, if we have to leave our culture behind. Because it's not true that white people have no culture or no ethnicity, we want to hear about all of it. But all of it, not just the folks who get to go on dinner cruises, but the ones who bus the dinner tables. It's time to tell the truth and figure out where did all this money come from, anyway, what and who has made this country great, and why are all these immigrants coming in great waves clamoring for resources they have never seen but were grown in their soil. These are gay and lesbian issues worthy of being included in our literature.

As writers, we have a choice: to perpetuate the lies or tell the truth. The lies are composed of censorship, exclusion, deliberately twisting history to support the Eurocentric view. As people whose human rights are threatened, it behooves us to support, encourage, and protect in all ways the telling of the truth with the potential to liberate us all. By clinging to any part of oppression, we fracture

---

3. Romo-Carmona references the issues surrounding the Joseph Beam prize at the conference as discussed in the introduction.

ourselves. Any one of us who is interested in a hierarchy of oppression loses. We lose a part of ourselves. Because we cannot buy a little oppression with our discretionary income, we buy all of it.

As a Latina lesbian writer, I am not using my specific culture to adorn my plain words. The color of my narrative is my narrative. The way it meanders through reasoning and fanciful flights is there not merely to entertain but to express how I have arrived at my understanding of the world. I presume to say that when writers of non-European heritage write in our own particular voices, it takes every ounce of strength to reveal the very center of what has been hidden in us for centuries. We bring forth a soul that dares to make itself visible in a battlefield. As for me, when I write or speak in my halting way, I draw from hiding my Popol Vuh. It has been translated and reinterpreted by my own colonized consciousness. That is the tragedy, perhaps, for a writer like myself who still seeks to speak her own voice in another tongue. But there are many Native writers who are here with us, those who have written and those who are emerging, writing in their own words. So who will you be? The soldier or the priest? The translator? The curator of antiquities?

Because of this almost forgotten heritage, it is important to unearth a new meaning for the observance of these five hundred years. The last half millennium has attempted to suppress all forms of protest and alternative expressions of life, love, and sexuality. In whatever form, we as lesbians and gay men of color have a connection with all social protest that clamors for freedom of expression. Our identity as political activists may be different from that of five hundred years ago, but let us not be arrogant. We may not have the last word on how life should be lived, and we certainly have a lot to say about how it shouldn't, beginning with our struggle against racism, sexism, and homophobia.

Survival Is the Least of My Desires

KEYNOTE ADDRESS

MARCH 20, 1992

I was asked to speak about survival. The difficulty for me is that survival is the least of my desires. I'm interested in a lot more than mere survival. And I do not feel old enough or smart enough to be able to tell other lesbian and gay writers how to survive, much less to send everyone out of this place feeling inspired, provoked, challenged, and determined—to convince people that we, as a community, are capable of so much more than endurance. What I do know is that we must aim much higher than just staying alive if we are to begin to approach our true potential.

I am part of a nation that is not secret but rarely recognized. Born poor, queer, and despised, I have always known myself one of many—strong not because I was different but because I was part of a nation just like me, human and fragile and stubborn and hungry for justice in an unjust world. I am past forty now. I have known I was a lesbian since I was a teenager, known I wanted to write almost as long.

My age, my family background, the region and class in which I grew up, and yes, my times—the political and moral eras I have come through—have shaped me. I was the first person in my family to graduate from high school, the first to go to college. It is hard for me to explain what an extraordinary thing that was: to be not only the first but for a long time the only one of my people to step outside the tight hostile world in which we were born. But I went to college in the early seventies, and I had the great good fortune of being there at a time when lots of other working-class kids were also confronting a world in which we were barely acknowledged. That experience spurred in me, as in many of us, an outrage and determination that questioned accepted barriers of authority, validation, rightness. I became convinced that to survive I would have to remake the world so that it came closer to matching its own ideals.

In college, I was involved in civil rights activism and antiwar demonstrations. I became a feminist activist when other people my age were marrying or joining the Peace Corps or starting careers. All those things that they were doing that I did not do shaped my life, what I thought I could do with my life. Understand me; I am one of those dangerous ones. I have never wanted to be rich. I have always wanted a great deal more. I have always wanted to remake the world, and that is a much greedier, far-reaching ambition than cash. I joined a small nation of would-be revolutionaries, queers and feminists and working-class escapees—dreamers, most of us, who wanted a world in which no one was denied justice, no one was hated for their origins, color, beliefs, or sexuality. Though it is rarely acknowledged, people like me have remade this world in the last few decades.

Let me be clear how much has changed in the short span of my life. Although there are few people who think of themselves as revolutionaries anymore, the world has been remade. Look around you. Apartheid is being dismantled, and Nelson Mandela walks the streets of South Africa. Until a few years ago, I could not imagine that happening. Russia is a new place; so is China. The communist bogeyman I was threatened with throughout my childhood is gone. The world is no less dangerous, and people are still dying for their origins, beliefs, color, and sexuality, but I find myself full of startled awe and hope. The rigid world into which I was born has been shaken profoundly. *Homosexual* is no longer a psychiatric disorder, and my lover and I actually married each other down at city hall in San Francisco last spring.

The world is a new place, but it still needs to be remade. We still need revolutionaries. It was more than ten years ago that the first person I knew personally died of AIDS. Last year I lost four more friends, four more of the many who should not have died. This last year my lover's ex-girlfriend turned up in jail after living on the streets for two years, my last aunt followed my mother into death by cancer, and I went through each day without health insurance, knowing that most likely, I, too, will die of cancer before I am sixty. Half of the people I know live without health insurance or the certainty of a living wage. The world needs to be remade. The brilliant, talented, young gay men and lesbian writers in my life earn barely enough to pay their rent, much less buy the time they need to write the books I want to read. We live, all of us, in the most impossible conflict, poor because of the work we choose to do, the lies we choose not to tell. Most of us know that sending applications to the National Endowment for the Arts or well-funded grants committees is like throwing a snowball into the sun. Our own organizations—our presses, magazines, bookstores, and writing programs—barely survive. Oh yes, the world needs to be remade.

If we, as writers, are to continue, we need more people of large ambition; people who refuse censorship, denial, and hatred; people who still hope to change the world—writers who see themselves as revolutionaries, who turn up at demonstrations or envelope-stuffing parties with the shadows under their eyes that prove how many nights they've gotten up, after a limited sleep, to hone their skills and dream on the page the remade world.

I have lived my life in pursuit of the remade world.

When I was twenty-two, I helped organize a rape crisis center. That same year, I was involved in starting a feminist bookstore, staffing a women's center, volunteering as a lesbian peer counselor, teaching a feminist anthropology course, editing a feminist magazine, trying to organize a waitress union, and organizing a lesbian-feminist living collective that became my family and home for eight years. I did all of that before I was twenty-four, telling myself that if only I could give up more sleep, I could get so much more done. These days, I look around and I think we need a few more people willing to give up a little sleep.

Except for the fact that I lived for eight years in that lesbian-feminist collective, I am like most other lesbians I know, the women I love. I have always written after everything else was done, in spare moments after filling in at the childcare center, or building shelves for the bookstore, or preparing grant applications, first for the women's center and then the women's studies department and then the magazines. I have worked with four feminist magazines. None of them still survive.

When I was twenty-four, I read everything written by lesbians—and when I was twenty-four, it was still possible. I rarely dealt with men, rarely contacted my family, was strictly nonmonogamous, wrote bad poetry when I was too tired to sleep, and taught myself, laboriously, to write fiction in short snatches of time stolen from my day job. I edited other people's writing for long years before I published my own. I didn't publish anything until I began to think I might be good enough. And to put it frankly, by my own standards, I am still rarely good enough. What I want—my ambition—is larger than anyone imagines. I want to be able to write so powerfully I can break the heart of the world and heal it. I want to write in such a way as to literally remake the world, to change people's thinking as they look out of the eyes of the characters I create.

I am and always have been completely matter-of-fact about being a lesbian. The statements of gay writers who defensively insist that they wish to be seen as writers first and gay or lesbian secondarily, who insist they simply happen to be queer, that being queer has nothing to do with what or how they write; the arguments that take place between those writers and those others who despise the first category, who take their sexual identities as their primary subject and the underlying factor for their aesthetic—those loud insistent arguments seem to me mostly intellectual, beside the point, and curiously old-fashioned. I have never imagined that there was any question about my sexual preference, and as a feminist, I know that my convictions shape what I write about, what voice I can manifest, and what kinds of characters I will imagine—what I can write at all. I am one whole person, one whole person who is a lesbian and a writer.

When I listened to Edward Albee speak at the second OutWrite conference in San Francisco in 1991, I kept thinking that the times and the ethos that had shaped his concept of who he was—both as a gay man and as a writer—were not so maddening as tragic. That it was first and foremost a waste that he had spent so much of his life in a defensive struggle to claim himself and his sexuality in the face of an ignorant and hateful public. Worse, it seemed that fighting so hard for that sexuality had left him bitterly ignorant of how interlinked the struggles for gay rights and human rights are, unable to see how much the struggle for other people's hopes is related to his own. If we are forced to talk about our lives, our sexuality, and our work only in the language and categories of a society that despises us, eventually we will be unable to speak past our own griefs. We will disappear into those categories. What I have tried to do in my own life is refuse the language and categories that would reduce me to less than my whole complicated experience. At the same time, I have tried to look at people different from me with the kind of compassion I would like to have directed toward me.

When I think about that generation of writers that Edward Albee is part of, I become more determined to remake the world. I work to make it possible for young queer writers not to have to waste so much of themselves fighting off hatred and dismissal of an ignorant majority. But to make any contribution to other lives, I know that I must first begin in the carefully examined specifics of my own. I must acknowledge who has helped me survive and how my own hopes have been shaped. I must acknowledge the miracles in my life.

Yes, I have been shaped as a lesbian and a writer by miracles— miracles as in wonders and marvels and astonishing accidents, fortunate juxtapositions and happy encounters, some resulting from work and luck but others unexplained and unexplainable. It was a miracle that I survived my childhood to finish high school and get that scholarship to college. It was a miracle that I discovered feminism and found that I did not have to be ashamed of who I was. Feminism gave me the possibility of understanding my place in the world, and I claim it as a title and an entitlement.

But feminism, for me, was not only about sex. Sexual desire was more problematic. When I was very young, I imagined that I would have to be celibate. I knew what I wanted from the first flush of puberty. I knew what I wanted to do with those girls in school. And all around me, I saw fear and death and damnation. You cannot imagine how terrified I was at twelve and thirteen. I decided I would become a kind of Baptist nun. That seemed a reasonable choice after my family moved to Central Florida and I sneaked off to the gay bar down near the Trailways bus station in Orlando, Florida. I took one look at those women and knew I was in a lot of trouble. I knew, pretty much from the beginning, what was going to happen to me. I knew I was femme, opinionated, bossy, completely romantically masochistic and that those girls were going to eat me alive.

So the choice was to be eaten alive or to become celibate.

It's a wonder there's a scrap of me left.

It was a miracle that I figured out what it was I enjoyed sexually that did not require my partner to be crazy drunk, to be violently angry, or to acquire permanent rights to my body just because she knew how to make me come. It was a miracle that I kept on writing fiction for my own satisfaction even when I truly believed in the women's revolution and was completely convinced it would never come about if I didn't personally raise money for it, staff the phones, and cook the protein dish for the potluck where we would all plan it. Miracles, incidental and marvelous, women and men, met at the right time or just past it but still soon enough to save me from giving up or doing myself more damage than I could survive.

I cling to no organized religion, but I believe in the continuing impact of miracles.

Finally, I have to tell you that it was a miracle I did not kill myself out of sheer despair when I was told I was too lesbian for feminism, too reformist for radical feminism, too sexually perverse for respectable lesbianism, and too damn stubborn for the women's, gay, and queer revolutions. That I am here now, writing and speaking and teaching and living out my own feminist ideals, is astonishing. I have changed nothing. The world has been remade.

I believe in the truth. I believe in the truth in the way only a person who has been denied any use of it can believe in it. I know its power. I know the threat it represents to a world constructed on lies. I believe in any trick that keeps you writing the truth is all right but that some tricks are more expensive than others. The one I have used most often and most successfully is that gambit in which I pretend that I am the only one person trying to get down my version of what happened. My writing becomes fiction soon enough anyway. The truth is wider than the details of what really happened in my life.

I know the myths of the family that thread through our society's literature, music, politics—and I know the reality. The reality is that for many of us, family was as much the incubator of despair as the safe nurturing haven the myths promised. We are not supposed to talk about our real family lives, especially if our families do not duplicate the mythical heterosexual model. In a world in which only a fraction of people actually live in that *Father Knows Best* nuclear family, in which the largest percentage of families consists of women and children existing in poverty, we need to hear a lot more about those of us who are happy that we do not live inside that mythical model. But I also believe in hope. I believe in the remade life; the possibilities inherent in our lesbian and gay chosen families, our families of friends and lovers; the healing that can take place among the most wounded of us. My family of friends has kept me alive through lovers who have left, enterprises that have failed, and all too many stories that never got finished. That family has been part of remaking the world for me.

The worst thing done to us in the name of a civilized society is to label the truth of our lives' material outside the legitimate subject matter of serious writers. We are not supposed to talk about our sexuality, not in any more than the most general and debased terms, our passions reduced to addictions or the subject of poorly thought-out theories of deviance and compulsion, our legendary loving relationships rewritten as the bland interactions of best friends or interlocking systems of dependence and necessary economic solutions.

I need you to do more than survive. As writers, as revolutionaries, tell the truth, your truth, in your own way. Do not buy into their systems of censorship, imagining that if you drop this character or hide that emotion, you can slide through their blockades. Do not eat your own heart out in the hope of pleasing them. The only hope you have, the only hope any of us has, is the remade life. It is the only way we will all survive, and trading any of us for some of us is no compromise. It is the way we will lose our lives, all our lives.

The second worse thing done to us is a thing we do to each other. We ask each other to always represent our sexuality and relationships as simple, straightforward, and lifesaving. We want to hear heroic stories, legends where the couples find each other in the end and go off into the sunset, with the one distinction that they are the same gender arm in arm and lip-locked into the next dawn. We need our romances—yes, our happy endings. But don't gloss over the difficulties and rewrite the horrors. Don't make it easier than it is and soften the tragedies. Don't pretend we are not really murdered in the streets or broken in the darkened bedrooms of the American family. We need the truth. And yes, it is hard when fighting for your life and the lives of those you love to admit just how daunting that fight can be; to acknowledge how many of us are lost, how many destroyed; to pick apart the knots of fantasy and myth that blunt our imaginations and stalk our hopes for families in which we can trust each other and the future. But if I am to survive, I need to be able to trust your stories, to know that you will not lie even to comfort.

I believe the secret in writing is that fiction never exceeds the reach of the writers' courage. The best fiction comes from the place where the terror hides, the edge of our worst stuff. I believe, absolutely, that if you do not break out in that sweat of fear when you write, then you have not gone far enough. And I know you can fake that courage when you don't think of yourself as courageous—because I have done it. I know that until I started pushing on my own fears, telling the stories that were hardest for me, writing about exactly the things I was most afraid of and unsure about, I wasn't writing worth a damn.

I write what I think are "moral tales." That's what I intend, though I grow more and more to believe that telling the emotional truth of people's lives, not necessarily the historical truth, is the only moral use of fiction. I'll give you an example. The historical truth about the child on whom I based my character Shannon Pearl is that she went on, a child of her culture, and lives that life still, as far as I know, back in Greenville, though the child I remember knew nothing about gospel music. I gave her that life to make a larger story. But what is emotionally true is that she was someone I thought of as squeezed down, her soul like a pearl compressed as tight and white as cold stone. Maybe the "truer" story of her life would be a better one than "Gospel Song," but I give myself the benefit of the doubt. This was the story I could write then, and it is as true as I could make it. Its veracity lies in the complexity of the character, that she is hated and hateful, that she is not a nice but a tragic person. I do not write about nice people. Neither is anyone I have ever cared deeply about. The truth about our lives is not nice, and acknowledging that allows me to make the people in my stories more whole, to truly honor those I have lost. It's something I am not always able to do as well as I would like. But wanting this in my stories is about wanting myself whole.

Some of my stories that read hard from the outside are much easier in the writing, stories fueled entirely by rage. Anger is easy. Most of my short story collection, *Trash*, was written in rage. If I'd done it more in grief, it might have been a better book, but I needed to work through the rage first. Sooner or later, though, if you keep pushing yourself, you begin writing stories out of more than rage, and they begin to tear you apart even as you write them. Oddly enough, that tearing open makes possible a healing not only in the writer but in the world as well. It is as if you were opening up scar tissue and allowing new growth. The easiest story for me to write is the one in which I sit down in front of the imaginary image of the one person I have always ached to say something to—my stepfather, or my mother, or my first lover—and I begin the story by saying, "You son of a bitch . . ." That's easy. I let the anger tell the story. The harder stories are the ones where I begin with grief or the attempt to understand, the stories that start with "I'm sorry," or even "I was so ashamed," or "Goddamn, I miss you so much."

I want hard stories. I demand them from myself. I demand them from my students and friends and colleagues. Hard stories are worth the difficulty. It seems to me the only way I have forgiven anything, understood anything, is through that process of opening up to my own terror and pain and reexamining it, recreating it in the story, and making it something different, making it meaningful—even if the meaning is only in the act of the telling. Some things are absolutely unjust, without purpose, horrible and blinding, soul destroying: the death of the beloved, the rape of a child—situations some of us know all too well. There was no meaning in what my stepfather did to me. But the stories I have made out of it do have meaning. More importantly, those stories do not function as some form of retribution. They are redress for all those like me, whether they can write their own stories or not. My stories are not *against* anyone; they are *for* the life we need.

It has taken me twenty years to be able to write what I write now, but what I wrote nineteen years ago was just as important. There's an essay by Ursula Le Guin that I love where she talks about the importance of women offering their own experience as wisdom, how each individual perception is vital.[4] That's what I believe to be the importance of telling the truth, each of us writing out of the unique vision our lives have given us. It is the reason I urge young writers I work with to confront their own lives in their fiction. Not that they must write autobiography, but that they must use the whole of their lives in the making of the stories they tell; they must honor their dead, their wounded and lost; they must acknowledge their own crimes and shame, feel the impact of what they do and do not do in the world of their stories. I tell them they must take the business of storytelling completely seriously. I want the stories I read to take me over, to make me see people I do not know as they see themselves—the scared little girl who grew up lesbian, the faggot child who loved and hungered for truth, the young dying unjustly and too soon who talk about death familiarly and make me laugh at my own fear. Each of us has our own bitterness, our own fear, and that stubborn tenderness we are famous for. Each of us has our own stories, and none of them are the same no matter how similar some of the details. Tell me the truth and I make you a promise. If you show me yours, I'll show you mine. That's what writers do for each other.

Write your stories any way you have to frame it to get it out, any time you can get it done. Use any trick. I want to know what it was that you looked at unflinchingly, even if you did not know what you were seeing at the time. If nothing else works, start by writing that story for me. Imagine me. I was born to die. I know that. If I could have found what I needed at thirteen, I would not have lost so much of my life chasing vindication or death. Give some child, some thirteen-year-old, the hope of the remade life. Tell the truth. Write the story that you were always afraid to tell. I swear to you there is magic in it, and if you show yourself naked for me, I'll be naked for you. It will be our covenant.

---

4. Ursula Le Guin, "The Fisherman's Daughter," in *Dancing at the Edge of the World* (New York: Grove, 1989), 212–240.

I tell people that I write mean stories, and I do—stories that tell the truth that I know and only the part I know because I don't know that much. I know about being queer in this decade, about the grief inherent in losing so many friends, so many memories, so many members of our precious remade families. I have no aunts left to tell me stories, and three-quarters of the young gay men whom I worked with and learned to love when I first began to write are gone, along with far too many of the lesbians.

AIDS and cancer have run through my community—not metaphors but death in wholesale numbers. Sections of my life have disappeared with the ones we have lost, and I feel great pressure to write the stories that would somehow preserve those times, those people, my friends: John Fox, Mary Helen Mautner, Allen Barnett, Geoff Mains, Vito Russo, Cynthia Slater, George Stambolian, and too many more to list in anything less than a massive memorial. Just my personal friends who have died, the list is too long. How can I not write mean stories? I don't have that child's easy hope for better times that fueled so much of my early stories. I have fallen in love with the hard side, with the women and men made tough by life and loss, who nonetheless have never lost their determined love for their own kind. If I am not mean enough to honor them, then I have no right to the stories.

I need you to write mean stories. I need you to honor our dead, to help them survive. More than ten years ago, I wrote a poem about a lesbian who died in Boston, a death I read about in the paper and knew immediately could have been my own. The death of a woman who "might not have been known to be a lesbian" but who, as I read her poem in public, I learned more and more about until I was certain that not only her death but her life could have been my own and that very likely she, too, would have wanted the mean story her life told. I made a mean piece of hope out of telling about her because I believe that if I died that death someone would sing my song, recount my story.

More and more of what I write now I write in homage to those we have lost. To do more than survive, that is what we need, what I need from you. I need you to tell the truth, to tell the mean stories, and to sing the song of hope. I need all of us to live forever and to remake the world. Listen again to the words of my poem, and remember the life it honors, the remade life denied to one of us:

Boston, Massachusetts, many years ago
a woman told me about a woman dead,
a woman who might not have been known
to be a lesbian.

No one is sure they knew that.
The cops didn't say that, they said
she was wearing a leather jacket, blue jeans, worn boots
had dark cropped hair and was new to the neighborhood,
living in an old brick rowhouse with three other women.
Said she was carrying a can of gasoline.
They did not say why,
a car waiting
a jar of sticky brushes.
Said she was white
her friends were white
the neighborhood was bad,
she and her friends were fools
didn't belong there
were queer anyway.
Said the young rough crowd of men
laughed a lot
when they stopped her
that she laughed back,
and then
they made her pour the gasoline
over her head.

Later, some cop said
she was a hell of a tough bitch

'cause she walked two blocks on her own feet,
two blocks to the all-night grocery
where another little crowd watched
going
    Shiiiiiiit!
    Will you look at that?
    Look at that!

I read about it in the paper—two paragraphs
I have carried that story with me ever since
wanting more, wanting no one to have to be
those two stark paragraphs.

We become our deaths.
Our names disappear and our lovers leave town,
heartbroken, crazy,
but we are the ones who die.
We are forgotten
burning in the streets
hands out, screaming,
    This is not all I am.
    I had something else in mind to do.

Not on that street,
always and only that
when there was so much more she had to do.

Sometimes
when I love my lover
I taste in my mouth

    ashes
    gritty
    grainy

grating between the teeth
the teeth of a woman
unquestionably known
to be a lesbian.[5]

5. Allison published this essay in *Skin: Talking about Sex, Class & Literature* (Ithaca, NY: Firebrand Books, 1994), 209–223; the final poem is "Boston, Massachusetts," which is in Dorothy Allison, *The Women Who Hate Me* (Ithaca, NY: Firebrand Books, 1991), 55–57.

Speaking a World into Existence

WORKSHOP PRESENTATION

MARCH 21, 1992

March is the windy season in the country I come from, a season of warm days and cold nights.[1] Or cold days and cold nights. Clouds, chased in from the Gulf of California, drop their load of moisture over the highest peaks in Arizona. Snow falls above seven thousand feet, but along the lower elevations of the Rio Grande, the fruit trees are beginning to blossom. And overhead, the sandhill cranes are in the early stages of their incredible migration back to the Arctic. You can hear them crying out as they wing their way above the bosque, the swath of cottonwood, Russian olive, and saltbush that grow for hundreds of miles along the sandy river.

The bosque is an ecological zone that houses great numbers of migrating birds and waterfowl, various reptiles, and small mammals, such as beaver and coyote. It's a fragile environment and, where I live, under attack by developers and the U.S. Army Corps of Engineers, who want to build bridges across the Rio Grande to speed the flow of traffic to and from the growing west side of the city of Albuquerque. Some of the most beautiful old cottonwoods

---

1. Janice Gould presented this speech at the panel "Language and Imagery of Lesbian Poetry." The panel also featured Rachel Guido DeVries, and Susan Sherman moderated. The program book describes the panel as answering this question: "What, if anything, makes poetry by lesbians lesbian poetry?" Gould published the speech (presumably slightly edited) in *Women's Review of Books* 9, no. 10/11 (July 1992): 12, with the title given here.

have fallen to the chainsaws, and their roots have been plowed under by bulldozers. The changes made to the bosque are irreparable.

By the time I hear the sandhill cranes over Albuquerque, they have been flying for some time from the Bosque del Apache, where they winter. And as I begin writing this essay on lesbian poetry, I am wondering why I fastened on these birds and this place as a way of getting into the material. Is it appropriate? Is that great chevron of birds heading north a symbol for my own desires to fly out of range, out of sight, far away? If so, am I being responsible to my own deeper instincts of ritual and renewal, or am I irresponsibly wishing not to stand up before a crowd of people who expect interesting, and possibly important, words? Or is the imagining of the bosque—that narrow strip along the river that has narrowed even more in "historical" times—is that threatened and naturally constituted area a symbol of other kinds of communities at peril in these hard economic and politically repressive times? How does the imagination work? Specifically, how does the imagination of a mixed-blood Native American lesbian in her forties work?

In some ways, asking that question is like asking where poetry comes from. What is the source of our imagery? What is the source of our language? People have been asking these questions since long before Plato. But probably in non-Western societies, those questions hold a lot less relevance than they do in this culture because what is assumed about how the world is constructed is based in an entirely different logic and experience of reality.

Plato could ask these questions because he had already decided that this reality is a mere shadow of the ideal. The first step in setting up a well-ordered society, he declared, was to create infallible standards of excellence and inferiority. Anything that smacked of fancy, blurred distinctions between good and evil, or suggested instability and mutability in the all-powerful divine was to be considered inferior and exiled from the state. And a mind that could separate, label, and categorize orders of lies and truth, fiction and fact, the real and the ideal, was superior to a mind that had not been trained to work in this way. Indeed, in Plato's *Republic*, the training of the mind had to begin in infancy, and the only way to do that was to constrain the oral tradition, to constrain the first tellers of songs and stories, those "casual persons" who tell the children "casual tales." And who were those "casual persons"? They were, of course, the children's mothers and nurses.

It is important to understand how deeply the oral tradition has been excised from Western culture and what that excision has to do with the valuing of one type of mind over others. We are carefully taught to distinguish not only between types of mind but between different states of mind, as we call them, between thought and emotion, between knowledge and imagination. The dream world, we learn, is a product of our ever-industrious fancy, which, like a workaholic, continues to figure out at night those things we couldn't deal with during the day. The dream, then, is a reflection of our psyches, not an actual world in which we can participate.

Yet in many tribal cultures, which are oral cultures, the dream is a source of knowledge and power. Among many American Indian tribes, for example, the dream could instigate life changes of enormous magnitude that could reestablish one's entire relationship to the community. Among California tribes, and especially in the desert regions along the old river systems where the tribes farmed for corn and beans, dreaming was a well-cultivated art. A child could dream of becoming a shaman, a ritual healer of the sick, with the help of one or another spirit creature, like buzzard, or tarantula, or homyavre, "the bug who causes the mirage."[2] A girl child could dream of becoming a great warrior and taking a wife. Or a boy child could dream of becoming a woman and of participating in the cyclical rounds of gathering and production that women practiced as the ground of community and well-being.

Such dreams were respected and adhered to, especially if they fit other patterns of behavior that parents could observe. And I

---

2. Malcom Margolin, *The Way We Lived: California Indian Reminiscences, Stories and Songs* (Berkeley, CA: Heyday Books, 1981), 115.

would guess that in those cultures that tolerated and even approved of the *berdache*, as the males who practiced female activities and wore female dress were called by anthropologists, there were oral roots to the tradition that explained the presence of the person who was considered to be "two-spirited," or of a third gender. Among the Navajo, for example, Nadle was such a person, created in time immemorial. When the men and women separated in the long-ago time, it is said, Nadle went between each group, satisfying both for a time and him- or herself as well, no doubt. For with the men, she was a woman, and with the women, he was a man.

Many gay and lesbian American Indian writers have looked to the tradition of the *berdache* as a source of power and inspiration. And to look to this phenomenon is to see it in the context of great and complex oral traditions whose stories emerge from time immemorial. These stories tell of a time in which the powers of life were very close to the surface of reality. The purpose of ritual, ceremony, and prayer is to open ourselves to that power, to bring into our everyday existence the knowledge and memory of that time, to reinvoke it and reparticipate in it. And the gate through which we enter the dream world, the world of time immemorial, the place of inception, conception, and perception, is language. For without language, there are no stories; there is no speaking and singing the world into existence.

Now, you may be asking yourselves, What has this to do with the language and images in lesbian poetry? I would answer that many of us writing today, especially if we are lesbians of color, have turned consciously or unconsciously to the roots of an older tradition. Consciously or unconsciously, we form our speech, which ultimately becomes our writing, along lines that invariably produce a world counter to the world our bodies painfully experience and inhabit.

The Western mind, through which we have been colonized and by which our land, labor, and lives have been robbed and exploited, is as uncomfortable with us as we are uncomfortable with it. The

Western mind has labeled our thinking illogical, random, evil, and superstitious. It has guarded itself against us by outlawing our languages, customs, dress, and sacred practices. And if you don't think this happens anymore, look at the recent Supreme Court decision about the ritual use of peyote in the case of *Employment Division v. Smith.*[3] The First Amendment does not protect members of the Native American Church in states whose legislatures have passed general drug laws prohibiting the use of peyote. Think about it: peyote and other sacred plants, such as tobacco, were given to and used by Indians since the first people emerged into this world or were breathed into existence by the creators. Their use helped us understand power and helped us access that power for the good of the people. The use of these plants clearly did not constitute the fetishistic, obsessive, and personal-use patterns that we see today or the first-contact Europeans would have found American Indians riddled with lung cancer and drug addiction.

I would suggest that any time a group of people participates in an antilinear thinking, any time a group of people practices customs and beliefs contrary to the norm, any time a group of people begins to speak negatively and unflatteringly of God and the state, any time a group of people organizes itself into a cohesive whole with a language that tells the truth as it knows it and experiences it—and calls that language art, poetry, song, sculpture, work, study, lovemaking, child-rearing, or what have you—then the powers that be order in the troops. And the troops stand guard, infiltrate, imprison, and in various ways attempt to control all of those who would subvert the "natural" order of things, the construction of the world as we know it today: patriarchal and imperious, bloated on its own self-importance, pompous, cruel, and dominating.

Lesbian images and language, especially the images and language of lesbians of color—because we have lost more than many

3. Robert Allen Warrior, "Forget 1492. What about 1992?," *Progressive* 56, no. 3 (March 1992): 18–19.

others—may be some of the most subversive texts being written today. It isn't just the challenge to the state's notions of normalcy as represented by someone like Jesse Helms. Our challenge to authority does not come alone in the area of reimagining and reconstituting our sexuality. For years now we have reconstituted on some level the family, the community, the schools, and perhaps even the military. The meaning and value of these institutions have come under scrutiny and reevaluation and change by those of us who have functioned in and survived them. We lesbian writers have taken it as our responsibility to articulate our survivals and transformations in this war on our integrity.

We represent a challenge to the Western way of thinking at a primal level. The more we tap into those tribal roots and quench our thirst on the milk and honey of our mother tongue, the more we can withstand the shock of living in this deadly and soul-annihilating system. We have to scramble their messages and learn to read the code we devise out of it. We have to go into the place of the great solitary vision of our own being—a being intimately attached to and integrated with the net of all being and beings—and humble ourselves and ask for a song, a vision, a dream, a language that promotes and heals, that nurtures and provides. We have to humble ourselves, perhaps before the little bug that causes the mirage or before the northern flight of birds, on whose shiny backs we may find the words that ensure our survival and the survival of those who come after us.

I'll Be Somewhere
Listening for My Name

KEYNOTE ADDRESS

MARCH 22, 1992

This speech, delivered in 1992, contains several instances of the word nigger. *Rutgers University Press does not condone usage of this word and does not reprint it without careful thought. In this instance, the word is used by an African-American gay man to express generational trauma of racism, LGBTQ violence, and AIDS.*

When He calls me, I will answer
When He calls me, I will answer
When He calls me, I will answer
I'll be somewhere listening for my name
I'll be somewhere listening.[1]

As gay men and lesbians, we are the sexual niggers of our society. Some of you may have never before been treated like a second-class, disposable citizen. Some of you have felt a certain privilege and protection in being white, which is not to say that others are accustomed to or have accepted being racial niggers and feel less alienated. Since I have never encountered a person of no color, I assume that we are all persons of color. Like fashion victims, though, we are led to believe that some colors are more acceptable than others, and those acceptable colors have been so endowed

---

1. At the plenary, Dixon sang these lines.

Melvin Dixon (*Photo credit: Courtesy of the Bromfield Street Educational Foundation records at the Northeastern University Library's Archives and Special Collections.*)

with universality and desirability that the color hardly seems to exist at all—except, of course, to those who are of a different color and pushed outside the rainbow. My own fantasy is to be locked inside a Benetton ad.

No one dares call us sexual niggers, at least not to our faces. But the epithets can be devastating or entertaining: We are faggots and dykes, sissies and bulldaggers. We are funny, sensitive, Miss Thing, friends of Dorothy, or men with "a little sugar in the blood," and we call ourselves what we will—as an anthropologist/linguist friend of mine calls me in one breath, "Miss Lady Sister Woman Honey Girl Child."

Within this environment of sexual and racial niggerdom, recovery isn't easy. Sometimes it is like trying to fit a size twelve basketball player's foot into one of Imelda Marcos's pumps. The color might be right, but the shoe still pinches. Or, for the more fashionable lesbians in the audience, lacing up those combat boots only to have extra eyelets staring you in the face, and you feel like Olive Oyl gone trucking after Minnie Mouse.

As for me, I've become an acronym queen: BGM ISO same or other. HIV plus or HIV minus. CMV, PCP, MAI, AZT, ddl, ddC. Your prescription gets mine.

Remember those great nocturnal emissions of your adolescent years? They told us we were men, and the gooey stuff proved it. Now in the 1990s, our nocturnal emissions are night sweats, inspiring fear, telling us we are mortal and sick and that time is running out.

In my former neighborhood in Manhattan, I was a member of the 4H club: the happy homosexuals of Hamilton Heights. Now it is the 3D club: the dead, the dying, those in despair. I used to be in despair; now I'm just dying.

I come to you bearing witness to a broken heart; I come to you bearing witness to a broken body—but a witness to an unbroken spirit. Perhaps it is only to you that such witness can be brought and its jagged edges softened a bit and made meaningful. We are facing the loss of our entire generation. Lesbians lost to various cancers; gay men lost to AIDS. What kind of witness will you bear? What truth telling are you brave enough to utter and endure the consequences of your unpopular message?

Last summer my lover Richard died. We had been lovers for twelve years. His illness and death were so much a part of my illness and life that I felt that I, too, had died. I'm just back from Florida, visiting his family and attending the unveiling of his headstone. Later this month, our attorney will file the necessary papers for the settling of Richard's estate, and I shall return to our summer home in Provincetown without him but not without the rich memories of our many years there. And he is everywhere inside me listening for his name.

I've lost Richard. I've lost vision in one eye. I've lost the contact of people I thought were friends. I've lost the future tense from my vocabulary, I've lost my libido, and I've lost more weight and appetite than Nutrisystem would want to claim.

My life is closing. Oh, I know all the clichés: "We all have to die" and "Everything comes to an end." But when is an ending a closure, and when does closure become a new beginning? Not always. It is not automatic. We have to work at it. If an end is termination, closure involves the will to remember, which gives new life to memory.

As creators, we appear to strike a bargain with the immortality we assume to be inherent in art. Our work exists outside us and will have a life independent of us. Doris Grumbach, in her recent book *Coming into the End Zone*, reminds us of the life of books: "Let the book make its own way, even through the thick forest of competitors, compelling readers by the force of its words and its vision."[2]

I am reminded of a poignant line from George Whitmore, who stuck a Faustian bargain with AIDS: If he wrote about it, perhaps he wouldn't get it. George, as you know, lost that battle, but his books are still with us. His two novels are *The Confessions of Danny Slocum* and *Nebraska*. His harrowing reporting on AIDS is called *Someone Was Here*. And now George is somewhere listening for his name, hearing it among us.

I am not above bargaining for time and health. And I am troubled by the power of prophecy inherent in art. One becomes afraid to write because one's wildest speculations may in fact come true. I wrote all the AIDS poems published in Michael Klein's *Poets for Life* before I knew I was HIV positive. I was responding in part to my sense of isolation and helplessness as friends of mine fell ill. And when I published the poem "And These Are Just a Few" in the *Kenyon Review*, I made a point of acknowledging the dead and those yet fighting for life. I'm sorry to report that of the twenty people mentioned in the poem, only two are presently alive.

As writers, we are a curious lot. We begin our projects with much apprehension about the blank page. But then as the material assumes its life, we resist writing that last stanza or paragraph. We want to avoid putting a final period to it all. Readers are no better.

---

2. Doris Grumbach, *Coming into the End Zone* (New York: W. W. Norton, 1991).

We all want to know what new adventures await Huck Finn or if Ishmael finally "comes out" following his "marriage" with Queequeg. As sequels go, I'm not sure the world needed Ripley's extension to *Gone with the Wind*, but consider *Rocky 10*, in which the son of the erstwhile fighter discovers he is gay and must take on the archvillain Harry Homophobia. Would the title have to be changed to Rockette?

Then there is the chilling threat of erasure.

Gregory, a friend and former student of mine, died last fall. On the day following a memorial service for him, we all were having lunch and laughing over our fond memories of Greg and his many accomplishments as a journalist. Suddenly his lover had a shock. He had forgotten the remaining copies of the memorial program in the rental car he had just returned. Frantic to retrieve the programs, which had Greg's picture on the cover and reprints of his autobiographical essays inside, his lover called the rental agency to reclaim the material. They had already cleaned the car, but he could come out there, they said, and dig through the dumpster for whatever he could find. Hours later, the lover returned empty-handed, the paper programs already shredded, burned, the refuse carted away. Greg had been cremated once again, but this time without remains or a classy urn to house them. The image of Greg's lover sifting through the dumpster is more haunting than the reality of Greg's death, for Greg had made his peace with the world. The world, however, had not made its peace with him.

His siblings refused to be named in one very prominent obituary, and Greg's gayness and death from AIDS were not to be mentioned at the memorial service. Fortunately, few of us heeded the family's prohibition. While his family and society may have wanted to dispose of Greg even after his death, some of us tried to reclaim him and love him again and only then release him.

I was reminded of how vulnerable we are as gay men, as Black gay men, to the disposal or erasure of our lives.

But Greg was a writer, a journalist who had written on AIDS, on the business world, and on his own curious life journey from his birth in the poor Anacostia district of Washington, DC, to scholarships that allowed him to attend Exeter and then Williams College and on to the city desks of our nation's most prominent newspapers. His words are still with us, even if his body and those gorgeous programs are gone. And Greg is somewhere listening for his name.

We must, however, guard against the erasure of our experience and our lives. As white gays become more and more prominent—and acceptable to mainstream society—they project a racially exclusive image of gay reality. Few men of color will ever be found on the covers of the *Advocate* or *New York Native*. As white gays deny multiculturalism among gays, so too do Black communities deny multisexualism among its members. Against this double cremation, we must leave the legacy of our writing and our perspectives on gay and straight experiences.

Our voice is our weapon.

Several months ago, the editors of *Lambda Book Report* solicited comments from several of us about the future of gay and lesbian publishing. My comments began by acknowledging my grief for writers who had died before they could make a significant contribution to the literature. The editors said my comments suggested a "bleak and nonexistent future" for gay publishing. Although I still find it difficult to imagine a glorious future for gay publishing, that does not mean I cannot offer some concrete suggestion to ensure that a future does exist.

First, reaffirm the importance of cultural diversity in our community. Second, preserve our literary heritage by posthumous publications and reprints, and third, establish grants and fellowships to ensure that our literary history is written and passed on to others. I don't think these comments are bleak, but they should remind us of one thing: we alone are responsible for the preservation and future of our literature.

If we don't buy our books, they won't get published. If we don't talk about our books, they won't get reviewed. If we don't write our books, they won't get written.

As for me, I may not be well enough or alive next year to attend the lesbian and gay writers conference, but I'll be somewhere listening for my name.

I may not be around to celebrate with you the publication of gay literary history. But I'll be somewhere listening for my name.

If I don't make it to Tea Dance in Provincetown or the Pines, I'll be somewhere listening for my name.

You, then, are charged by the possibility of your good health, by the broadness of your vision, to remember us.[3]

---

3. *Callaloo* published a selection from this speech in 2000 with the same title (Melvin Dixon, "I'll Be Somewhere Listening for My Name," *Callaloo* 23, no. 1 [2000]: 80–83); it also is included in *The Melvin Dixon Critical Reader*, ed. Justin A. Joyce and Dwight A. McBride (Jackson: University Press of Mississippi, 2010).

What Fiction Means

KEYNOTE ADDRESS

MARCH 20, 1992

I have something to confess right here up front. Tonight I feel utterly at home. You might think we're in a magnificent wedding cake ballroom full of chandeliers and debutante pretensions. But I spring from a long line of Baptist tent preachers, brothers and sisters. This might look like a Formica podium, but it can become a pulpit so quickly—especially on a Sunday like this; there's just something about Sundays. I feel overwhelmed with my ancestors' spirits. I know I'm supposed to be polite and witty and not offend anybody. But what I really want to do, ladies and gentlemen, moved by the spirit and talent and all the grace and bravery I feel in this room, is "testify," brothers and sisters!

We have so much to say to each other and the world. And as Melvin Dixon just eloquently suggested, we have too little time to say it. Sentimentality should be put aside. It's time to talk about real feelings. It's time to overcome shame, time to tell the truth about our riding out the current plague by writing our way through it.

We are subject to an epidemic still unmentioned by our president. We are governed by politicians proudly unwilling to spend money on researching its cause and cure. Since it first infected Haitians and urban gay men, right-wing legislators are glad to let the virus freely prune those populations.

But let's not get stuck in plain old anger. Anger, brothers and sisters, is a kind of B minus emotion. Anger just bumps you along the

Allan Gurganus. (*Photo credit: Photo by Robert Giard, copyright Estate of Robert Giard.*)

sidewalk. You keep hitting your head and belly while blaming the world. Anger is self-destructive and an amateur's emotion. What we need—and what we all have in our every true sentence—is not mere anger, fellow sexual outlaws, but rage.

Mere anger lets us blame ourselves for our trouble, our history. Rage remains as clear as gin. Rage lifts us up out of the petty woes, including our own mortality. It can make us each a weather satellite. Rage lets us understand that—in the noun *homosexual*—what scares America most is not even the *homo* part. No, it's those closeted three letters: *sex*. From the Salem witch trials forward, America has been terrified of its unadmitted muscular sexuality. And America is terrified of us because we have the muscle and the nerve to see sex as a bonus, not a curse. And we've had the nerve to fight for our right to it, my brave brothers and sisters and my sisters who are brothers and my brothers who are sisters.

As witnesses and poets, as novelists and journalists, we've been battling this disease and that bigotry for more than a decade. As a result, each of us is stronger than most people in the world. We have already survived the fire. We have already survived tribulations that would stop most of our straight brothers and sisters in their tracks. We have seen beautiful kids age a lifetime in two months. We have stood by bedsides. We have changed the sheets. In terms of experience, we are in the stratosphere already. Fellow writers and supplicants and survivors, we are in the stratosphere with our immortal early brothers and sisters: Walt Whitman, Virginia Woolf, Gertrude Stein, Langston Hughes, Tennessee Williams, Oscar Wilde, Michelangelo, Willa Cather, and Caravaggio. The list goes on and on and on: Marcel Proust. Yes. James Baldwin. Absolutely. Zora Neale Hurston. Noël Coward. E. M. Forster.

When I was in the fifth grade, I discovered a novel called *Robinson Crusoe*, and it remains one of the greatest novels ever written. Of course, it's about a man who washes up on an island alone, a man who is cut off from the civilization that made him, a man—like every man and woman in this room—who, instead of despairing, recreated civilization on an island alone and independent.

And after you'd made your island secure, after resigning yourself to an invert's sovereign isolation, do you remember the night you stepped into your first gay bar and saw women dancing with women and men dancing with men? It was as if we had walked through the looking glass and had discovered—each on our separate islands—how many hundreds of thousands and millions of islands combined to form a continent. That joined land mass is here in this room tonight, these hundreds of souls who have given so much to a culture that still grossly undervalues our kind. Well, let me tell you, brothers and sisters, this culture needs us more than we need it.

Yes. Let's tell the truth here. Let's not hold back. There is so much to say. And so little time to say it.

We are each on our separate quest. And when you get home and sit down at your desk come Monday—and I hope it will be on Monday, not next Thursday—I want you to do what I intend to do come Monday morning, which is to unpack not only your energy, not just your intelligence, not only your imagination, but the imagination of that person sitting on your right and on your left now. And I beg you to know that you are not just telling your own story. You are telling our story, and you're telling it, not simply for us and you, but for them. If not for them now, then for later.

There is a kind of beauty and truth in a story that is so much larger than any single intelligence. If you trust your own beginning and middle and end, it will lead you to a kind of wisdom beyond wisdom. The Sphinx's riddle, the central question, the key to all wisdom is simply that people are born, they mature, they age and die. And no sector of American society knows that better than we do now. We, each of us, have a winter black outfit and a summer black suit, stylish and slenderizing but funeral suitable. We, each of us, have become amateur nurses and professional mourners before our time. I, for one, am sick of bad news. I am sick of baring my soul and having my straight friends pat me on the back while seeing this as somehow my responsibility, as somehow our fault. I want to tell stories, not just about us, but about everybody, but I can only do that by starting with the "me" in "us" and ending as the "us" in "me."

In time, the others will understand that what has happened in this country in the last twelve years is the greatest civilian groundswell since abolition helped end slavery. What the current American administration has not done, American citizens have managed. History will remember this and us and our advance-guard angels. We will be named in literature because we refused to stay quiet and passive and polite. We have conquered self-blame, my fellow satellites of angel rage. I know you; you know me; my work is your work. We must read each other, support each other. We must nurse each other. We must bury each other—remember each other and praise each other, in ways bitchy and not. My beloved fellow queers, my sister-brothers and brother-sisters, world without end, our job is turning trouble into meaning, making even a disease yield light and beauty.

There's been something about this weekend that has retired all my usual white-boy, academic jargon. I can't tell you how liberated I feel. Do you know what I mean? There's a sense that we are not simply putting together careers, brothers and sisters. I don't want a career. I want a mission.

I don't want to write mere entertainments. I want to write out of my own experience and out of my own life, a new Bible, a Bible that is useful and, as Melvin Dixon says, useful long after I am so much fog on a coffin lid. I am putting my note in my bottle, on my Robinson Crusoe island, and sending it out into the salty world. And I am goddamned if I am going to pretend to be something I am not. My power, my voice, and the power in your voices come precisely from what society sees as our flaws. Maybe the AIDS crisis will finally prove to straight people that gay people don't spend all their days in gyms and all their nights in bars.

There's a wonderful moment in Oscar Wilde's *The Importance of Being Earnest*. Wilde, that great genius of the late nineteenth century, wrote plays so fresh that a hundred and some years along, they're not merely contemporary—they're futuristic. Let me give you a little sample. Miss Prism, the aged tutor of young Cecily, says, "You must not speak slightingly of the three-volume novel, Cecily, for I wrote one myself in earlier days." Cecily replies, "Did you really, Miss Prism? How wonderfully clever you are! I hope it did not end happily? I don't like novels that end happily. They depress me so much." And Miss Prism responds, "The good ended happily, and the bad unhappily. That is what fiction *means*."

There are people who will tell you that everybody in this room is bad, but I feel such goodness. And there are people who will tell you everybody out of this room is good, but I feel such careless badness there. What are we to make of this inversion?

What are we to make of a society that calls us perverted while offering as exemplars Mr. Kennedy Smith and Clarence Thomas, who will be ruling on our sexual behavior decades from now? These are straight guys who just happened to get caught. And they both then got off scot-free. Unlike Mr. Wilde's fatal years in jail.

The good end happily; the bad unhappily. A complicated notion.

I'm proposing that we invert inversion, brothers and sisters. I'm proposing that we recognize how divinely equipped we are to be writers and artists and moral guides. I am proposing that if you understand what masks are, you understand what identity is (and nobody understands masks better than we who've had to hide all our lives). This is the first day of gay liberation, ladies and gentlemen, and we owe it to all the heroes who've led us till now—many of whom are here today and some of whom will not be here next year. We want to say to them, you will be remembered. We want to say to them, we will build on your example. We want to say to them, your book is a new Bible to us. And your example is pure and hallowed. And you exist in religious relation to our continuing lives.

As artists, we are divinely equipped with sensitivity to style and humor, but we mustn't be mere minstrel entertainers. We mustn't specialize in tuxedoed soft-shoe routines. We mustn't settle. We must go for the complicated truth of being alive in the age of AIDS.

I would like to end by quoting from my own work. And if that seems immodest, it's because I'm trying in my own way to write the same Holy Bible you are. The Bible has many chapters, but it's all Bible, brothers and sisters.

In this particular story, "It Had Wings," a retired lady in her eighties who sold formal clothes to ten mayors' wives is home on

Elm Street on a given Sunday.[1] Her sons are grown and scattered, and she's doing dishes looking out at her own backyard when a naked angel, male, falls near her picnic table.

Interested, she wanders outside wearing her terry cloth robe and slippers, carrying her breakfast mug. She does what anybody would do for an angel, especially a beautiful, pale, uncircumcised angel. She pours warm milk into his angel mouth. And by helping him stand on her barbecue pit, she allows him to ascend once more renewed to heaven. I'm choosing this tale for obvious reasons. There are angels sitting on your left and right who are about to ascend, brothers and sisters. And we have to help them on their way. Angels are among us. You know who you are, and you will know them when you see them. I see them everywhere. We have so much to teach. We have so much to tell. We have so much to celebrate in the community gathered in this room. In a few minutes, you'll take your suitcases and backpacks and laptops elsewhere. And it will never be the same. And it will always be the same. And when you're alone again on your desert island, remember all the rest of us on ours, making it up as we go.

God knows we have subject matter. We have so much to tell the others, if only they could hear us—if only they might understand some of what we've already experienced. In my little story, the aided angel has just ascended into heaven, and the widow wanders back into her cottage, back where she first saw him from her kitchen sink:

> She finishes the breakfast dishes just in time for lunch. This old lady should be famous for all she has been through: today's angel, her scattered sons, her years in sales, she should be famous for her life. She knows things. She has seen so much. She's not famous. Still, she keeps gazing past her kitchen's café curtains, keeps studying her own small tidy yard, the anchor fence, a picnic table, new

---

1. "It Had Wings" was first published in the *Paris Review*, no. 98 (Winter 1985): 12–16. It is collected in Gurganus's collection of short stories *White People* (New York: Vintage, 2000).

Bermuda grass, the barbecue pit. Hands pressed to her sink's cool ledge, she leans nearer a bright window. She seems to be expecting something, expecting something decent. The kitchen clock is ticking, a nearby dog barks to calm itself. And she whispers, mostly to herself, "I'm right here, ready. Ready for more."

Can you guess why this old woman's chin is lifted? Why does she breathe as if to show exactly how it's done? Why should both her shoulders, usually quite bent, brace so square just now? She is guarding the world. Only nobody knows.[2]

---

2. This is adapted from Gurganus's "It Had Wings."

The Gift of Open Sky to Carry You Safely on Your Journey as Writers

KEYNOTE ADDRESS

OCTOBER 8, 1993

I would like to begin my part of this evening by giving you a moment of silence to honor the memories of my dear friends and mentors Audre Lorde and Pat Parker, Black Dykes who died of breast cancer. They have given so much to us and named themselves proud queers long before it was chic to do so. We all are able to write partially because they wrote doors open for us. I invoke their powerful spirits to join us this weekend.

In my language, we say "Megwetch" to mean thank you—Megwetch Nidi Shinook. I have the honor of welcoming you to OutWrite in Boston, where I hope we'll all get laid. I'm not supposed to announce my room number over the microphone.[1]

This is a particular honor for me as a First Nations lesbian activist because I'd expect that many of you don't know about my work, which I define as activism. Writing happens in the cracks of my life. My books are shed snakeskins of my fierce journey toward justice and safety for my people. Though I've been a proud femme Dyke for twenty-seven years, my first concern as an activist is for them. This separates me profoundly from the gay community, which, for the most part, is indifferent to our prisoners of war, the conditions of our lives, and the facts of our existence. We have the highest infant mortality rate in the Western Hemisphere and

---

1. The audience laughed uproariously here.

Chrystos. (*Photo credit: © Lynda Koolish.*)

the highest teenage suicide rate in the world, and the average life span for a Native Nations woman is forty-six years. This year, I will celebrate my forty-seventh birthday with a passion that may be hard for you to imagine because I am the survivor of the death of five lesbians in my family circle from breast cancer, all of whom are Women of Color. And of the sixty original members of Gay American Indians in San Francisco, only ten have survived because of AIDS. I write from a desperation of survival that sees privilege as a barrier to our unity. I don't write to buy a BMW or to be famous. I write literally against the enormous machine of erasure and genocide that is this country's final solution for Native Americans. I would suggest to you that, as we queers become more politically active for groups other than ourselves, we will lose more and more of our complacency, and the United States will have a final solution for queers as well. I am at war with heterosexual colonialization as surely as I am at war against greed and ignorance.

Traditionally, in our Nations, Two Spirited persons were very sacred. Our rules were various. We mediated disputes between men and women, gave names, acted as healers and philosophers and dreamers. In some of our Nations, these roles are active today. As an example, my good friend Wesley Thomas is a traditional Navajo, or Diné, Nádleehí who is honored and respected among his people. His mother weaves dresses for him. Most of us have been deeply wounded by dominant culture because we've never experienced this kind of love. We can use this understanding to create writing and art, which will bring more love to our lives. We can speak the truth of our battles and use this power of words to claim our natural place in human life.

As writers, we have very serious responsibilities to honor our connections to each other and to our home and mother, the Earth. Writing is not a right or an ego trip but a profoundly sacred act. We must be very careful in what we create, continuously examining the meanings of our acts and our metaphors. Words can be used to demean, to justify injustice, to confuse, and to attack. As colonized people, and each of us is colonized, we have a womandate to examine our own hearts as we write. I'm sure all of you have written scathing replies to ex-lovers as I have, but we don't publish those because we understand that it doesn't heal.

That is our work here—to heal all the splits and divisions among people. Because we live outside of gender clichés, we are uniquely qualified to do this work. We need to keep our minds alert and honed. I joke that I'm a "honosexual" because I have such good sharp facts. We have the opportunity now, unique in written Western history, to engage our passion in the struggle for equality, a concept that has never been actualized against the zombies of Columbozo colonialization. We face dangerous phrases and words that must be deconstructed. The concept of "political correctness" has been abused until our natural understanding of justice has become lost and an embarrassment.

We know that discrimination and abuse are morally wrong, but the ruling corporations find it inconvenient for us to have a conscience, and they set about to destroy our common sense with glitzy advertising lies, mockery, and co-optation. Because we don't agree with the myths of what little girls or boys are made of, we are dangerous to the status quo. I believe it is very silly to want to be accepted by the so-called mainstream. I think they need to be accepted by us. They have a long, hard job ahead of them.

Another phrase that is a tool of oppressors is "ethnic cleansing." I could not believe it when I first heard that phrase roll out of a newscaster's mouth. I posit to you that there is no such thing as clean murder. These phrases are con artists whose job is to convince us to accept injustice. As long as we butcher language ourselves, such as using the word *blind* to mean ignorance or insensitivity, we are cooperating with our oppressors. When we hold events in inaccessible places or charge rates that could buy a bag of groceries, we imitate the very people whose aim it is to eliminate us. What People of Color, the aged and the imprisoned, those with disabilities share with us as queers is our outsider status. When we fight only to have our own private privilege, we are abusing our comrades and denying our sacred role as healers. These issues that I am naming are often dismissed as tiresome. I challenge you to think about what it means when equality and mutual respect are considered boring.

One of my particular jobs is to spread the word about Norma Jean Croy, a Native lesbian who remains incarcerated though her brother has been freed on the grounds of self-defense in the same incident.[2] This is a reflection of the fact that the prison business is blatantly sexist and racist, routinely forcing women and People of Color to serve double and triple time compared to white males. I have petitions and a donation can to which I would appreciate your attention. Lest you think that I'm abusing the privilege of this speech by speaking of Norma Jean Croy, I'd like to remind you that she will not be on the six o'clock news or discussed in the *New York Times* and, so far, has not been embraced by the media.

---

2. Chrystos spoke about Croy's case during a conversation she had at Out-Write 93 with Cheryl Clarke. During that conversation, she said,

Norma Jean Croy is a lesbian Native woman, prisoner of war at Chowchilla. Her brother "Hooty" was freed on the same charge a while ago in self-defense. How the U.S. injustice system works is that if you're on death row, you have access to appeals automatically. Hooty was on death row, which is a different legal status, which is why he is now free. Norma Jean was not on death row, and so she doesn't have access to the same legal framework. The other part of it is that People of Color and women always do two to three times more time than other prisoners. The prison system is extremely sexist. They will deny most lesbians parole because they have not reformed (because part of the prison system is still the idea that a woman should not be leaving the prison as a lesbian).

So there's still enforced drugging and putting lesbians in the hole and all kinds of stuff like that. Norma Jean has done fourteen years of time for slugging a white man clerk in a convenience store. Dan White did seven years for killing two politicians. So that tells you something of the kind of racism that we're dealing with. So at the Press Gang table, which is in the mezzanine, I have petitions which you can sign for Norma Jean Croy to be released. We're trying to embarrass the government into releasing her, which is also what we're up to with Leonard Peltier. I hope you've all written letters to Clinton about him. There's a donation basket, and I'm going to go over there now to sign books.

Because she is invisible, because I have not done hard time, I need to bring her into our circle tonight.[3]

I would like to close with a poem I wrote for the place where I live—to give you the gift of open sky to carry you safely on your journey as writers:

Before Me the Land & Water Open

their arms tender sisters who have kept my place
Watched each spray of racing birds
Woven them into the still air for me to catch
a shimmering glint
The blowsy pine grows tall
as the distant mountains we call home
Mischief of the eyes is sweet
Silver slate the sound ruffles my hair
Roots I've packed for years settle in this meadow
delicate with brambles, broom
bright yellow suns I call beach daisies
These are the variations of green & gold
I keep deep within my hands
These never same astounding clouds drift through my eyes
in bleached conversations with strangers
These are the leaves & berries who marry me in delight
This is the earth I carry in a corn husk pouch
against the brutal light of clapping hands
Here is the path choked with driftwood I trace
to watch the sun go down over mountains whose wildflowers
have caught & pressed my heart

---

3. Norma Jean Croy was released on March 20, 2005, after nineteen years in prison (largely due to activists making her case an international issue by speaking in Europe).

Fly through these words sharp as
a deep blue & rust swallow
that wavering branch is
waiting for you.[4]

Megwetch.

---

4. This poem appears on page 50 in Chrystos's collection *Fugitive Colors* (Cleveland: Cleveland State University Poetry Center, 1995) and carries this dedication: "Especially for Barbara Cameron Nation Shield."

An Exceptional Child

KEYNOTE ADDRESS

OCTOBER 8, 1993

I have always wondered at the ways how things that are perceived can be transformed by labels. I had my first lesson in that when I was quite young. When I first went to school, I was labeled an exceptional child. I don't know who decided that, and I'm not sure why I was first given the test that said I was so exceptional. As such, I was valued. I was even regularly studied by psychologists at Boston University (BU) who wanted to understand the ways I interacted with the world and how I saw it. Exceptional childhood is a pretty wonderful thing; it's full of attention and rewards. After all, I had a whole group of adults who wanted nothing more than to play with me in their laboratory every Saturday just because I was so different from the other kids, because I had such promise and they wanted to learn how to nurture that promise.

At some point, and I honestly can't remember what happened to create this change, my label was altered. I was no longer an exceptional child. I became instead a psychiatric client; rather than the warm greetings at BU, I now had to go to regular sessions with a cold doctor whose purpose wasn't to study and encourage me but to control me and teach me restraint. The world is a much different place for a pediatric psychiatric patient than it is for an exceptional child. I promise. Just listen to the sounds of those words and tell me that you can't hear there's a difference in what they mean. The world alters the way it responds to you. Your parents go from bragging about you to all their acquaintances to whispering about you

John Preston. (*Photo credit: © Robert Diamante.*)

with only their best friends and closest relations, those who might understand. You go from having a sense of entitlement and accomplishment, even if you didn't seem to have to work for it, to having a sense of shame and guilt. Your behavior changes without your knowing it. Rewards are traded in for punishment, and you don't even know why. You discover that you are no longer delightfully spontaneous and exuberant. Now you're acting out and being hostile. You're left humbled and humiliated, wondering what's wrong with you that you cause all this trouble. It was not a comfortable transformation for a young boy to make. I assure you of that. It taught me a great lesson though. It taught me to avoid being noticed, to avoid, as much as I could, accumulating any new labels; those labels can get you. But there were some new labels that weren't all that bad. At least not at first.

I took one of them on right here in this very hotel. This is the place where a traveling salesman from Hartford, Connecticut, relieved me of the truly onerous burden of my adolescent virginity. The Park Plaza was called the Statler then, over thirty years ago. And I put myself in the path of this man, who was only too happy to talk to this boy about his sexual problems, except the man didn't want to label the sex as the problem. He thought the virginity was. So we got rid of that in the night that still kindles the fire of my imagination; my loins were lightened. And I learned that there were some men, at least, who thought this new label that I was acquiring could be a lot of fun. I tell you, I can still hear that traveling salesman laugh with pleasure and with sheer joy.

And there were some labels that I thought were inalterable. Whatever other problems I had, I grew up believing that I belonged to my hometown of Medfield, Massachusetts, not far from here. My mother's family had lived there for generations, and little old people would stop me on the street and tell me that they saw my grandfather's face while they pinched my cheeks. And they were telling me that I belonged. They were telling me I was of Medfield. Maybe I had some secrets to keep, but they weren't as important as being a valued member of my community.

College was different. Being from a rural community wasn't so hot for my classmates and the faculty of the socially elite and academically dysfunctional school I attended. My heavy working-class accent was labeled vulgar. I was told that. I was told I was vulgar. I was so disgraced by my classmates that I spent most of my freshman year in my dorm room losing that accent. It is one of the true, true disappointments of my life that I succeeded. I know I now talk like some kind of wussy public television person. I have lost the rich accent of my family, the people who created Medfield, the people who ran its trains and started its screening store and built its houses. I feel I have betrayed them when I hear myself in a recording.

It is intriguing, though, that other people can bring it back. Only a very few. I can get that accent back with my brothers. When we kick back, and we have a few beers, there it is; my voice has suddenly transformed, and it sings with the sounds of the Charles River Valley and Vermont mountains and all the rest. This is the voice that no one wanted to hear when I went to college. God, I loathe the people who dared to make me devalue that music. I. Loathe. Them. I loathe them, and their fake Oscar Wilde witticisms, and the way they self-importantly suck their fucking sherry in the faculty lounge, and the way they had taken away a Massachusetts boy's sense that he belonged.

I hate them for other reasons. I hate them because they also told me to be guilty about sex. My traveling salesman had been followed by a line of men and boys with whom I laughed and had great fun. I met many of them right outside this very door in Park Square in Boston. We were looked after by a gaggle of drag queens. We were loved by our governesses. They carefully observed the other people we met, and they would not let us go away with suspicious characters, and they would never ever let us go away with men who were suspected of carrying syringes. We were the exceptional children who would come out at an early age, and we were to be nurtured, cared for, not to be put in danger.

Our lives were not perfect then. And there was strain from the hiding, but we did find one another. My traveling salesman taught me many lessons, and my new friends carried them on. I was taught to talk and tell stories. I was told that it was important to listen to people for advice, for warnings, because they could entertain. The story seemed to weave connections between us. I realized they were similar to the family histories that my parents would tell, those endless recitations of ancestors that had seemed so boring to me when I had to listen to them night after night, until I realized that they were the stories that made those old people point at me out on the streets in Medfield and gave me the message "You belong." I carried the stories men told me between sheets, and I valued them. They had character; they had substance; they were history.

At least I valued them until I got to college. There I found other men who were just as sexually interested in me but who were even more interested in shutting me up. I was a danger. I had an air about me of availability. It horrified the professors I would meet in the gay bars when they saw how well I had learned the lessons of my traveling salesman. They told me to stay away from them. At least they told me that after they'd had their way. When they would talk to me, they violated the tradition of my traveling salesman: they never laughed.

I remember once I went to a professor and asked him if we couldn't talk about this sex we each had. I had, much to his horror, discovered him standing in a dark corner of a bar downtown. I thought this meant we had a bond. That's what my drag queen guardians had taught me. I asked him if there wasn't some advice he could give me on how to handle this torturous life on campus. Well, he said it was simple. I had two choices. I could lie the way he did and find a woman who would be generous enough to marry him for the sake of public presentation as he had, and life would be good, with the occasional lapse like the one that I had witnessed. Or I could keep on being someone who went to the gay bars, and I would end up a hopeless drunk who would commit suicide in a few years. That was the lesson he had for me. It was in one form or another the lesson every gay faculty member gave me. I can only thank whatever powers there are that I had the voice of my traveling salesman in my memory, that there was someone who enjoyed sex, someone who was gay, who was happy, whose very existence proved that assholes like that professor could be wrong. There weren't many other voices telling me that, and there were no voices telling me to speak myself. In fact, that horrible accent of mine was the reason I was counseled never to be an English major. It was a label to which I was told I should not aspire. The head of the department told me I would not fit in because I was so, well, vulgar sounding, and those stories about my family that I'd heard so often of men and women coming to Massachusetts from the cold steps of Nova Scotia and the mountains of Vermont, better forget them. They would label me forever if I kept on telling them. That is, unless there was a New England poet in there, of course, but it was so highly unlikely; they were all in the Ivy League.

It is one of the strangest facts of my life that I accepted that advice, that I also went out and got a job at the local newspaper to earn my spending money covering local politics. I was not the right kind of person to be one of the students who published one another in the campus literary magazine, but I was the one who got paid to attend the city council meetings and then record what happened from my new community. What I find strange is that I never put the two things together until quite recently. I never thought it was weird that I'd been barred from literary classes but that I could earn some money and, it turned out, some respect in the community by doing a good job communicating. And I must admit with some glee that I realized I learned a great deal more by being a journalist than I ever would have if I had taken those assholes' classes in fine writing.

But I did not have that label, author; I was just a news writer. I finally found my voice in gay activism in the late sixties. And it was finally my own voice. I became one of the first waves of people who worked to establish a community out of the rubble of our personal experience. I was driven to do it because of a lover's suicide, because of the ruin of the lives of the gay men my own age, because the silence that enabled those deaths and that destruction was intolerable. I did it because I no longer gave a fuck whether my voice was the right kind or if my actions were proper; I did it because the cost of not doing it was too high. What we were doing was very simple. We were taking the label that had been slapped on to us by psychiatrists and politicians and religious fanatics—the label that said we were sick, deviant, and damned—and we were saying no. We were beautiful. We were angry. And we were our own future.

Our revolution was a revolution of labels and emblems and slogans, just words, but we knew the danger of not speaking them. I was honored by my group in Minnesota to become the speaker. It was decided that I would be the person who would give the talks, make the points, argue the questions. It was my role in our evolving community to change the words and the way the words were used. That was the first time I understood the power of the role of the writer in his or her community. I understood that I was being asked to invoke the alchemy that would alter the way that we looked at ourselves—from being the hated to becoming the vital.

I just went to the National Lesbian and Gay Journalists Conference in New York, where a man came up to me and told me he had heard me speak on his college campus more than twenty years ago. I can't remember the occasion all that clearly, but I remember the school was much like the one I had gone to myself, the one that has stolen my accent and made me feel guilty about sex. I remember I told the gay and lesbian students that they must not let that happen to them, that they must not let their speech be taken away from them. Now so many years later, at least one man told me that I had saved his life with those words. I loved him for it. And I thought my traveling salesman would have been very proud of me.

And even when I began to assume the label of "writer," I did it in a very circumspect way. I began being a writer by avoiding the arenas where real writers acted out. I wrote pornography. I was still concerned about hiding. I figured no one would notice this transgression because I thought no one noticed who wrote pornography. I forgot the fans. I forgot that there were readers. And I learned very quickly, much to my shock, that there was a population of people out there, and never make the mistake of thinking that it was only men, who wanted the threads of communities to weave them together. Mr. Benson became their icon. I also learned that those readers would follow my threads even when they wove the rich spangled costume for Franny, the queen of Provincetown, the personification of every drag queen who protected me every night I was on the streets of Park Square.

It was after the response of the community that I realized I was a real writer, and I was a writer with as much power as I wanted to grasp. They wanted me to have all of it and give them the voice that would come from it. The early readers of my books and the few critics who saw in them what I was doing—the changing of the labels that I was insisting upon, changes that demanded that a drag queen could be a hero, that a man in leather could fall in love—helped me understand.

I moved to Maine fourteen years ago, and there were lots of reasons for my move. At least one of them was the evolution of a writing that seemed to dominate the gay lit scene at a certain time. What was labeled our new voice frightened me because it was so narrow. I wasn't sure my own voice was strong enough to survive these labels, which seem very limited.

It all felt too familiar. It felt like an attempt to found a new academy. I have learned to just distrust academies, of course, and besides, this one didn't look all that appealing. The old one had aspired to Oscar Wilde witticism; this one wanted to emulate Ronald Firbank.[1] There were some invitations to join; I had an audience after all. I must speak to becoming a real writer, but I was out of there back to my roots—Ronald Firbank, no way.

When I came back to New England, I discovered yet a new silence. My move was my attempt to find a way for a gay man to go back to a community like Medfield and be part of it without hiding, without guilt. I thought Portland, Maine, would be a place where that could happen. One of the first nights I was in the city, when I was still living in a motel room, a bit frightened to make the commitment of actually renting an apartment, I turned on the television set and saw a report on gay life in Maine. The only person who was willing to appear on television would do so only if he

---

1. Ronald Firbank was a British novelist inspired by Oscar Wilde.

appeared in silhouette, hidden. That was a challenge to me. I vowed to stand up and become the writer for the gay community in Maine. I began to write about my own life in a small city—far, far from the fast track—and I began to interview people who had lived in Maine all their lives. I was heartbroken every time I would bring out my tape recorder. The other person would say, "But no one is going to care. No one is interested in my story." I wanted to know who lied to them. Who had lied? Because I knew someone had. Because when that tape recorder would go on, those men gave me novels. I would hear these epics of human resistance and endurance: of men who had taken up arms to save their own lives from roaming gangs of homophobes, of men who had lost their jobs because they loved one another and were then thrown into exile, of women who endured the double labels of "woman" and "lesbian" to be heard in city hall and the state capitol. And I wrote; I wrote about them as much as I could. And I published their stories as often as I could. I thought that many of them would resent this—the invasion of their privacy—but they didn't. There had not been a writer like me in that community in Maine before. I was doing the work of reflecting their importance, of bringing their story into categories that had new labels, not shame but pride, not guilt but affirmation. That is my role in my community now: to be the writer, to tell the stories, to speak the truths.

When I do reflect on that new label for myself, I wonder about those people who would run from it. When I listen to harangues about the limitations of being a gay or lesbian writer, I'm shocked. This is not a limitation. This calling to be the voice of one's community is not a degradation. It's an anointment. How could anyone rather be drowning in sherry in the academy than listening to the people on your street, in your own neighborhood, who thank you for articulating their lives? Where's the sense of proportion here? Who's choosing the labels, and for what reasons? Who's being hurt?

Toni Morrison did not just win the Nobel Prize because she believed that universality was found in the lives of white, straight suburbanites in Fairfield. Morrison won the Nobel Prize because she loved her people and insisted, demanded that their stories be told. She won the Pulitzer Prize because her audience insisted, demanded that the stories of African Americans throughout U.S. history were worth telling, that her contribution to her community was to tell them in the finest possible way. That is why we are writers in our community. She created writings breathtaking and so finely wrought that it could not be denied. That should be our goal. That certainly was the gift that Morrison has given to this world—to give what had once been dismissed as anecdote and folklore a new label, to force it into the ranks of literature, as though it had never been.

I have often been told that to be a writer was somehow less important than being an activist. It was another lessening of my label, but the advent of AIDS ended that nonsense. My role as a writer during the time of AIDS began by my being a sentinel, alerting people in Maine about what I had seen in New York and San Francisco, what I knew was coming to our small state. Then I became a teacher, giving speeches again, this time on risk reduction and ways to avoid stigmatizing the disease. I wrote and I wrote and I wrote all about it until I was no longer the outsider, but I became part of what is now one of my most burdensome labels: a person with AIDS. That diagnosis was what shut me up. Finally, I became, honestly, a victim of my disease. I was silenced. My life was so tied up with a concept of being a writer that when my life was threatened, I had no ground to stand on. It was only through the writing that other people had done that I saw a way out of my despair. It was through writing that I could come back to life. And once I was back, I took my writing to other people with AIDS. I took my skills of writing to other people with AIDS. I took down the letters they dictated to be read after they died. I recorded their struggles in the press. I promised them I would be their scribe who would put out their stories to be read and heard as best I could. I was always amazed by how clearly they understood the slogan of the AIDS movement: silence equals death. It is a statement that reverberated through the whole experience with the wisdom of all lesbians and gay men, all of us who were taught by our guardian angels in drag that to not speak is to be erased.

That led me to the work of creating anthologies, a task that has dominated my life in the past few years. I discovered that one could call into being a chorus of voices around issues in teams. Those voices could become a symphony. I could become the conductor, and creating anthologies as diverse as *Hometowns* and *Flesh and the Word* has been an exercise in community. As I've worked with hundreds of writers, I've always tried not to stifle their voices but to help them find their voices. Not to silence them but to show them the ways they can make themselves be heard. It has been of special importance to me that these anthologies have always carried new voices, that there are always writers who are represented in these handsome volumes who have not been read before. I remember too well those faculty lounge lizards, and the way they longed for the power of the gatekeeper, and the way they would misuse that power.

I can't deny that I have that role now, that there are some who wanted to be in my anthologies, who would like to be, but I'll be damned if I'm going to be the one to tell them they shouldn't be heard. If my books are not their arena, then I'll do my best to find them another. That's really why I write my column in *Lambda Book Report*—information is power. My one sustained role as a journalist in college proved that to me.

I've tried to take it further with a project of my own where I work with young writers who have a specific goal, not so much to rewrite their writing, to edit it too heavily, but to make the introductions, to present their work to an audience, to help them make the connections. I think this is the least that a successful author owes to his or her community. It is our obligation to work with our young because if we don't, we're leaving them vulnerable to the snakes of the would-be academy who will try to shut them up.

All of this is me taking my place in the proud tradition of New England, which I'm reclaiming for myself, yet a new label. I'm often asked now why I live alone and how I could do that in a world where pseudopsychologists label anyone not in a monogamous relationship as someone who has the dreaded "issues with intimacy." I am now old enough to begin to assume the role of a New England curmudgeon, and therefore I now allow myself a response, which is to shoot back, "I got a dog."

But as I grow older, my Yankee heritage has become more obvious in other ways. I have learned more about how my forbearers lived in love. And I discovered that in every single generation of my family, at least those of whom we have any record, there has always been a good bachelor uncle. I have learned as much as I can about my own uncles. I have talked to my relatives about them. I have come to see that my role is now, as a now accepted writer, to emulate my uncles. It's a liberating experience that their example frees me to indulge and become a curmudgeon. But the good bachelor uncles offer another model in addition to that one. The boys on my father's side of the family have one man in particular who was the favorite of us all. Let me tell you about him and the gifts he gave me because this is the gift I think I owe to our young writers.

My parents and their siblings used to pool their money in the summer, and together they would rent a cottage in New Hampshire. One night I was in bed, listening to the rambunctious adults, playing cards and drinking and laughing in the front room. The night sky in the mountains of New Hampshire isn't polluted by the reflected light of any city. It is dark; it is deep; it is broken only by the brightest stars. I was awake and looking out the window into that darkness when I suddenly saw a light moving down the road; it came closer, and I suddenly realized it was my uncle. A city man, he had assumed that there would be cabs to meet him at the train he had taken up from Boston. But of course, there were none in rural New Hampshire, and there was no phone in our cheap rented cottage. He couldn't call to get a ride. So he had walked five miles from the station in the dark New Hampshire night, his way illuminated only by his cigarette lighter. I ran to the door and yelled to everyone that he was here. He was here. The other kids were put back to bed after the excitement died down, and I refused to go. I climbed up on my uncle's lap, and I remember to this day the wondrous belief that he had come all this distance for me, just for me. I fell asleep, resting on his potbelly that night, and I do not remember ever being happier.

That was the kind of gift that my bachelor uncle gave me. My traveling salesman from Hartford was in the same tradition. It is the tradition that let me become a writer. My traveling salesman laughed at my stories. My uncle listened to what I had to say. My uncle used to take me on walks, and I can't remember the content of any of our conversations, and I suppose I was a brat, but I don't remember that. I remember walking endlessly through the forest of New Hampshire and Massachusetts, and I remember talking forever, and I remember him listening. He never told me I was acting out. He never told me I was a brat. My uncle was the one man would never let me forget that I was an exceptional child.

Aversion/Perversion/Diversion

An Excerpt

KEYNOTE ADDRESS

OCTOBER 10, 1993

If you could speak to a few hundred gay writers, what would you say? I found myself sitting over my notebook pondering the problem; the fact is, I don't know if I'm in a position to answer it any better than anyone else. What do I have to say that would be of interest, much less be of use, to a twenty-one- or twenty-two-year-old gay Asian woman desperately seeking a venue that will be sympathetic to her short stories? What do I have to say that would interest at the same time, much less be of use to, a fifty-seven-year-old gay Latino writer who is returning to playwriting after more than ten years of teaching and activism that in his own words "simply swallowed up all my writing time"? I know both of you are out there because I've talked to you both on separate occasions in the last six months.

What do I have to say of interest, much less of use, to a well-known gay Black writer of novels in his late forties who, because of IRS difficulties dating back to delinquencies when he was nowhere near as well known, is living at about the same level of financial security as the other two? What do I have to say that would interest at the same time, much less be of use to, a twenty-eight-year-old gay white poet whose first collection of poems has just been accepted by a publisher, putting a fair amount of energy into gay-oriented literature up till now—only the editor who has been so

Samuel R. Delany. (*Photo credit: Photo by Robert Giard, copyright Estate of Robert Giard.*)

vigorously promoting gay writing there has just gone over to another publisher so that the poet is afraid, and with good reason, that his book, though it will indeed finally come out, will be swallowed up without any of the special attentions a book needs to make any sort of dent at all in the minds of people who pay attention to such things? I know both of you are out there too because I had brunch with one and drinks with the other less than a year ago.

But now the question must include itself—why these specific little stories? And what is their purpose? What's accomplished by mentioning these individuals that couldn't be accomplished just as easily by talking about some ideal average gay writer, not quite male, not quite female, not quite white or Black or Latina or Asian? I'd hope that the specificity reminds us that no such average exists. It's a way of suggesting the range of gay writers. And I hope the specificity also suggests the realization that no range I could choose is itself exhausted. If, for instance, I took all my examples from Asian lesbians—one twenty-two and looking to publish; one thirty-five and from a position as a creative writing teacher at the University of Illinois, wondering how she will get her second novel to place; one fifty and writing romances under a pen name; and one working in France at age seventy-one, a poet who writes primarily in French—what do I have to say to these? What do I have to say to these gay writers?

Well, I hope one could hear echoing behind it all the times people have chosen their exemplary gay writers from a list of white males: one, two, three, or thirty, or three hundred of them at the same time. Some among you are sure to find yourself troubled by the fact that the range of gay writers as suggested wholly by a list of Asian lesbians is certainly no more characteristic than the range suggested by the usual list of white males, even as one celebrates the difference from the usual, the forcing of attention to where it is not usually directed. The point, of course, is that uncharacteristic stories always have their troubling side. As they force us to consider the characteristic briefly, I'm saying that one cannot recognize or celebrate the uncharacteristic without remembering what is characteristic.

I have assumed today that you have asked me here as a storyteller; there is, of course, a tale.[1]

* * *

So another tale—in this case of a muscular Puerto Rican with curly black hair, whose work shirt bore a name we'll say was "Mike" in yellow stitching across the gray pocket. He wore a green

---

1. Delany told four tales as a part of this speech—one about a young white man at the Cameo, one about a woman named Carla, a third about early sex/gender experiences of his daughter, and the fourth included here. Delany gave a similar speech in 1991 at Rutgers University. That speech is included in its entirety in *Longer Views: Extended Essays* (Hanover: Wesleyan University Press, 1996).

jacket with a green and yellow knitted collar to the same theater where I met the first young man I spoke of. Across the back, yellow letters spelled out "Aviation Trades High School," from which, I presume, he must have graduated sometime over the three and a half years I knew him.

Mike was as regular a visitor to the theater as I was. He was handsome, in a bearlike way. From a couple of quiet approaches, however, I'd gathered he was not interested in me. From time to time, I would see him sitting in various seats in the balcony or orchestra. Nearly as frequently, as I walked up or down between the lobby and the balcony, I would pass him, sitting on the stairs toward the top, sometimes leaning forward, forearms across his knees, sometimes leaning back, elbows on the step two above and behind.

Once, after I'd stopped paying much attention to Mike, I was sitting a few seats away from another Black man in green work clothes and dilapidated basketball sneakers. Knees wide against the back of the seat in front of him, he was slouched low in his chair, watching the film.

Mike, I noticed, was slouched equally low in the row ahead, one seat to the right.

Then something moved near the floor.

I glanced down—to see a hand. Under the seat and behind the metal foot of the ancient theater chair, it looked rather disembodied. But the fingertips now and again brushed the rubber rims and black cloth uppers of the man's right sneaker. Glancing at the top of Mike's head, then down at the man's foot—the man seemed oblivious to what was happening—I realized Mike had reached down between the seats and was playing with the man's shoe.

"Ah . . . !" I thought, in all the self-presumed sophistication of my own sexual experience. "So *that* explains it!" And four or five times over the next few months, I noticed Mike now in the balcony, now in the orchestra, at the same practice with different men.

This was back in the years when today's ubiquitous running shoe was just emerging as *the* casual fashion choice. As is more usual than not, I was at least a year behind most other people, and it was only that week that I broke down and got my first pair—in which, I confess, I never ran in my life.

They were a conservative gray.

One day I stopped at the Cameo and, on my way to the balcony, passed Mike sitting on the steps. Several people stood near the top, watching the movie; I stopped behind them, largely to watch them.

Minutes later, I happened to glance down. Mike's hand was on the step, the edge of his palm against my shoe sole. I was surprised because till then, I had considered myself outside his interests. My first and most innocent thought was that his hand's straying to that position had been an accident, even while more worldly experience said no. Precisely because of what I knew of him already, while it might have been an accident with someone else, his hand's resting there could only have been on purpose, though his attention all seemed to be down the stairs.

I tried to appear as though I was not paying any attention to him. He continued to appear as though he was not paying any attention to me. I moved my foot—accidentally—a quarter of an inch from his hand. His hand, a half minute later, was again against my shoe. Again—accidentally—I moved my foot a quarter of an inch closer, to press against his fingers, and two of his fingers, then three—accidentally—slid to the top of my foot.

In ten minutes, Mike had turned to hold my foot with both of his hands, pressing it to his face, his mouth, leaning his cheek down to rub against it.

To make the point I'm coming to in all this, I must be clear that I found his attention sexually gratifying enough so that I continued to rub his hand, his face, his chest, his groin with my shoe until, at last, genitals loose from his gray work pants, he came— and, over the next three weeks, when we had some four more of these encounters, I came as well during one of them.

We do not even have a term for the perversion complementary to fetishism. The myth of the sexual fetish is precisely that it is solitary. Its assumed pathology is the fact it is thought to be non-reciprocal. A major symptom of the general insensitivity of our extant sexual vocabulary is that as soon as fetishism is presumed to move into the realm of reciprocity, the vocabulary and analytical schema of sadomasochism take it over, and to me, this seems wholly to contravene common sense and my own experience.

Mike and I became rather friendlier now, when we were not directly engaged in sexually encountering one another. If we met outside the theater on the street, we said hello and nodded. If we passed in the theater stairwell, we might exchange brief small talk. There were no words at all, however, about what we were doing. It was clear to me that Mike did not want to flaunt his practices before the other patrons, with some of whom he was rather friendlier than he was with me. Among the theater's younger clientele were a number of hustling drag queens and pre-ops: their teasing and joking could be intense. And these were the people who, in the theater, were Mike's conversational friends.

Running shoes, at least the brand I'd bought at that time, do not last as long as they should. Soon it was time to replace them.

I thought of Mike.

By now, though, I'd glimpsed him several times get as involved with other men's running shoes or sneakers as he could from time to time with mine. I felt nothing but empathy and goodwill toward him. But clearly some excited him more than others. The specifics of his preference, however, I hadn't been able to piece together. How, I wondered, do I ask about such a thing? How do I put such a question into language?

Not much later, when I was getting up from my seat in a legitimate Forty-Second Street movie house where I'd gone to see some genre horror film, I saw Mike—also leaving. We smiled across the crowd and nodded to each other. I decided the best thing to do was to be as open and aboveboard about my curiosity as possible.

"You know," I said as we joined each other walking toward the lobby, "I've got to get a new pair of sneakers one of these days soon. What kind do you think I should get?"

He seemed not to have heard me. So I persisted: "Is there any kind you like particularly—some kind you think are the best?"

Mike stopped just inside the lobby door. He turned to me, a look blooming on his face that, in memory, seemed a combination of an astonishment and gratitude near terror. He leaned forward, took my arm, and whispered with an intensity that made me step back: "Blue . . . ! Please. . . . Blue!" Then he rushed away into the street.

I'd expected an answer at the same level of fervor I'd offered my question. But I confess, that afternoon, with an anxiety that, somehow, seemed not all my own but borrowed, at Modell's Sporting Goods I purchased a pair of blue Adidas.

Two days later, when I wore them to the theater, however, Mike was not there.

Nor did I see him on any of my next dozen visits.

After a few months, I realized he had dropped the place from among his regular cruising sites. Three times over the next year, I glimpsed Mike in his green jacket with the yellow letters, now on a far corner under the marquis at the Port Authority bus terminal, now by the subway kiosk at Seventy-Second Street, now with his hands in his pockets, hurrying down Forty-Fifth Street toward Ninth Avenue. But I never saw him in the theater again. I've wondered if our encounter in the second movie theater had something to do with his abandonment of the first: I can only hope that, among his friends, he might be telling his version of this tale— possibly somewhere this evening—for whatever didactic purposes of his own.

A few years ago, however, when I first wrote about Mike to a straight male friend of mine—a Pennsylvania academic—he wrote me back: "If you can explain the fascination with licking sneakers so that I can understand it, you can probably explain anything to anybody!"

My first thought was to take up his challenge, but as I considered it, I realized all I could explain, of course, was my side of the relationship. I'd found Mike desirable—well before I had known of his predilections. Using some formulation by Lacan, "One desires the desire of the other," it seems easy enough to understand that if Mike's desire detoured through a particular focus on my sneakers, it was still *his* desire and therefore exciting—perhaps not quite as much, for me, as it would have been if it had focused on my hands, on my mouth, over all my body, on some aspect of my mind, or on my genitals, but it was exciting nevertheless.

As I thought about it, it occurred to me that, in similar environments, I'd actually observed many hours of fetishistic behavior by any number of men over the years, though most of those had involved work shoes or engineers' boots in specifically S&M contexts—so, therefore, I knew something quite real about that behavior. But at the same time, I'd spent perhaps less than a single hour talking about that behavior with any or all of the men involved, including Mike.

That meant there was a great deal I *didn't* know.

What could I explain?

What could I not explain?

Even though I'd responded sexually to Mike, I could no more speak for him than I could speak sexually for any of the very few women (eight, by my count) I had gone to bed with—or, indeed, for any of the many thousands of men.

* * *

The gay experience these days is specific and individual. For every one of us has always resided largely outside of language because all sexuality, even all experience, largely resides there. What has been let into language has always been highly coded; that coding represents a kind of police action. Even while it is decried in the arena of politics, it is often among us in the academic area of gay studies, for example, unnoticed.

I've tried to bring up these specific and troubling tales to help cast into the light the smallest fragment of the context of not gay experience in general—for as I hope my tales suggest, there is no such thing—but just to eliminate the context of the tales that I am now in the process of telling for that, that's how the tales relate to each other.

If, when we take as our object of study, say, some lines by Shakespeare or Whitman to a boy, citing the contestation of other homophobic scholars, or when we examine some profession of love to another woman in a letter by Emily Dickinson or Eleanor Roosevelt or Willa Cather, contested equally by still other homophobic scholars, or the coded narratives of Melville's wide world of navigation, or Oscar Wilde's London, or Thomas Mann's tourist town of Venice, or Djuna Barnes's wonderfully sophisticated Paris—if we take these tales and assume that we are not dealing with a code that in every case excludes a context at least as complex and worrisome as the ones I have here gone to such narrative lengths to suggest, then I maintain we are betraying our object of interest through a misguided sense of our own freedom by an adoration too uncritical of that wonderful, positive tale.

We all perhaps adore, but what I hope worries you, what I hope troubles you, is a sense of the appropriateness of these tales. The here and now of what certainly most of us will experience as a liberating occasion is what suggests that even with the surge of linguistic freedom that has obtained since 1968 and with the movement toward political freedom that has been in motion since the Stonewall riots of 1969, what is accepted into language at any level is always highly coded and heavily policed. Those strictures relax or tighten at different places and in different periods.

The relaxation never means that the policing or coding has somehow been escaped. Sexual experience is still largely outside language, at least as language has constituted on any number of levels. Because both today and in earlier times what of the sexual that was allowed into language is notably more than what was allowed in during that period of extraordinary official prescription any of us over forty can still remember, we must not assume that "everything" is *ever* articulated; we are still dealing with topics that were always circumscribed by a greater or lesser linguistic coding and at a greater or lesser social policing. But even as we recover ourselves in this moment of general inclusiveness, I hope for at least a few moments, I've been able to maneuver some of you into thinking, "Is this what Gay Identity is supposed to be? What does all this sneaker looking, drunken undergraduate mischief, and little girls urinating in a fountain in the park and another sob story of a hapless drug user have to do with *my* sexuality, my Gay Identity?" For certainly raising that question was precisely my intention. I said these tales were to trouble. And the troubling answer I would pose is fundamentally as simple as any of the stories themselves:

Quite possibly not much.

The point to the notion of Gay Identity is that in terms of a transcendent reality, concerned with perception of sexuality per se (a universal similarity, a shared necessary condition, a defining aspect, a generalizable and inescapable essence or experience common to all men and women called gay), I believe Gay Identity has no more existence than a single, essential, transcendental sexual difference between men and women. Which is to say, I think the notion of Gay Identity represents the happily only partial congruence of two strategies, which have to do with a patriarchal society in which the dominant sexual ideology is heterosexist.

In terms of heterosexist oppression of gays, Gay Identity represents a strategy for tarring a whole lot of very different people with the same brush: Billy, Mike, my perpetual virgin—at least, that is, if the people with the tar believe in transcendent differences between males and females. (For those are precisely the people who historically have contrived to keep male homosexuality not talked of and lesbianism trivial.) And if, on the other hand, they simply believe deviance is deviance, then it includes as well you, me, Carla, and Hank. The tar is there in order to police a whole range of behaviors—not only in terms of the action that is language but also in terms of the language that human actions themselves must generate, including the language of the stories.

Now in terms of gay rights, Gay Identity represents one strategy by which some of the people oppressed by heterosexism may come together, talk, and join forces to fight for the equality that certain egalitarian philosophies claim is due us all. In those terms, what we need these stories for is so that we don't get too surprised when we look at—or start to listen to—the person sitting next to us. That person after all may be me, or Hank, or Mike, or Carla, or anyone else I've spoken of this evening. In those terms, Gay Identity is a strategy I approve of wholly, even if, at a theoretical level, I question the existence of that identity as having anything beyond a provisional or a strategic reality.

That is to say, its place is precisely in the politically positivist comedy of liberation we began with—but probably nowhere else. The reason the partial congruence between the two strategies is finally happy is because it alone allows one group to speak, however inexactly, with the other. It allows those who have joined together in solidarity to speak to those who have been excluded, and to me, even more important, it allows the excluded to speak back. That very partial congruence is the linguistic element of the conduit through which any change, as it manifests a response by a vigorous and meaningful activism, will transpire.

From time to time, I have been accused—and have always taken it as praise—of trying to put the *sex* back into *homosexuality*. Here, not as a matter of nostalgia, but to facilitate an analytical and theoretical precision, I am trying to trouble the notion both of what we aver and of what we are averse to, in its perversity and its diversity—or if you will, through occasional appeals to the averse, I am trying to put a bit of the perversity back into perversion.

I hope many of you so inclined will welcome it. And to all of you this afternoon, love, luxury, justice, and joy.

Less Than a Mile from Here

Keynote Address

October 10, 1993

I want to thank the people who made me what I am today. And there's some dispute about what the hell that is. A loud Black woman. But the people who helped me were my family, and I think families get a bad rap a lot of the time. My family helped create the person who I am able to be today. And I feel very fortunate that some of them are here: my cousin Allen White, who still lives in the house less than a mile from here where we kind of grew up together. He's featured on page forty-seven of my new book of essays, Allen. My young niece Alicia, who's too young to be in the book yet, but take a look at her. My other young niece Atia. She's featured, I think, on page twenty-nine of my book; she's just made it.

They still live less than a mile from here where I grew up. Less than a mile from here is very near and, at the same time, very far away. Less than a mile from here is still in my head existing in the 1950s and 1960s, with jumping juke joints and women and men and flashy clothes, working the streets and loud music. It was also poverty, knife fights, and police brutality. The difference in this neighborhood today is we're not allowed to see those things. Gentrification has put a new face on the neighborhood; upper-middle-class lesbians and gay men now cruise the streets, looking disdainfully at the house I grew up in because it doesn't fit their standards of elegance. But inside that house are the people who made me who I am. They're the people I write about in

Jewelle Gomez. (*Photo credit: © Lynda Koolish.*)

my books. And I write about them because they are heroic in their everyday life, surviving the routine discouragement and deliberate oppression that faces the working class and that faces people of color in this culture. They are heroic. It is from them that I learned to write and learned to have hope. It is from them that I learned about anger and what to do with it. It is from them that I learned style and grace and cooperation. These are the people of my universe. Still, even when I'm writing about universes very far removed from here, you will find them on the pages of all of my books. These are the people who I think deserve to be mythologized for surviving and surpassing. And I say that not because I think they are alone in their extraordinary nature. Almost all of us have some such people in our lives somewhere, maybe blood related, maybe not, but they must exist somewhere. Or we probably couldn't have made it to this room today.

The Nobel Prize committee, in announcing the award for Toni Morrison, said, "Toni Morrison gives life to an essential aspect of American reality in novels characterized by visionary force and poetic import."[1] These people I grew up with taught me that I am an essential aspect of American reality, as are we all. And that being a visionary force, whether in your family's survival, whether in your lesbian and gay communities' survival, or whether in just your artistic survival, you must have visionary force in order to reach any kind of sense of fulfillment. And by visionary force, I mean a couple of very specific things. And perhaps they're not exactly the same things that the Nobel committee was thinking of. One of the elements in visionary force for me is anger—anger at injustice, not just anger that you specifically did not get what you wanted, but anger at the ramifications for others like yourself who may not have gotten what they wanted.

And even when you did get what you want, anger and understanding, how many others never will? A book contract, a book tour, is that what you want? Good. Be angry if you can't get it, and be angry if you do. When I hear a lesbian or gay author say, as I did several times this weekend, "Oh, I had no problem with my publisher about the lesbian or the gay content," I know they are deluding themselves. They don't see themselves as part of a continuum of authors who've already taken the heat. They don't see themselves as part of the years of rejection and the continual rejection, the one space that was made for them to be acceptable. Nor do they ever think about those others who will not be accepted because the accepted authors have been used to create a canon to exclude everybody else.

Not one of us is out here by ourselves, no matter what we think—not me whose triumph is in selling copies of my books in the thousands or others whose triumph is in selling copies of their

---

1. Toni Morrison won the 1993 Nobel Prize in Literature; the prize was announced on October 7, 1993. ("Toni Morrison," NobelPrize.org, October 7, 1993, https://www.nobelprize.org/prizes/literature/1993/press-release/.)

books in the hundreds of thousands. I know that most of you probably don't think much of me is angry. I think I don't get to talk about that very much. But anger is constantly the fuel that feeds the work that I do, keeps me thinking of myself as an activist, and keeps me writing. And I like to think that it keeps me clean. When I was in college, I was the editor for a couple of years of the Black student newspaper here in Boston at Northeastern University. That was in the late sixties. The name of the newspaper was *Panga Nyeusi*, which I was told—I personally don't know (I took French)—but in Swahili, I was told, loosely translated means "off the pig."[2] On the cover, we had a picture of a saber held by a muscular arm. It was another statement we were making. I think from the moment that I worked on that project, I never had any intention of evolving into a contented Democrat.

In the late sixties, I worked for the public television station here in Boston, WGBH, which had the—I don't want to call it foresight because mostly I think they were afraid of rioting—idea to create a Black weekly television show called *Say Brother*, which is still on the air. And I was on the staff of the show, which was one of the first Black weekly television shows in the country. And that was an incredibly pivotal experience for me as a young Black woman, learning that there was value in being Black in this country. And then being able to tell millions of viewers (Black, white, of all nationalities) who had, you know, television, anyone who had a television could just turn it on and find out, that—I felt that was valuable. That was one of the most significant things to happen to me.

---

2. The credited translation of *Panga Nyeusi* is "black saber." For more information, see "Panga Nyeusi Collection," Northeastern University Library, accessed October 1, 2021, https://repository.library.northeastern.edu/collections/neu: cj82nr31d; and "African American Activism and Experience at Northeastern University," Northeastern University Library, accessed October 1, 2021, https://blackactivism.library.northeastern.edu/organizations/.

What also happened was one of our producers said, "Well, you understand that if we really begin to do our jobs properly—that is, really define what's going on—they'll put us off the air," and he was right. 'Cause they did. Not because we did a show in which we filmed riots against Black people in New Bedford and had film of a car speeding away after they had shot and killed a young Black man, not because of that show, but because we did a show in which we brought together five of the perhaps six Black media producers in the entire country and had them on television talking about what it meant to be a producer in the media as a Black person, and their responsibilities, and how they felt torn by their responsibilities as a Black person and the betrayal of the media. Boy, they put cartoons on channel two quicker than I've ever seen. Our show was off the air.

This helped me see myself in the context that the media did not want me to see myself in the context of. And it made me angry, and I was not less angry when the community fought and got the show put back on. There's no reason to be less angry. In raising the importance of anger, I want to stress something that is not productive, and that is bitterness. Anger and bitterness are two very different things. And I feel like we need to think about that a lot as we keep butting our heads against the publishing world, the editorial world, both mainstream, straight, and gay. I may be angry at commercial publishers that have a very narrow space for lesbian and gay literature that doesn't include me or other writers like me. But realistically, I know this is a capitalist society, and they can define the marketplace any way they want to. Being bitter does not help me. Being bitter just gives me frown lines, and I am not in favor of them on me. (I actually liked them on my girlfriend—but not on me.)

More importantly for me is to look at situations like that and see what is it that we learned from that when we examine what we've come to look at. In this conference, every other panel seems to be having a discussion about it: the competition between small and large presses. What do we learn from that first? I have to say, it gives me the opportunity, as I did earlier, to congratulate the small presses and the feminist presses that for thirty years have provided the nurturance and a forum for women's and for lesbian voices where no one else would do that.

And because we are in a capitalist society, they will continue to do that because of the nature of the marketplace. It's important to support small presses and feminist presses, and now the gay presses that have really begun to blossom, because there will never be room for all of us in the central marketplace. And I don't necessarily think that's a bad thing. Some of the things I have to say, just like the things I had to say when I worked at channel two—why should they publish them? 'Cause I'm telling them how I feel about them. And sometimes it's not very nice. Why do I want them to publish me? I think there's room for all of us. The voices out here will fill up as many pages, as many publishers, as many computers as we can produce in our factories.

Another element I feel contributes to seeing ourselves as a visionary force is our capacity for joy. The potential for joy is what keeps us at our typewriters when we know our royalties will never come together to make a down payment on a house. The potential for joy is what keeps small press publishers up working on manuscripts when they weren't even able to pay themselves this week. The potential for joy is what makes a young dyke brave enough in the early seventies to send her manuscript to a major commercial publisher with her own name on it.

It's not simply the idea that it's going to be a name that will appear on shelves across the country, but it's a sense of the real joy that will come back to you when people read your words. We must hold on to that capacity for joy. We must continue to see that potential for joy as we become old and jaded. And that's one of the things that conferences like this can do: make you feel old and jaded. You come to this conference, and it's suddenly like a networking meeting. It's like wheeling and dealing. You would think the moguls from MGM and Paramount were here, the way some people are working the corridors. I come here 'cause I get to, like, sit on a panel with other writers whose work has meant something to me. Nine years ago, I reviewed a book by Jenifer Levin, and she was not happy with my review. I was on a panel with her yesterday, and that was one of the greatest joys 'cause she and I got to express our issues together as part of a whole, not as two parts fighting each other—and to see again, to use the word that they like to use now, to revisit, the joy that both of us knew was going to be there when we started writing.

Another contributing factor, I think, to a visionary force is a political eye. Now I know I'm on shaky ground here because a lot of you want to be just artists, not politicians—just want to write. But I will say this quite frankly: whether you click off right now or not, as long as you are a human being, you are a part of a political interaction. You cannot get away from it. I don't care what you write about.

I don't care if you are a woodsbeing writing in isolation in Maine or Edmund White sitting on the Champs-Élysées. Politics is the interconnective tissue, whether you are willing to acknowledge it or not. The trick is knowing and using that knowledge, knowing and learning from it. As writers and editors and publishers and readers, we are in a position to use that political awareness to postulate a more inclusive, more just world. Not by creating didactic or goody-two-shoes characters—that is not what I'm talking about. I am not talking about, and I think I have been misread as implying, that we need to create simply good lesbians or good gay men. What I am actually saying is, using our political eye, we can approach our writing and, just as importantly, the business of writing with integrity. We can think about the differences between us with integrity and face them. Not necessarily say, "I agree with everything you say, Jewelle, because, you know, gosh, you must know everything," but I say, "I'm trying to listen to what you're saying. I don't know that I agree. I don't agree. Will you listen to what I have to say?" And then see if I do.

An interesting discussion came up in two panels while I was here: What's the question of white writers creating nonwhite characters? This is a discussion that has come up in every writing event, conference, convention, coffee klatch, whatever, that I have been to. And the thing that's frightening to me is ultimately, a year later, ten years later, I don't see things have changed very much. I think it takes a political consciousness to recognize that we do not live in a monochromatic society. Very few of us do. I mean, there may be some people here who do, somewhere in an isolated circumstance of their town, but our society is not monochromatic. There is nothing in this society, there is no book on any bestseller list, there is no painting in the museum of modern art, there is no statuary in any museum in this country created by a U.S. citizen that was not informed by the multicultural nature of this society.

I will say that it does take courage to try to reflect that in your work. If you want to start at a small place, make it a walk-on character. I'm not asking you to write *Native Son*. I'm asking you to think about what you're saying. When you create a character, create a series of characters who interact with no one who is any different from the one main character. I'm asking you to think about what you do when you create a novel in which all the bad guys are white. What happens when you create a place? And this is what it is—a place of exclusionariness, where your world is simply defined by your own single consciousness. This is the exact same place that we have been fighting against all of our lives. The singular consciousness, one person's single experience, is just that. It has meaning in the ways it relates to all others, in the ways that it relates to the people like you and the people not like you. It does take courage to write outside of our experience.

I like to aspire to being a visionary force. And I like to think that most writers want to be a visionary force. I don't know that that's true. Perhaps it's something I'm imposing on people. But it is something that I've always associated with writers, from the first writers I ever read as a kid. I started reading dime novels and actually all the books that my great-grandmother got secondhand from the secondhand store, including James Cain, who wrote *Mildred Pierce* and *The Postman Always Rings Twice*. I mean, people are not running around talking about James Cain as a visionary force in literature or this country, but he was; he had a real deep vision. He ended up creating some female characters who are unforgettable and helped shape who I am today by sheer virtue of that influence. His visionary force is very clear in the body of his work. By approaching the writing and the business of writing and thinking, we can be a visionary force. By taking on a sense of integrity about the power of our words, we simply become it. It's not as if we need to do anything much more different than ask the questions and then stretch when we look for the answers and not take the answer that pops right out.

When I first started writing in the lesbian/gay community, I wrote mostly for newspapers like *Gay Community News*, *womanews*, and the *New York Native*.[3] These publications were the social and political lifeline of our community. And for me, journalistic training was the best there was. And I still believe it's the best there is for any genre of writing. It gave me the skills to meet those deadlines, even when I had to extend them just a little bit. But it also gave me the training to think about what the reality was in relationship to what I was actually reading. In the sixties, that was a very important lesson. When I worked at WGBH, we used to get wire copy and have to interpret what they were really saying about riots, what they were really saying about economics in Black

---

3. The 1970s and 1980s witnessed a flourishing of independent feminist and gay newspapers, including the three listed here: *Gay Community News*, based in Boston, Massachusetts, published from 1973 until 1992, with a short revival during the 1990s in conjunction with OutWrite. *womanews* started in Gainesville, Florida, as a radical feminist newspaper in the mid-1970s and then moved to New York and published monthly through 1991; archived copies of *womanews* are at the University of Florida ("WomaNews: Gainesville's Feminist Newspaper," University of Florida Digital Collections, accessed October 1, 2021, https://ufdc.ufl.edu/UF00076708/00001) and online at "WomaNews," JSTOR, Reveal Digital, accessed October 1, 2021, https://www.jstor.org/site/reveal-digital/independent-voices/womanews-27954026/. The *New York Native* published biweekly from 1980 until 1997; archives of the *New York Native* are at the New York Public Library.

communities, because they were saying one thing and meaning something else. Working with the lesbian and gay media helped me go back to that political eye, that value of discerning where you're being lied to. And that's the most important quality you can have as you read a daily newspaper or watch any TV. The United Press International and the Associated Press will lie to you. And when we forget that the media lies, we forget ourselves, we forget the realities that we know.

Our presses, the feminist presses, the small presses, taught us: they will lie to us. They lied to us in every book that they published that didn't bother to mention the gay character who we knew was embedded in the text—or created a Black character who sounded exactly like the white characters in the interest of cosmopolitanism, as if the thoughts in their heads were exactly the same as the white characters. They will lie. And we need to remember that. We need to bring more probing skepticism to our work and to the business of our work. Then we will come closer to that visionary force.

Now I'm going to say the dreaded F-word that was actually spoken earlier today, and that is feminism. My name is Jewelle, and I am a Black lesbian feminist, which is sort of like being a socialist but more. And one of the questions that the organizers asked me was, What is lesbian and gay literature? And I have a basic principle from feminism that helped me make a decision about that, and I thought it was going to be like a long part of the talk, but basically, lesbian and gay literature is what we say it is. I mean, if they can start defining us, why shouldn't we define ourselves? It is a feminist vision that helped bring us here today as lesbian and gay writers and editors and publishers—we must not forget that. It was all the movements that came before the lesbian-feminist movement that brought us here today. And we should not forget that. And not only should we not forget it; we should learn to use it. It's one thing to just simply quote it and say, "Yes, I know that," but what is it that you learned? What is it that you do differently now? Because you understand the oppression of women in this society and the exclusion of women and people of color and poor people from this society. What is it that you learned that makes you do things differently at this conference? If you don't feel you're doing anything differently at this conference because of these lessons, I would find that very upsetting. I would find it very upsetting because it means you haven't really fought a lot. I actually know that it is true because people are doing things differently and I've seen it. I've seen it in the panels. I saw it in the dance. You could definitely see that people were different and treating each other differently. And a dance floor is a dead giveaway. Social situations are a dead giveaway as to how well or how not well we are treating each other.

I mean, I actually know bars in New York. Fortunately, they're closed now, which, you know, white people would leave the bar and not come. If we played the wrong kind of music, too much Black music, lesbians would disappear.

Think about where you place yourself philosophically, and you can help make the decisions of your everyday life. You can help make the decisions about what kind of characters you want to create—what kind of essays you want to write, what kind of topics you want to cover. Not just the topics that they're going to ask you to cover, but when you're going to write an essay about something that somebody thinks you would never be interested in writing about. If you find yourself creating a philosophical stance, you will get more and more curious about everything and not be satisfied with what's right in your realm. A month or so ago, I was in residency in Jacob's Pillow up in Massachusetts.[4] I had to go out and do a reading, and they sort of shifted around really quickly and found a place for me to read at a place called the Mount. And I thought, *Oh, great. A lesbian bar.* I'll just rush right over there. I got there and discovered it was actually Edith Wharton's mansion. That's cool with me. And they're in the

---

4. Jacob's Pillow is an internationally recognized dance festival and incubator of new work in dance, located in Becket, Massachusetts.

middle of this big restoration thing. And you know, since they got the movie, they're really raising money for this restoration and whatnot. So I read from my novel, and I had to say right away—'cause I didn't want the audience, which clearly was there for Edith, not for me—I let them know right away that I was going to be reading from a Black lesbian vampire novel and hope they would kinda, like, try to stay with me. And they did. And they did to the point that the executive director of the restoration called me when I got back home and said, "I'm going to try to get a grant because I would like you to, you know—how do you feel about Edith Wharton?" I said, "Well, I liked her library. Marble was always cool with me." She said, "I'm going to try to get this grant. So I would like you to read her work and next summer do a presentation on Edith Wharton." And I said, "Heck yeah, I'm down." Because Edith Wharton is a woman who was writing, like, from a very privileged economic position in the United States, and she seems related to me—she's a woman who struggled. It was easier for her to write because she had money. She had this Mount, which was quite lovely. But she was still a woman writing. And I'm interested in looking at what she was writing about and seeing where it says something to me and where it does not. And I do that as a Black lesbian-feminist. And it makes it interesting to me. I may read it this morning 'cause the only thing I remember from her is *Ethan Frome*, and I may read her and find her boring as hell. I understand the movie is boring, but I'm going to see it. I know having a feminist vision makes me curious about doing something like that. It does not mean I'm going back to read all the classics, so don't get nervous. It is having a feminist vision and a philosophy, and I'm going to say this one more time: that helps us decide where we hold our events, and the right decision is not to hold them in any accessible places.

I don't want to belabor it, but I have to say it one more time. We went through this in the seventies. We've got bookstores in our community that spend every penny they can to make their stores accessible. We should not be making this mistake in the nineties, and I know we will not make it again next year when we come back.

Given all of that political stuff, you know, I will say that a friend of mine, Marita Golden, has edited a couple of anthologies that I had the good fortune of being included in, and we did a reading recently, and she says (and I believe it) that ultimately the reason we as writers do any of this—you know, forget the politics, forget the money, you know—is, ultimately, we want to be loved.[5] And I think that's true. We want to put our vision of the world out there and have people love us. We want people to applaud and say, "We think you are great." I will tell you it will never happen—I mean, really deeply happen—until you start to think about what those words and what those images are that you're putting out there; until you, here's another word I've worked on, contextualized to them politically, the love coming back does not mean a whole heck of a lot.

May Sarton said we must make myths of our lives in order to bear them.[6] I also believe that that's true. The mile away from here is actually a very attractive little area right now. I know how much money people pay for rent in some of those houses. And I know how much the money they pay for rent is not met by the money that they make to stay in those houses. And that's less than a mile from here. The burden of economic oppression and all the other oppressions, which I believe grow out of economic oppression, is almost unbearable, and we must make myths of our lives in order

5. In addition to being a noted anthologist, Marita Golden is an award-winning novelist and the founder of the Hurston/Wright Foundation.
6. May Sarton (1912–1995) was a popular novelist, memoirist, and poet, known particularly in lesbian communities for her 1965 lesbian novel *Mrs. Stevens Hears the Mermaids Singing*. This paraphrased quotation is from her 1968 memoir *Plant Dreaming Deep* (New York: W. W. Norton, 1968), 151. The original quotation is "We have to make myths of our lives; it is the only way to live them without despair."

to bear them. When I write and I speak of my family who is living that mile away from here still—and it's actually like a foot, a couple of feet away from me now—I'm not just writing about them. I'm writing about you. I'm writing about the people whom you grew up with, the children whom you have, the children whom you don't have but used to know, who grew up and are still out there. When I write about that family and I try to make heroes of them, I'm trying to make a hero of myself, and I'm trying to make heroes out of all of you.

Two Poems

"The Bridge Poem" and "A Pacifist Becomes Militant and Declares War"

Audre Lorde Memorial Lecture

October 10, 1993

The Bridge Poem[1]

I've had enough
I'm sick of seeing and touching
Both sides of things
Sick of being the damn bridge for everybody
Nobody can talk to anybody without me   Right

I explain my mother to my father my father to my little sister my little sister to my brother my brother to the White Feminists the White Feminists to the Black Church Folks the Black Church Folks to the ex-Hippies the ex-Hippies to the Black Separatists the Black Separatists to the Artists and the Artists to the parents of my friends. . . .

---

1. Kate Rushin gave the first Audre Lorde Memorial Lecture at OutWrite 93, less than a year after Lorde's death on November 17, 1992. Unable to secure an audiotape of this event and with Rushin's recollection that she read from her new collection of poetry, *The Black Back-Ups* (Ithaca, NY: Firebrand Books, 1993), we include two poems from that collection.

Then
I've got to explain myself
To everybody

I do more translating than the U.N.

Forget it
I'm sick of filling in your gaps
Sick of being your insurance against
The isolation of your self-imposed limitations
Sick of being the crazy at your Holiday Dinners
The odd one at your Sunday Brunches
I am sick of being the sole Black friend to
Thirty-four Individual White folks

Find another connection to the rest of the world
Something else to make you legitimate
Some other way to be political and hip
I will not be the bridge to your womanhood
Your manhood
Your human-ness

I'm sick of reminding you not to
Close off too tight for too long

Sick of mediating with your worst self
On behalf of your better selves

Sick
Of having
To remind you
To breathe
Before you
Suffocate
Your own
Fool self

Forget it
Stretch or drown
Evolve or die

You see   it's like this
The bridge I must be
Is the bridge to my own power
I must translate
My own fears
Mediate
My own weaknesses

I must be the bridge to nowhere
But my own true self
It's only then
I can be
Useful

A Pacifist Becomes Militant and Declares War

In the old days
I'd see lovers
Strolling and laughing
I'd watch them and smile
And almost let myself wonder
Why I never felt the way they looked

Now I walk down the street with you
And simply because you are always a woman
I get this teetering feeling

Your sudden
Street corner kiss
Accentuates my hesitation

And I realize that in order to care about you
I have to be everything that is in me

Your laughter underscores the
Sick sinking feeling in my stomach and
I know once and for all
If I walk away
Hide from you
I keep on running from myself

Sometimes
When you kiss me on the street
I feel like a sleepwalker
I feel like I just woke up
And I'm standing on a ledge
Twenty-stories high

And I don't know how in the hell I got here
I say to myself
I say Fool
Why don't you go home and act right
You don't have to be here
Pretend it never happened
Pretend you never felt a thing
Except maybe a nightmare
Or maybe it was a salty, half-shell dream

Go home and act right
But what for
I can never go back
To what never was
I can't force myself into
Somebody else's image

And If I love you
Even just a little bit
I have to love the woman that I am
I have to reach down deep inside
I have to stand and show myself
I have to walk in the world
There is never any going back
Only going forward into the next day
And the day after that

Your full-length street corner kiss
Is seasoned with excitement
And rebellion

O.K.
Then I'm a rebel
I'm a crazy colored woman
Declaring war on my old ways
On all my fear
My choking
My cringing
My hesitation

I break my fast and admit
That I am hungry
I am hungry to care
To become careless
Careful

So I'm a rebel
Get ready for the insurrection
Get ready for the
Rebellion
Uprising
Riot of my kisses

We Have to Fight for Our Political Lives

KEYNOTE ADDRESS

MARCH 3, 1995

Publishing and activism are two areas in my life that have become critical and where I've been doing a lot of work and that have truly been life transforming for me. The larger theme I'd like to focus on is the need and really desperate need that we have to get our voices out. And because of the swing toward the Right, it's very critical that we keep talking, that we don't allow ourselves to be silenced, that we get our stories in print—no matter where, whether it's a magazine, a book, a newspaper; whether you are xeroxing pages and stapling together and handing them out somewhere; whether it's fiction, nonfiction, poetry, whatever—that our voices be heard, that we get them out to save our own lives, to save the lives of other people who are struggling and in pain. And the wonderful thing about it is that we can do it with style. We can do it with true emotion, and we can do it with beauty.[1]

One of the most rewarding things about my job at *Essence* is the really subversive ways that I am able to effect change, even if they're just baby steps kind of change. My goal there, being a staffer, is just to be able to be my true Black lesbian self and to be able to make change that will change people and the way they think. And since I have five million people available to me, to

---

1. At this point, Villarosa told a three-minute story that described how editors work with writers, and that was both warmly received by and illuminating to the audience.

change the way they think is really often a daunting task.[2] The other part of my job is to roll up my sleeves with a group of other women because we work in a collective way to slide in often radical politics around gender, sexuality, and even for a Black magazine, race.

Essence is the only large magazine for Black women; we feel really responsible in a serious way to move the race conversation forward. So between those hair and makeup tips, we really try to give serious discussion, political discussions, on very serious topics, from discussions of *The Bell Curve* to prison reform to environmental racism.[3] We also run some really wonderful, and I think subversive, articles about lesbian and gay issues.

This is our Whitney and Bobby cover, which is, you know, we don't have to say it out loud, but it's problematic on a number of levels.[4] But in it, I really was proud to get an excerpt of E. Lynn Harris's second book, *Just as I Am*, and to have it in the context of reads about romances.[5] When readers opened up the magazine without any explanation, just as a natural thing, we had a gay male love story. I really, I really treasure that. Then in our June issue of last year, we had this cover of Halle Berry. And we had a piece written by Nadine Smith called "Homophobia, Will It Divide

---

2. Five million people is the estimated audience of *Essence* in 1995.

3. Published in 1994, *The Bell Curve: Intelligence and Class Structure in American Life* by Richard J. Herrnstein and Charles Murray argues that the "cognitive elite" drive the divisions within the United States; relying on mean IQ data, the authors draw conclusions about cognitive abilities based on race, with Asian and white Americans performing the best. The book was widely debated and condemned by progressive thinkers and activists.

4. Whitney Houston and Bobby Brown. Houston was widely rumored to be in a lesbian relationship at the time of the cover of *Essence*. In 2019, Robyn Crawford confirmed her relationship with Houston in her memoir, *A Song for You*.

5. E. Lynn Harris (1955–2009) was a popular African American gay male writer whose novels centered Black gay men living "in the closet" or "on the down low."

Us?"[6] It was really a serious discussion in honor of the March on Washington, the Gay Games, and lesbian and gay issues. I'm really proud that we got that in. In an upcoming issue in June, we're having a piece about fathers raising their children, and we have, without any huge fanfare, an article about a gay man who's raising his son. That's the work I'm most proud of. To explain lesbian and gay issues to a mainstream heterosexual Black audience and also to introduce our readers to some really wonderful, gifted writers whom they may not know about, that's my day job.

Now, I also have this other thing that's happened to me, and it's around activism, which is at least as important as the work I do at the magazine. It's part of my life now. First, I would really like to give praise to the people who did it before me and who have done it longer than me and who have done it really wonderfully and have influenced what I'm doing now. When I wrote my coming out article with my mother four years ago, I really had absolutely no idea that I would be thrust into the limelight the way I have been. And I really had no idea about the real demand and true hunger for a visible symbol of Black lesbianism. Being that visible symbol has been almost utterly consuming. As a writer, and even more behind the scenes as an editor, I really had no idea what it would be like. I've had some frankly shocking experiences along the way in these four years. One thing I've learned is that it is critical that we as writers use our skill and our position as members of the out community to make that link between other oppressed communities and the gay community. And this is difficult, frustrating, and often painful.

And I'm going to speak about it from the standpoint of the Black community. And as we all know, the right wing is out to get all of us, and it's regardless of race, gender, or sexuality. We have to really understand that; we have to drive that point home. We have to drive it home as writers. We have to stop being good, trying to

---

6. Nadine Smith was one of four cochairs of the 1993 March on Washington; she is now the executive director of Equality Florida.

be good little boys and girls and saying, "Please, please give us a place at the table." We have to question who's on the invite list. If we're going to go to that table, we need to say, "I'm going to bring a few uninvited guests to the dinner party."

And this is often hard because we've been suckered into believing that equality is this scarce commodity, this scarce little pie, the dessert at the dinner party—and that there's only a limited, limited amount, and not everybody can have some, so there's not enough to go around. So if one group gets some, then another group can't have any. We have to, I mean, break it down to that level in print, we have to talk about it, and we have to even explain it that way because it's such a hard thing to get. It's such a hard notion. And I saw that really in a straightforward and difficult way about two or three years ago. We were doing an action at city hall around Hattie Mae Collins. For anybody who doesn't remember, Hattie Mae Collins was a woman, a Black woman in Oregon, who was murdered by racist skinheads. When she and her gay roommate were in the house, the skinheads threw a firebomb in the house, and she burned to death. There was little press around this. It was in Oregon, and so we were wanting to get the word out in a national way. So a group of us went to city hall, a mixed-race group. So we're doing our little thing, not a big turnout. On the side was a group of Black journalists, many of whom lived in New York and I knew. I was really glad to see them. I said, "Hey, bring that reporter's notebook and that microphone over here to what's going on with this Black woman. Did you know a woman was murdered? A Black woman was murdered." And they said, "No, we didn't hear; what happened?" As I explained to them that this Black woman was killed—she burned to death, racist skinheads—and they were starting to move over. And then I said, "You know, she was a lesbian." And they're dismissive. It was very weird. We got into this discussion that was like, "She was a Black woman. She was murdered. She was a lesbian, she was a Black woman, she was a lesbian." And it turned out to be this frustrating day.

At that point, I wasn't equipped to handle it any differently. And so I just kept insisting she was a Black woman, and it wasn't working, but I couldn't move them. And it was almost as soon as I said "She was a lesbian," then her blackness, which should have been the most obvious part of her, disappeared. She became just somebody, and it was somebody whom they couldn't relate to. Since then, I've learned to take a different tact and to be able to explain these issues more clearly and without so much anger.

I was able to confront it again at the University of Cincinnati. This was just three weeks ago. I was to speak to a student group. Before I got there, the group called me in a rather casual way and said, "Oh, by the way, you're going to have six bodyguards there because, you know, there's been a death threat from the Klan." So I was like, "Oh, OK"—thinking, "OK, Whitney Houston, *The Bodyguard*, the movie." No. What I did was, this time, I didn't panic. I called a lot of activists whom I knew from Sarah Schulman to Mandy Carter to the Klan Watch to the Black student groups on campus to local politicians.[7] I just was hysterical telling everybody about this and asking, What should I do? What should I do? So the word really got out. I got on the radio, and the group was like, "You know, maybe you shouldn't talk about that so much." I was like, "Did you know that the Klan has threatened us?" I mean, I was really open about it.

So when I got to the actual event, it was packed. And it was bad. People were really there. And they were really impressed by those bodyguards too. People were there, they said, to watch my back. There was a group of Black people sitting kind of segregated and a group of lesbian and gay activists, many of whom have had to organize around the antigay legislation in Cincinnati. It was the

---

7. Mandy Carter is a longtime southern activist. She is one of the founders of the National Black Justice Coalition and Southerners on New Ground; she worked on many campaigns to challenge and unseat Jesse Helms, as well as other nationally significant projects. Klan Watch was a project of the Southern Poverty Law Center.

Black group that was madly militant and like, "Don't touch her." And then it was like, you know, this whole wonderful group that often I don't get when I go to speak. The wonderful part about it was afterward. When I called to check in on them, the groups between them made pacts; the lesbian and gay group made a pact that next Christmas, when the Klan raises its stupid cross in the town square in Cincinnati, the white lesbian and gay activists were going to come and support the Black people who are there year after year. The next week at the meeting of the lesbian and gay group, those Black people who were sitting there like this were at that meeting because they said, "Don't let the Klan mess with anybody." Because it was such a dramatic incident, I was able very easily to make that link: the Klan is usually out trying to lynch Black people, and here they are. *Lynch* was the word they used: to lynch lesbian and gay people. You can see that link. It was clear. I didn't have to keep driving it home over and over. People understood it. Not all of the work that has to be done can be by those of us who are Black lesbian and gay people to the Black community. Today I really want to challenge white lesbian and gay activists to do some long-range thinking around this. I know some of it's happening—but to even drive it home further and to really push harder on this, to really begin to do more and use different strategies to forge ties with communities of color.

Often it works. In Seattle last summer, there was an antigay initiative started by the Oregon Citizens Alliance. They infiltrated Washington, and there was an antigay piece of legislation that was trying to be put on to the ballot for a vote. There was very poor planning by the white activists. The right-wing Oregon Citizens Alliance easily came in and started going to the Black churches and saying, "Hey, these gay people are nasty. They're trying to take away your rights, blah, blah, blah, blah." It was very late in the game that finally the Black activists were called in. And the people were mad. They were like, "You should have come to us sooner, but blah, blah, blah, blah." But they still rallied around this. And I was brought in to speak around my job at *Essence*, to speak to communities of color. And it was really wonderful what happened. I mean, it was very difficult. I was on Black talk radio. I was at the church group. I was at the community center, and there was always, or often, a minister with me, a straight Black minister, and we talked about religion. We talked about it. That ballot initiative never even got on the ballot. A tremendous tie was forged between these communities. It's important for white lesbian and gay activists to do the work of listening to angry Black people, straight and gay, so that we can figure out ways to strategize against the right wing.

It's also important for all of us, especially those of us who are not from communities of color, to study the ways in which the right wing has historically used the same strategies over and over to keep oppressed groups oppressed. We have to make these links both in print and in public; they always use the Bible against groups they don't like. To keep blacks enslaved, this was what they used. It's clear. I looked it up myself in my little Bible: "Slaves be obedient to those who are your earthly masters with fear and trembling in singleness of heart as to Christ, not in the way of eye service as man pleasers but as servants of Christ" (Eph. 6:5). That was what they used to keep slaves enslaved. To condemn lesbians and gay men, they use 1 Corinthians 6:9–10, which reads, "Do not be deceived neither the immoral nor idolaters nor adulterers nor homosexuals nor thieves nor the greedy nor drunkards nor revilers nor robbers will inherit the kingdom of God." And we have to challenge that. I, on my own, looked up to see if "homosexual" had really been in the King James Version of the Bible, and of course it hadn't. It said "effeminate." This is something we have to challenge. We have to challenge in print. And we also have to explain it in a way that people who are religious can hear.

The other thing the right wing does is always accuses us, whoever it is that they don't like, of being hypersexual; Black men and women were told we were hypersexual in order to justify slavery. This comes from a slave trader's journal from the 1600s. This is how he described African culture: "Negro nature is so craven and sensuous in every fiber of its being, so deeply rooted in immorality are Negro people that they turn in revulsion from any sexual relation, which does not invite sensuous embraces." Another account of African women on slave ships characterized them as "hot unconstituted ladies." From the sixteenth to the nineteenth centuries, Black women were repeatedly and randomly sexually victimized and had no control over their sexuality or fertility. While white men raped their way through the slave quarters to justify this brutal behavior, they perpetuated the myth that Black women were oversexed savages and insatiable, but doesn't that sound familiar? Doesn't that sound familiar to what they say about gay men? I don't even have to make that link any clearer, but here's an aside, is that lesbians also get it; you know, here we are complaining about lesbian bed death, and then the right wing is calling us hypersexual. I was speaking to a group, and there was this young woman, and I know she wandered into the wrong room or something. I don't know what happened. So she raises her hand really tentatively. She says, "You know, you spoke so eloquently, and your job is so great. Before you spoke, I thought all lesbians did was have sex." I just did a Kate Clinton, and I said, "Oh, don't have time."

Another key strategy that the right wing and the Christian Right use is to pit groups against one another in terms of economics. Even though one-third of all Black people are poor and one-third of all poor people are Black, we are being told that as Black people, we are the ones getting all of the privileges and all of the opportunities. This is a long-term strategy, but it's also heating up more and more around the discussion of affirmative action. Now, as lesbians and gay men, we know that this has been used against us; anybody who has looked at those videos like *Gay Rights, Special Rights* and *The Gay Agenda* knows this is true.[8] The video

---

8. *Gay Rights, Special Rights* and *The Gay Agenda* are two videos produced and widely distributed by the right wing in the 1990s to attack gay and lesbian communities.

makers used our own statistics, collected for marketing purposes, against us with the message of "Why do you need special rights if you're so rich and chic?" These are strategies that have been used against us that we have to learn to dissect in print, and to really analyze, and to really refute.

The other thing is there are activists of all colors, but especially activists who are not from communities of color, who can really learn from some of the issues that the activists of color have struggled with during the civil rights movement and some of the arguments used internally and also some of the mistakes that were made. It is not a new situation in the struggle for rights to wonder if fringes of the community should be kept out of a public march. In the 1963 March on Washington, folks were asked to put on their Sunday best suits and dresses—and we're talking women in dresses, not the guys—in order to look presentable to the mainstream. Bayard Rustin, who was the openly gay architect of the March on Washington, was downplayed in his role in order to elevate A. Philip Randolph, who was a heterosexual man. He really took a back seat. That was a mistake, but that was something that was hotly debated at the time. We should go back and read that debate to really think about it, to really include it in writings, as we try to sort through our own issues along the same line. You know what I mean. I don't know if I can hear one more time, "Should drag queens be able to march in the March?" Like we could stop them.

We've also had to struggle with the idea that "Do we stand behind somebody just because they're a member of our tribe?" This is another painful, bizarre public lesson that we Black people learned with Clarence Thomas. When he was first up for the confirmation (to the U.S. Supreme Court), many Black people were skeptical about him, right from the start. But once he began to be attacked by the mainstream white media and also by white women, then Black people were unable to deal with the public spectacle of a Black man being brought down in public. So people who were not even really for him really started being more for him as a reaction. Other people just froze—caught up in indecision around what to do from the many confusing points of view. Ultimately, of course, we've paid the price for this.

As gay people, were really struggling with this, to be specific, around David Brock most recently, who was an openly gay man, and we don't know what to do with him.[9] Is this man our ally? What do we do? Does he have any place in the movement at all? But as we sort through this issue, we can look at communities of color that have already been through this struggle for guidance. These subjects are very difficult, but they are the ones that right now—around issues of race, around gender, and around sexuality—are the most contentious, which makes them the most interesting in print. But it's also vital that we struggle with them for ourselves. Sorting through these issues is difficult. And I want to say this really from my heart: I know that writing is a difficult process. It's often lonely; it's often frustrating. And I really want to encourage you not to be discouraged. And at many points along the way, you will be discouraged. You will be frustrated. You will be staring at an empty sheet of paper, at an empty computer screen, and just know that you can do it. You need to do it. You really have to do it at this point. And I want to share with you that a lot of people think, "Oh, you got that book. It's so big. It was such a snap." That book was ten years in the making.[10] And for me, it was worth the wait because I was ultimately able to do something that was political, that was openly political, with a foreword written by Angela Davis and June Jordan. It has one long chapter, and then many other points interspersed in the copy issues, dealing directly with lesbian health concerns. It's openly pro-choice. It talks about racism and discrimination against the

9. From an audience question, Villarosa clarified in the speech who David Brock is with this statement: "He's a writer for the *American Spectator*. He's the infamous person who called Anita Hill 'slutty.'"
10. Linda Villarosa's book *Body and Soul: The Black Women's Guide to Physical Health and Emotional Well-Being* was published in October 1994.

poor. It talks about problems with the health-care system, and it talks about alternatives to mainstream medicine. However, it took me so long to get the book into print because I was discouraged in a really profound way and often a crushing way in that ten years on that long road. Don't let that happen to you, and don't let anybody ever tell you you can't write. Over and over, you might hear those negative voices, and maybe they're your own voice, but don't listen; block them out. But one caveat is to make sure you really can write.

One thing that helps is really to study good writing. One way you can study it, and just know that I am now going to openly plug my best friend's new book, is to read Jacqueline Woodson's *Autobiography of a Family Photo*. That is good writing. To improve your own writing, do it every day. Just do it. Get down there with that typewriter and do it no matter how tired you are. You're bone tired. You're beyond bone tired—just write. Just practice that craft because that's what it is. It is a craft. If I had listened to any or all of the people who had told me I couldn't write, I don't think I ever would have even written a paragraph, much less a whole book. I'd probably be curled up in bed somewhere sucking my thumb. My supervisor at my first job told me that I had no writing talent. I realized even then that, although I was crushed, it wasn't about my talent. It was about my mechanics. I wasn't getting the mechanics. I wasn't doing something right. It wasn't me. It was just the process that I hadn't quite gotten down. So I encourage you to study that and to really learn it so you feel comfortable with it. Also, seek out criticism, seek out sensitive criticism, and listen to it, and be willing to revise.

Don't let people tell you that your story or your idea has already been done. Hell, everything's already been done. Our challenge now is to look for unique ways to tell different stories, or sometimes tell the same story in different ways, to tell stories that are slightly different. Who cares if the themes have already been covered? That hasn't ever stopped anybody else from being published. Mary McCarthy obviously has already talked about the Catholic girlhood to womanhood thing, but that didn't stop Anna Quindlen from getting a book deal. Charles Murray has his book *The Bell Curve* in print even though Adolf Hitler has covered that race-in-genetics story before.

Now the idea that we can't have more lesbian and gay books because there are already enough books is a crock, and it feeds into the false notion and fear of scarcity. There is no scarcity. It's like, and I hate to use an Eddie Murphy joke, but it's like that video—or maybe it was a skit—he did where he was this one Black person on the bus, and as soon as he got off the bus, it was all white people, and when he gets off the bus, then all of a sudden they start handing out money on the bus, there's a huge party, and they're serving drinks on the bus. That's what we, those of us who are not involved in the publishing industry, think, but there is no scarcity.

Don't listen to people who tell you that our stories are not universal. Craziness. Why is the story of bisexual vampires surviving through the ages written by heterosexual white women more universal than a Black lesbian vampire character in Jewelle Gomez's novels? There should not be this big difference. It's all about the comfort level of the generally white heterosexual acquiring editor who is making the decision. I was asked, and I'm asked still repeatedly, What can white women get out of a Black women's health book? And I have a really great pat answer down. I say, "Listen, you can read it exactly the way Black women for years have read books that are supposed to be about mainstream women's health. These books are written by white women, usually doctors. All the contributors inside, if there are any, are white women; the illustrations and photographs are white women. You can weed through this as a Black woman and find what you need," but that's what white women need to do with my book.

On the other hand, we also shouldn't be too discouraged by investing too much power and negativity into the individuals who publish books. There are some lesbians and gay men, wonderful people out and not out, as well as cool heterosexuals who really are looking out for our stories and have some of the same goals we have in mind. I was told by so many people that I would never be able to have a Black women's health book that dealt openly with lesbian issues. I don't know how many people told me that. So the first day I met my editor, I was in there ready. It was the first thing I was going to ask her. So I'm like, "How do you feel about us having a chapter on lesbian health and having lesbian concerns in the book?" And she turns around and she reaches on her bookshelf and says, "I edited this book, *The Lesbian and Gay Parenting Handbook*." So it was fine. It worked out fine.

In order to get our messages and stories in print, we really have to support each other. Even as writers, we're often put in situations where another writer is pitted against us. I don't know how many times that I have been asked if Evelyn C. White, who is a good friend of mine, and I are in some kind of feud because she's a Black lesbian who also has a health book. Hers is a book of essays. Mine is more of a self-help book. Over and over, I am asked that. Now, why would I possibly be in a feud with an ally? She is somebody who inspires me, who supports me, who I support. We reach out to each other. We hold each other's hands. We do that long-distance whining on the telephone. We're not in a fight, because we both understand how necessary the material that we're putting out is and how important it is and affirming and desperately needed. I'm not jealous of her. I need her; I need her in my life. That's what we have to do. We really have to try to watch each other's backs.

Finally, I want to encourage you to take your talent as writers and activists and do something and do it right now. Now is the opportunity because we are in the midst of a real crisis, and to use a medical metaphor, we got a fever. Now there's a fever, and a fever signals illness, but it's usually a good sign that the body is trying to fight. The body is trying to fight back, fight for its life. And that's what we have to do. We have to fight for our political lives. We have to fight now. We have to fight for the lives of ourselves, and we have to fight for the lives of others, and by others, I'm talking about otherness in a very broad sense. That means we have to take those stories that we have, and we have to tell them from the heart and from the gut. We have to write the truth with courage and with conviction. Ask yourself one question: How am I going to use my special voice and my unique experience to create change?

On Pretentiousness

KEYNOTE ADDRESS

MARCH 3, 1995

Pretentiousness, overstatement, rhetoric and histrionics, grandiosity and portentousness are, as much as they are also tropes of fascists and demagogues everywhere, American tropes, gestures of habitual florid overstep common among those practitioners of American culture to whom I have always been most instantly attracted.[1] It is an aspect of American history and the culture we have developed that I am keen to possess, to transform for my own purposes: the writing of declarations, constitutions, epics, manifestos. Consider chapter 18 of de Tocqueville's *Democracy in America*, which is entitled "Why American Writers and Speakers Are Often Bombastic" and which is remarkable for its insight, less for its French antidemocratic softness:

> I have often noticed that the Americans, whose language when talking business is clear and dry, without the slightest ornament, and of such extreme simplicity as often to be vulgar, easily turn bombastic when they attempt a poetic style. They are then pompous, without stopping from beginning to end of a speech, and one would have supposed, seeing them thus prodigal of metaphors, that they could never say anything simply.
>
> The reason is easily pointed out.

---

1. Kushner's full speech is included in his book *Thinking about the Longstanding Problems of Virtue and Happiness: Essays, a Play, Two Poems and a Prayer* (New York: Theatre Communications Group, 1995), 55–79.

Each citizen of a democracy generally spends his time considering the interests of a very insignificant person, namely, himself. If he ever does raise his eyes higher, he sees nothing but the huge apparition of society or the even larger form of the human race. He has nothing between very limited and clear ideas and very general and vague conceptions; the space between is empty. . . .

Writers, for their part, almost always pander to propensity, which they share; they inflate their imaginations and swell them out beyond bounds, so that they achieve gigantism, missing real grandeur. . . . Writer and public join in corrupting each other. . . . Finding no stuff for the ideal in what is real and true, poets, abandoning truth and reality, create monsters.

I have no fear that the poetry of democratic peoples will be found timid or that it will stick too close to the earth. I am much more afraid that it will spend its whole time getting lost in the clouds and may finish up by describing an entirely fictitious country. I am alarmed at the thought of too many immense, incoherent images, overdrawn descriptions, bizarre effects, and a whole fantastic breed of brainchildren who will make one long for the real world.[2]

When I began work on *Angels in America*, I felt that the outrageousness of the project I was attempting—offering itself like a fatted calf to critics who loved to feast on pretentiousness and grandiosity; I felt that this selfsame pretentiousness and grandiosity was my birthright as an American, and rather than pointing to some serious deficiencies and flaws in my character (although such deficiencies and flaws undoubtedly exist and are complicit in all of this), my artistic obstreperousness indicated to me, on good days, that I was heir, no matter how puny an heir I might be, to a literary tradition that had produced some of my favorite books.

Chief among which was, and still is, *Moby Dick*—we know de Tocqueville never met Melville, but he might have been describing him in advance. I have always loved the daring, the absurdity, the

---

2. Alexis de Tocqueville, *Democracy in America*, trans. George Lawrence, ed. J. P. Mayer (New York: Harper Perennial Modern Classics, 2006), 488–489.

frequently hair-raising success and occasional hair-raising failure, the passion, and the onrushing grandiloquent devouring reckless-ness of Melville's writing. It gives me license to try anything.

Melville's first taste of critical disregard came with his book *Mardi*, which is, in my opinion, one of his greatest, clearly a warm-up for *Moby-Dick*, which also failed critically. In *Mardi*, a fictional Polynesian archipelago, called Mardi, is a stand-in for the entire world. The book begins as a slightly fantasticized version of Mel-ville's early, successful South Sea adventures; but winds of meta-phor, the heritage of English literature and contemporary national and international politics, soon fill his sails and blow the author, by about a fourth of the way into the book, out of the realm of realism and into a new kind of entirely literary, philosophical, symbol-laden book-of-a-book—a planet on the table.

The novel is deliriously endless; in chapter 180, we encounter a character who is the Mardian Homer or Virgil or Dante, and his sufferings to produce his masterpiece, an epic called *Koztanza*, are described. But clearly Melville is writing about himself, in a perfectly splendid lament over the high-wire perils, the anxieties suffered by a writer—even a great writer—tilling the vasty fields of pretentiousness:

> Sometimes, when by himself, he thought hugely of [his book] . . .
> but when abroad, among men, he almost despised it; but when he
> bethought him of those parts, written with full eyes, half blinded;
> temples throbbing; and pain at the heart—He would say to him-
> self, "Sure, it can not be in vain!" Yet again, when he bethought
> him of the hurry and bustle of Mardi, dejection stole over him.
> "Who will heed it," thought he; "what care these fops and brawlers
> for me? But am I not myself an egregious coxcomb? Who will read
> me? Say one thousand pages—twenty-five lines each—every line
> ten words—every word ten letters. That's two million five hundred
> thousand *a*'s, and *i*'s, and *o*'s, to read! How many are superfluous?
> Am I not mad to saddle Mardi with such a task? Of all men, am I
> the wisest, to stand upon a pedestal, and teach the mob? Ah, my
> own *Koztanza*! Child of many prayers!—in whose earnest eyes, so
> fathomless, I see my own; and recall all past delights and silent

agonies—thou may'st prove, as the child of some fond dotard: beauteous to me; hideous to Mardi! And methinks, that while so much slaving merits that thou should'st not die; it has not been intense, prolonged enough, for the high need of immortality."[3]

Pretentiousness is risky; a vast, amorphous, self-generative anxiety comes with the equally vast and amorphous territory one has chosen to cover. One is highly susceptible to ridicule and possessed of such a number of flanks that it is impossible to protect them all. Since the size of one's ambitions is laid bare for the world to see, being thin-skinned is a predictable consequence and symptom of pretentiousness: one's skin is, after all, so painfully stretched over such a very large area. Implicit in grandiosity and pretentiousness is an unslakable desire to embrace everyone. The impulse to make work that contains the world surely stems from an infantile impulse to swallow it, whole, and to be universally adored for having done so. These desires are even more doomed than the desires you develop as an adult, and to carry the appetite of an infant into middle age is to risk a certain indignity, to say the least (the way, for instance, that this speech attempts simultaneously a self-defense and a self-critique and is, I fear, tangling itself up in knots). We pretentious writers of the Left share this unfortunate flaw, of being excessively thin-skinned and rapaciously greedy, with other control freaks, people we'd probably rather avoid any association with—Rush Limbaugh, Bob Dole, Adolf Hitler . . .

Pretentiousness is, I sometimes think, a form of hysteria that manifests itself as listing, cataloging—manifests itself in a panicked strained effort toward the encyclopedic, lest the important ideas, which the pretentious writer doesn't feel she or he truly or deeply comprehends, escape while writerly attentions dazedly malinger over some bit of inconsequence.

---

3. Herman Melville, *Typee, Omoo, Mardi* (New York: Library of America, 1982), 1262.

But the joys of pretentiousness are more alluring than its humiliations are forbidding. It is as de Tocqueville says a profoundly democratic gesture, or failing, though not entirely as he understood it. Pretentiousness is in one sense a Promethean, protean liberation of the imagination, and anyone is capable of it, provided we pretenders can inure ourselves sufficiently to the shame that is heaped upon us when we are caught in the act of pretending. Pretentiousness consists in attempting an act of bold creation regardless of whether or not one has sufficient talent, emulating the daring of which only genius is truly capable—daring to see how close to the moon we are capable, all our insufficiencies and limitations notwithstanding, of soaring. Embracing pretentiousness as a trope, as a stratagem and a tool, becoming ironically aware rather than ashamed of grandiosity, enables us to make literary and perhaps political hay out of the distance between what we would like to have done and what we have actually accomplished. The success and the failure both are part of the story—the success celebrating our gloriousness, the failure nobly demarcating our tragedy, but in both glory and tragedy, we pretenders are fabulous.

Pretentiousness is camp, it is drag, and perhaps this is why it's most resplendently at home in the theater. Pretentiousness, *if it's done well*, performs a salutary parody of carving out, in the face of the theorilessness and bewilderment of our age, metanarratives, legends, grand designs, even in spite of the suspiciousness with which we have learned, rightly, to regard metanarrative: by pretending that such grandeur is still possible, we acknowledge how absolutely necessary, and indispensable, an overview, a theory, a big idea still is. Such pretense will have to do, until the real thing comes along.

People fundamentally lacking a sense of humor when confronted with pretentiousness miss the irony and the fun and are left with flared nostrils indignantly aquiver at the *tastelessness* and the *presumption*. Invariably, such people are themselves guilty of pretention and are drearily unaware of it.

To make political art is always to risk pretentiousness because you can only ever fail to formulate answers to the questions you pose, if those questions are big enough—and really, if they aren't, why bother posing? To make overtly political art, you must, I think, always declare more than you can prove and say more than you can know: you must speculate and so risk the pretention all participatory political discourse is heir to. C. L. R. James values this most in Melville: the fact that Melville arrives at a place of self-confessed unknowing, that his art goes beyond his powers to explain, addressing issues of such depth that "to explain would be to dive deeper than Ishmael can go."[4]

I suppose I am speaking here specifically of a tradition of public art that consciously engages itself with civic debate, a tradition of writing that, presumptuously, aspires to position itself among other grand American texts, each of which is not without its over-reach. The Declaration of Independence is pretentious. So is the Constitution.

For all that I have publicly decried the dangers of assimilation-ism, for all that the assimilationism of the lesbian and gay Right infuriates me, I have long been guiltily aware of the extent to which my work and even my politics betray an assimilationist pen-chant for "the accumulated wisdom of culture," evident perhaps no place as clearly as in my ardent embrace of pretentiousness as my birthright as an American citizen, third generation ambiva-lently and only partially enfranchised—because queer—eternally implacably diasporan inhabitant.[5]

---

4. Herman Melville, *Reburn, White-Jacket, Moby-Dick* (New York: Library of America, 1983). This line is from the end of chapter 41, "Moby Dick." The text is available from Project Gutenberg, accessed October 1, 2021, https://www.gutenberg.org/files/2701/2701-h/2701-h.htm.

5. This paragraph follows a longer disquisition by Kushner in the full speech on the work of Leo Bersani and Ulysse Dutoit in their book *Arts of Impov-erishment: Beckett, Rothko, Resnais* (Cambridge, MA: Harvard University Press, 1993), 91.

Recognizing the accumulated wisdom of culture as a repressive ideological apparatus is easy to do—read one of Bill Bennett's books, if you really hate yourself—but a radical rejection of aforesaid culture is more difficult.[6] Embedded in this culture is a history tending, though not deterministically, not without struggle, toward some plausible, workable, realizable version of radical, pluralist democracy. In American history and culture, there is a liberal individualism that a radical anti-individualist progressivism relentlessly critiques and reshapes: a nonviolent, pragmatic revolutionary politics predicated on a collectivity of individuals reinventing themselves into something new; a social and economic justice emerging, fitfully; and for all our arrant and arid puritanism, a sensuality and socialism of the skin. In American millenarianism, I see the anticipation of the break that will finally come when, even in this hard-hearted, bloody, and mistrustful land, necessity finally submits, to borrow from Akhmatova, and steps pensively aside.

I see the contradictory motions of this politics in Melville; it's why he turns me on. Let me read you two passages from his novel *White-Jacket*. These follow close upon one another in the book: "Depravity in the oppressed is no apology for the oppressor; but rather an additional stigma to him, as being, in a larger degree, the effect, and not the cause and justification of oppression."[7]

This is formidable wisdom, arrived at in 1853; no one in Washington, DC, today seems capable of it. But only a few pages later, Melville delivers himself of this vatic, imperial pronouncement: "We Americans are the peculiar, chosen people—the Israel of our

---

6. During the Reagan administration, William Bennett chaired the National Endowment for the Humanities from 1981 until 1995 and then became the secretary of education. His 1992 book, *The Devaluing of America: The Fight for Our Culture and Our Children*, synthesizes his experiences in national policy work and conservative views through a full-throated attack on American liberalism.

7. Melville, *Reburn*. This line is from the end of chapter 34, "Some of the Evil Effects of Flogging." The text is available from Project Gutenberg, accessed October 1, 2021, https://www.gutenberg.org/files/10712/10712-h/10712-h.htm.

time—God has given us, for a future inheritance, the broad domains of the political pagans. . . . The rest of the nations must soon be in our rear. . . . With ourselves, almost for the first time in the history of the earth, national selfishness is unbounded philanthropy; for we cannot do a good to America but we give alms to the world."[8]

Here is something more congenial to the drafters of the Contract with America.[9] Melville at moments such as these reminds us that pretentiousness, again, is an expression of a certain luxuriousness, and hence perhaps of privilege, and it is also an expression of aggressive power, of dominance—in this case, of a hegemonic Manifest-Destiny-huffing-and-puffing that drowns out the truths and the histories of noncitizens, of which the writer is otherwise remarkably sensible. Both truth and also the lies state power tells itself are present in Melville; like Whitman, he contains multitudes. This naked, exposed working through, this public-arena-wrangling, is the cultural inheritance (more multiracial, multigendered, multipreferenced an inheritance than the Right has ever understood) I cannot bring myself to abandon. Do I, in this reticence, betray myself as, God forbid, a liberal?

We can balance the spectacle, from the assimilationist camp, of one prominent gay citizen recently visiting a large Catholic midwestern campus, ostensibly for the purpose of critiquing the church's homophobia, and in the process complimenting Joseph Cardinal Ratzinger for his "usual intellectual acerbity and indeed intellectual honesty," while the *New York Times* reporter covering the speech enthuses over the speaker's politeness, in the process equating ACT UP's anger with Operation Rescue's[10]—or another

---

8. Melville, chap. 36, "Flogging Not Necessary."

9. Contract with America was a set of Republican legislative initiatives championed after the large Republican win in the 1994 midterm election during the presidency of Bill Clinton.

10. Kushner refers to Peter Steinfels article about Andrew Sullivan's visit to the University of Notre Dame: Peter Steinfels, "Beliefs," *New York Times*,

prominent gay citizen, one I admire a lot and who really should know better, offering the readers of the *New York Times*' op-ed page his opinion that ACT UP and GMHC share "some of the blame" for the fact that far too many of us have stopped practicing safe sex.[11] ACT UP bashing, in fact, seems near epidemic these days. Let's hope we aren't witnessing in such instances the beginning of an old bad propensity for progressive people, when confronted with triumphant political evil, to take careful aim and shoot themselves in the feet.

We posit against these any politics, any theory that galvanizes action, that produces common cause, that is not self-defeating: perhaps, even, half-facetiously, half-seriously, a politics of literary pretentiousness, in which a book, or a play, muddled though it may be, is willing to sacrifice form and coherence in a determined effort to escape the library and become literature no longer—to become, instead, life. That this effort is also doomed, because writing will always remain writing, doesn't mean that the ultimate struggle is doomed or that writing has no contribution to make to a practical politics, to a ready response to the current unbelievable onslaught. The yearning displayed in pretentiousness may have its political uses, for one of the greatest dangers in times of reactionary backlash is that the borders of utopia appear to have been closed. When even bodily necessities are denied us, we can too easily surrender the necessity of aspirations, dreams, hope—the future. Isn't any art that seeks to inspire or provoke or excite yearning likely to be in some fashion pretentious? And for a *sexual* politics, as our politics must necessarily be, is pretentiousness and its concomitant stirrings of no interest to the excesses of desire?

A politics that seeks to dismantle normalizing categories of gender; that seeks to retrieve a history from a violently enforced forgetting; a politics that seeks enfranchisement not only for new

February 18, 1995, sec. 1, p. 9.

11. Kushner refers to a February 26, 1995, op-ed in the *New York Times* by Michelangelo Signorile, "H.I.V.-Positive, and Careless," sec. 4, p. 15.

kinds of citizens but for sexuality itself, that seeks to introduce fucking and sucking, licking and smelling, kink, sleaze, clits and dicks and tits and assholes and the games people play with them into the previously chaste temple of democracy; and even more daring still, a politics that seeks a synthesis between desire and transformation, that seeks some union between the deepest recesses and cavities of the human heart and body and soul and the sacrifices and responsibilities building communities and movement, building progress and power entails: this politics needs its writers, and it's writers had better be capable of extravagance, had better not be tame.

Oh well, who knows, really? Talk about pretentiousness!

I'll wrap up with Blake, that most unpityingly pretentious or rather *grandiose* of poets—because it can't really be called pretentious if it was dedicated to you by angels: "I pretend not to Holiness; yet I pretend to love. . . . Therefore dear reader, *forgive* what you do not approve, & *love* me for the energetic exertion of my talent."[12]

I promise you I will love you all for the energetic exertion of yours.

---

12. William Blake, *Jerusalem. The Emanation of the Giant Albion*, William Blake Archive, "Plate 3. To the Public," accessed October 2, 2021, http://www .blakearchive.org/copy/jerusalem.e?descId=jerusalem.e.illbk.03; the full manuscript is available online at William Blake Archive (website), accessed October 2, 2021, http://www.blakearchive.org/copy/jerusalem.a?descId=jerusalem .a.illbk.01.

Heroes and Saints from *Downtown*

CLOSING PERFORMANCE

MARCH 5, 1995

The first place that I went to when I was coming out
Was the great Latino watering hole
Circus Disco!
Tried to get into Studio One,
But the doorman asked me for two IDs.
I gave him my driver's license and my J.C. Penney card,
But it wasn't good enough.
Hey, what did I know,
I was still wearing corduroys.

Circus Disco was the new world.
Friday night, eleven-thirty.
Yeah, I was Born to Be Alive.
Two thousand people exactly like me.
Well, maybe a little darker,
But that was the only thing
That separated me from
The cha-cha boys in East Hollywood.
And I ask you,

Where are my heroes?
Where are my saints?
Where are my heroes?
Where are my saints?

First night at Circus Disco
And I order a Long Island ice tea,
'Cause my brother told me
It was an exotic drink
And it fucks you up real fast.

The bartender looks at me
With one of those
"Gay people recognize each other" looks.
I try to act knowing and do it back.
Earlier that year,
I went to a straight bar on Melrose.
And when I asked for a screwdriver
The bartender asked me
If I wanted a Phillips or a regular.
I asked for a Phillips.
I was never a good drunk.
And I ask you,

Where are my heroes?
Where are my saints?
Where are my heroes?
Where are my saints?

The first guy I met at Circus Disco
Grabbed my ass in the bathroom,
And I thought that was *charming*.
In the middle of the dance floor,
Amidst all the hoo-hoo, hoo-hoo,
To a thriving disco beat,
He's slow dancing
And sticking his tongue down my throat.
He sticks a bottle of poppers up my nose,
And I get home at five-thirty the next morning.
And I ask you,

Where are my heroes?
Where are my saints?
Where are my heroes?
Where are my saints?

Sitting outside of Circus Disco,
With a three hundred pound drag queen,
Who's got me cornered in the patio
Listening to her life story,
I think to myself,
One day
I will become something
And use this
In an act.

At the time I was thinking less about performance
And more about
Las Vegas.
And I ask you,

Where are my heroes?
Where are my saints?
Where are my heroes?
Where are my saints?

A guy is beating the shit out of his lover in the parking lot of Circus Disco.
Everybody is standing around
Them in a circle,
But no one is stopping them.
One of the guys is kicking and punching
The other guy, who is on the floor
In a fetal position.
And he's saying,
"You want to cheat on me, bitch?

Get up, you faggot piece of shit.
Get up, you goddamn faggot piece of shit."
It was the first time I saw us act
Like our parents.

I try to move in,
But the drag queen tells me
To leave them alone.
"That's a domestic thing, baby.
Besides, that girl has AIDS.
Don't get near that queen."
And I ask you,

Where are my heroes?
Where are my saints?
Where are my heroes?
Where are my saints?

I get home early
And I'm shaken to tears.
My mother asks me
Where I went.
I tell her I went to see a movie
At the Vista.
An Italian film about a man
Who steals a bicycle.
It was all I could think of.
And she says,
"That made you cry?"

I swear,
I'll never go back to Circus Disco.
I'll never go back to Circus Disco.
I'll never go back to Circus Disco . . .
But at Woody's Hyperion!

Hoo-hoo, hoo-hoo.
I met a guy there
And his name is Rick Rascon
And he's not like anyone else.

No tight muscle shirt.
No white Levi's.
No colored stretch belt.
He goes to UCLA and he listens to Joni Mitchell.
Is that too perfect or what?
He comes home with me
And we make love,
But I'm thinking of him
More like, like, a brother.
And I know, I know.
We're gonna be friends
For the rest of our lives.
And I ask you,

Where are my heroes?
Where are my saints?
Where are my heroes?
Where are my saints?

Starting working at an
AIDS center in South Central.
But I gotta,
I gotta,
I gotta
Get out of here.
'Cause all of my boys
All of my dark-skinned boys
All of my cha-cha-boys
Are dying on me.
And sometimes I wish

It was like the Circus Disco
Of my coming out.

Two thousand square feet
Of my men.
Boys like me.
Who speak the languages
Who speak the languages
Of the border
And of the other.
The last time I drove down Santa Monica Boulevard
And I passed by Circus Disco,
Hardly anybody was there.
And I ask you,

Where are my heroes?
Where are my saints?
Where are my heroes?
Where are my saints?
Where are my heroes?
Where are my saints?

Remembrances of a Gay Old Time

When I was a kid, I was always puzzled by those passages in the Bible that simply presented genealogies of otherwise unknown people, all those series of *begats* that seemed so mysterious and unnecessary.[1] But after all I've lived through in the last fifteen years, I understand the imperative need to record names, to keep lists of the dead, to inscribe something about them on a quilt or on the page or on a gravestone. I've come to see that those lists of names, which I used to skip over in the Old Testament and in Homer, far from being some annoying caprice on the part of those first authors (themselves unnamed, paradoxically), are the essence of literature.

We are all here to do honor to the memory of our friends. A few of them were writers, even fewer published, but most of them, like people everywhere, even the most powerful, are in danger of being swallowed up by oblivion unless we do something to name them; record their quirks, even their faults; cull a bit of their wisdom; memorialize their pain; do justice to their struggle; capture their moments of bliss.

I suppose since most gay people were not brought up by gay families, and most gay families do not bring up queer children, there is very little of the usual handing down of traditions from

---

1. *Harvard Gay & Lesbian Review* published this speech in the Summer 1996 issue, pages 7–10.

mother to child, from grandfather to granddaughter. Worse, since so much of gay socializing is still based on the mating game, there is less intergenerational contact in our world than there is in theirs. When I was teaching at Brown in 1990 and 1991, for instance, most of my lesbian and gay students had never before met and talked with an older gay person; in Paris, where I live now, I'm turned away from most gay bars for being too old.

Of course I realize that there are projects all over the country for preserving the archives of gay men who have died from AIDS; I know that in smaller towns, gays and lesbians of all ages socialize with one another, partly out of necessity, perhaps since there's often only one bar in town, but eventually out of genuine enthusiasm; in most cases, I also know that the lesbian community tends to be a lot less ageist than the gay male community, but nevertheless, I insist that even if normal lines of communication were open between the generations, AIDS has presented us with a major rupture in that transmission, one that we writers are called upon to compensate for.

Because so many men of my generation are dead, I frequently talk to guys in their twenties and thirties who ask me about what Brad Gooch has referred to with the title of his new novel, *The Golden Age of Promiscuity*, which is also a book about the much-maligned Robert Mapplethorpe and is an effort to defend him against the trivializing and demonizing that he underwent in the recent Patricia Morrisroe biography. People want to know not only about the sexual spree of the 1970s, say, but also about the lesbian and gay communes of that decade, or the beginning of lesbian and gay publishing, or the representation of queers in the movies. More subtly, they want to untangle the exact relationship that obtained back then between feminism and gay liberation, of Black liberation and gay liberation. Or they want to know about the successful fight in the early 1970s to declassify homosexuality as a neurosis in the American Psychological Association. Or they want to find out about the early days of the Gay Academic Union.

Fortunately, we are living through a vigorous period in the production of serious and adventurous lesbian and gay history writing. The Center for Lesbian and Gay Studies in New York, headed up by one of the great gay historians, Martin Duberman; Joan Nestle's Lesbian Herstory Archives; the creation of a new lesbian and gay study center in San Francisco, the first ever in a public library, which will house the papers of Randy Shilts and Harvey Milk;[2] the important collection of contemporary lesbian and gay manuscripts being assembled at Yale, where the late, much-lamented historian John Boswell taught and wrote with such passion and brilliance about gays in the Middle Ages;[3] the continuing achievements of the pioneer gay historian Jonathan Katz, who has never been affiliated with an institution and who has supported himself with odd jobs all these years as he has written volumes of gay American history and his recent book on "the invention of heterosexuality"[4]—these are just a few of the names that spring to mind. The late Randy Shilts did studies that have already become *the* history of gays in the military, as did Marianne Humphries and Allan Bérubé. George Chauncey produced a fascinating history of "gay New York" as it was at the beginning of the century. Richard Plant has written about gays in the concentration camps.

And then there are all the biographies of lesbian and gay artists, thinkers, doers: books that not only depict the homosexual life of earlier periods but also give us heroes and heroines or even villains—in any event populate the past with familiar faces where before there had been nothing but blank picture frames. There have been recent biographies of Djuna Barnes, for instance, and Willa Cather and Marguerite Yourcenar and Mary Renault. In the

---

2. The James C. Hormel LGBTQIA Center in the San Francisco Public Library.
3. Yale Research Initiative on the History of Sexualities.
4. Jonathan Ned Katz, *The Invention of Heterosexuality* (New York: Dutton, 1995).

last two years, there have been four new biographies of Thomas
Mann. I just read Tony Heilbut's excellent biography of Mann, in
which he talks openly about Mann's largely unconsummated
homosexuality and the real-life background for *Death in Venice*
(apparently the model for Tadzio was Count Wladyslaw Moes,
who in the 1960s, fifty years later, recalled that an "old man" had
watched him attentively in Venice when he was ten).[5]

If I mention my own biography of Jean Genet, I do so only
because it is the one I know the best. To me, there was nothing
more fascinating than tracing out the evolution of Genet's attitude
toward homosexuality, for instance, from his youthful shame and
defiance in the 1930s and his total lack of solidarity with other gay
men, to the point that he encouraged fellow thieves to rob and
beat up gay men—to the very different attitude he assumed in the
1970s, when he concluded that homosexuality could predispose
someone toward revolutionary politics. He was sufficiently irri-
tated by the Black Panthers' repeated references to their white male
enemies (especially Nixon) as "faggots" or "punks" that he made
strong objections, which caused his ally, Panther leader Huey
Newton, to issue his groundbreaking essay "The Women's Liberation and Gay Liberation Movements, August 15, 1970." Newton
said that "through reading and through my life experience and
observations" he knew "that homosexuals are not given freedom
and liberty by anyone in the society. They might be the most
oppressed people in our society." Newton called for the freedom
for each person "to use his body in whatever way he wants." He
said that although some homosexuals were not revolutionary, others were: "maybe a homosexual could be the most revolutionary.
When we have revolutionary conferences, rallies and demonstrations, there should be full participation of the gay liberation movement and the women's movement." I can remember when Newton

---

5. Anthony Heilbut, *Thomas Mann: Eros and Literature* (New York: Knopf,
1996).

issued that statement, but until I did research for my biography, I had no idea that Genet had influenced Newton's thinking.

What I'm trying to suggest is that since there is little direct, intergenerational oral transmission of gay culture, we writers—whether we are poets or novelists or historians or biographers or sociologists—have a crucial mission to keep our culture alive, especially since AIDS has wiped out most of the male members of a key generation, the very Stonewall generation that legitimized the idea of such a culture in the first place. And of course, I'm also acknowledging that, since Stonewall, an immense part of the past has been recovered and brought to light, a past that had never been known at all to earlier generations because few people were researching queer history, and no one was publishing it. I'm thinking of Foucault's *History of Sexuality*, for instance, of Dover's *Greek Homosexuality*.

More narrowly, I want to talk about our need to remember and celebrate the earlier writers who have influenced us. Acknowledging our debt to them does credit to them but also to us, since tracing out our spiritual heritage gives us a weight, a tradition, a resonance that all alone we do not possess. I think it must help a visionary, experimental lesbian novelist like Carole Maso know that she is part of a tradition of like-minded women, such as Willa Cather, Virginia Woolf, Djuna Barnes, and the poet Elizabeth Bishop, especially in a period as vulgarly commercial and unadventurous as our own.[6] I know that Alan Hollinghurst is quick to honor this descent from such writers as Ronald Firbank (Hollinghurst edited *The Unknown Firbank*) and E. M. Forster (although *Maurice* was not published until 1970 and the stories in *The Life to Come* till later still). Before Hollinghurst published *The Swimming*

6. Carole Maso is the author of ten books. At the time of this speech, she had received significant support for her work, including grants from the National Endowment for the Arts and a Lannan Literary Fellowship, and published four books, *Ghost Dancer*, *The Art Lover*, *AVA*, and *The American Woman in the Chinese Hat*.

Pool Library, serious gay male fiction of great artistry had almost died out in England; luckily, Hollinghurst could look back to the 1910s and 1920s and take up where Firbank's *Concerning the Eccentricities of Cardinal Pirelli* and Forster's gay stories and *Maurice* left off. Certainly, the pleasure for me of editing *The Faber Book of Gay Short Fiction* was to bring to readers works such as Denton Welch's story "When I Was Thirteen" and Henry James's "The Pupil" or the love scene from James Baldwin's *Just above My Head*—fiction that had never been read in a gay context or that had mysteriously remained unknown.

But for me, the most important gay writer of the past has always been Christopher Isherwood, whom I had the chance to meet in the late 1970s and who became my friend in the early 1980s. I was lovers in 1978 with Christopher Cox, another member of my writers' group, the Violet Quill, and he was working for the famous composer and musical critic Virgil Thomson, who was already in his eighties at that point. Anyway, Virgil had lived in France for fifty years and was a great cook and had written two operas with Gertrude Stein and seemed to know everyone. When Isherwood came to New York with his lover, the much younger Don Bachardy, Virgil naturally invited them over to dinner—and somehow Chris and I were also invited.

Isherwood was as inspiring as a man as he was a writer. So many writers I've met I've liked—in fact, I agree with Proust that writers are the best company—but most of them don't resemble their writing very closely. But Isherwood had the same graceful sense of humor linked to the same unvarnished truth telling that I'd always admired in his writing. His response to flattery, for instance, was a great roar of laughter; there was not a pretentious bone in his body. When I had been a teenager and in my early twenties, there were very few gay books that crossed my path. I now know of course that there were quite a few important gay books in print, including Gore Vidal's *The City and the Pillar* and the novels of John Horne Burnes, but the only ones I came across were the journals of André Gide and his memoir *If It Die*; James Baldwin's *Giovanni's Room*; John

Rechy's *City of Night*, which I read in installments in little magazines as it was coming out; and Isherwood's groundbreaking novel *A Single Man*. What was remarkable about Isherwood's book was that, unlike Rechy's or Genet's fiction, it wasn't about marginal people—hustlers, pimps, thieves—but rather about an Englishman, a professor living in Los Angeles whose lover has recently died and who seeks solace with another expatriate, an Englishwoman who lives nearby. There is no effort to apologize for homosexuality or place it in a medical context, no plea for compassion from the heterosexual reader, no suggestion that a gay man's life is more or less rewarding than that of his heterosexual colleagues and neighbors. The protagonist has his problems, including a nagging feeling that when he drives his car or teaches his classes, he's a robot, but these problems are not linked to his condition as a homosexual.

If I mention this novel of the early 1960s now, thirty years later, I do so because I wish to remember Isherwood's contribution. Not only did he write gay fiction and memoirs of an extreme lucidity and eloquence, but he also shed before anyone else the excess baggage of shame, psychoanalysis, and religion. I suppose the authoritative English biography that is being written now about Isherwood will determine how he managed to be so many steps ahead of everyone else, but I would hazard that he must have been affected by two factors: his contact with the first gay liberation movement in Berlin in the 1920s—the movement of Magnus Hirschfeld that was wiped out by the Nazis—and his later contact with the homophile culture that sprang up in California after the war, the period of *One* magazine, the burgeoning gay world that had been born during the war and that was nurtured by beach hedonism. To be sure, Isherwood did not admit in print that he himself was gay until his 1970 memoir about his parents, *Kathleen and Frank*, but he had already written superb gay fiction in such books as *Down There on a Visit*, *The World in the Evening*, and *A Meeting by the River*, as well as his masterpiece *A Single Man*.

Before I met Isherwood, I had been writing very differently. I can see my own work as a gradual and uneven movement away from a totally imagined kind of writing with an emphasis on a strict formal organization and an invented content and an ironic tone toward an autobiographical fiction that generates its sparks, if it does, through its tone of veracity and sincerity and its conformity to the natural trajectory of a life, my life.

Vladimir Nabokov had been my first great influence, and my first two novels, *Forgetting Elena* and *Nocturnes for the King of Naples*, were written under his spell. *Elena* is a very coded novel, but already in *Nocturnes*, there was some homosexual content, partially autobiographical but largely wish fulfillment.

Then I met Isherwood and I wrote a nonfiction book, *States of Desire: Travels in Gay America*. In it, I began to experiment with a technique that Isherwood had pioneered—a gradual self-disclosure, a flirtatious unveiling of the self, but in my case, I was coy not because I was afraid of complete candor but because I was searching for a device that would make the reader want to continue reading what was necessarily an episodic, fragmented travelogue. What Isherwood responded to in his book, however, was its political content, which he emphasized in his very generous blurb. The year was 1980, and we'd just lived through the Anita Bryant days; Isherwood was supremely aware of its full extent of religious bigotry and homophobia in the United States, and he knew just how lethal these sentiments could be.

I suppose all my work could be seen as existing in a dialectical relationship between Nabokov and Isherwood, and the relationship has never been a simple one. Nabokov cannot be pegged as an irresponsible aesthete; his brother was gay and died in the Nazi camps, and his wife was Jewish, which caused the Nabokovs to flee Germany for France and eventually the States. His hatred of fascism is evident in *Bend Sinister*, in *Invitation to a Beheading*, in many short stories, and in the scornful details about bullies and despots in all his postwar work. Nor can Isherwood be read as merely a political activist; he was at least as influenced by quietist Vedanta philosophy as by progressive politics, and his work was sober and reserved in the English tradition of E. M. Forster.

Moreover, at a certain moment, I felt Isherwood's understatement and control were linked to an internalized homophobia, a desire to appear masculine in the stiff-upper-lip English fashion. Fifteen years ago, when I was still making pronouncements about the gay sensibility, I declared that the true gay style is elaborate, even over-wrought and high metaphorical. My theory was that a chaste style like Hemingway's (or in our day Raymond Carver's) that spells nothing out and leaves everything up to the reader's interpretation is a style appropriate only to the dominant culture; the reader can only draw the conclusions he or she already has learned, and those conclusions are necessarily conservative or at least familiar. An elaborate style that spells everything out like Proust's or that rei-magines everything through extended metaphors like Genet's is appropriate to queers, since they want the reader to think new thoughts and feel her or his way into entirely new moral and psy-chological sympathies.

But a lot has happened in the last fifteen years. Gay and lesbian life has been mainstreamed, and even our values have become less separatist; I suppose the fact that gay marriage and adoption by lesbians and gay men have become the current hot issues shows the full extent of our real or attempted integration. Moreover, the very growth of gay culture—an expansion that can be sampled by look-ing at the growth of the gay bibliography in any bookstore or by the success of OutWrite, for instance—this growth means that our literature can explain less, can lower its voice, can speak casually.

At least it can speak casually to the converted, to an audience that is already gay or sympathetic. Genre fiction, humorous fic-tion, small-press fiction and nonfiction can address themselves to sophisticated lesbian and gay readers without seducing or explain-ing. Most of the year, I live in France, and if a recent visit to the States has taught me anything, it's that homophobia is still raging in the United States. I was appalled to discover how homosexual marriage and the possibility that Hawaii might legalize it have become a political football for the Christian Right. On C-SPAN at the time of the Iowa caucus, I watched one Republican candidate after another enter a church during an antigay rally and publicly sign a pledge to protect heterosexual marriage and family values against the satanic specter of homosexual marriage. One speaker even dug up a 1972 radical gay text that had called for multiple gay marriages! Horrors! Every time the word *lifestyle* was uttered in ominous tones, I knew exactly who was being evoked.

When I think of launching a mainstream lesbian or gay novel before such a nation, I remind myself that every effect must be calculated or at least conscious. I at least certainly intend to make my work as honest and in their face as it's been since I first published *The Joy of Gay Sex* in 1976. I do not subscribe to the conservative, assimilationist, low-profile principles of books such as *A Place at the Table* or *Virtually Normal.*[7] I do not want to melt into the crowd, because I know the crowd wants to lynch us. I do not want to disassociate the gay movement from drag queens and leather boys, partly because I don't want to be one of those dull normals normaling about—I identify too closely with drags and once used to be a leather boy—but mainly because I know that bigoted straights hate a middle-class gay man or woman much more than they hate a drag queen. Straight people made *La Cage Aux Folles* a huge hit; straight people are worked up to a frenzy about homosexual marriage. Because middle-class gay life is more objectionable to straights than is marginal lesbian and gay life, a book such as Isherwood's *A Single Man* will always be more disturbing to straight readers than *Our Lady of Flowers*. I am calling for defiance, for self-assertion, but I want every lesbian and gay author to be aware of the consequences and to know that we're playing a dangerous game with high stakes.

---

7. The gay publishing "boom" in the 1990s included conservative and reactionary books like *A Place at the Table* by Bruce Bawer (New York: Simon & Schuster, 1993), which argues that "radical gay activists" contributed to homophobia, and *Virtually Normal* by Andrew Sullivan (New York: Knopf, 1995), in which Sullivan dismisses the views of gay liberationists and calls for a synthesis of liberal and conservative approaches to homosexuality.

My excitement has carried me far from my subject, which is memory. I suppose I was led into this political excursus inevitably by the memory of Isherwood, who even now, ten years after his death, is my model, my interlocutor, my sparring partner. But if I think about my artistic and personal debts, I must not forget my contemporaries either, especially the members of the Violet Quill. The group itself met only less than a dozen times in the late 1970s and early 1980s, but our informal, friendly contacts preceded the club by many years (Robert Ferro and Andrew Holleran were college friends in the 1960s; George Whitmore and I met at a reading in the mid-1970s and were briefly lovers; Ferro and Michael Grumley were lovers, as were Chris Cox and I), and even today I remain in close contact with Felice Picano and Holleran, the only other members who are still alive.

This group has been resented and attacked by other gay writers partly because of its very success. What's important to remember is that before 1978, the modern gay literary movement scarcely existed. A few nonfiction books such as those by Dennis Altman or C. A. Tripp's *The Homosexual Matrix* or Donn Teal's *The Gay Militants* had been published, as well as that landmark feminist work, Kate Millett's *Sexual Politics*, but gay male fiction became a recognizable movement only in 1978 with the publication of Larry Kramer's *Faggots*, Holleran's *Dancer from the Dance*, and my own *Nocturnes for the King of Naples*, the least noticed of the three and the most modest seller. (On the West Coast, the first volume of Armistead Maupin's *Tales of the City* and Paul Monette's *Taking Care of Mrs. Carroll* were published in the same year.) Suddenly, American critics and readers were being asked to take notice of gay male fiction that wasn't apologetic, that showed (at least in Kramer's, Maupin's, and Holleran's books) not just a gay man or a gay couple but a whole gay population with its bars, its dialect, its folkways, and its watering places. Kramer was even confident enough to criticize the gay community for its promiscuity rather than apologize, as earlier books had done, for our very existence. Soon, Ferro, in *The Family of Max Desir* and *Second Son*, was able to take up the theme of the gay son's fight to be accepted on his own terms, with his male lover by his side, by his conservative Italian-American family. Grumley, in a posthumous novel, *Life Drawing*, broached the delicate subject of Black and white men together. Chris Cox, who became an editor at Ballantine, published many gay writers, including the haunting fairy tales written by Patrick Merla, for many years the editor of the *New York Native*. Our friend Vito Russo read to us at one of our meetings excerpts from the book he was writing, *The Celluloid Closet*, about the depiction of lesbians and gays in the movies. Our friend, the editor Michael Denneny, brought out an oral history of a contemporary gay love affair called *Lovers*. George Whitmore was one of the first journalists to give real-life accounts of the first people with AIDS before he himself died of AIDS. Now Picano has given us a sweeping epic about the 1970s and 1980s, before and after the onset of AIDS, in his novel *Like People in History*. I've just read Holleran's new novel, due to be published next summer, which is a dark, powerful account of the loneliness and isolation of a survivor, someone who has left New York, outlived his friends and parents, and now must make do with radically diminished expectations.[8]

I hope this brief overview of the work of the Violet Quill members will dispel the notion that all we could think about was Fire Island and tricking; if that is the image we projected, the stigma is due to Holleran's *Dancer from the Dance*, which is clearly the most beautiful gay novel of our times and the one more likely to be read a hundred years from now. Our enemies suggest that we represented an arrogant New York hegemony, but we just happened to live in New York; that we crowded our rivals out of the field, but the field didn't exist before we came along; that we used our cunning and power mongering and money to get where we got, but I was a humble ghostwriter writing college textbooks, Whitmore was a secretary, Ferro and Grumley were

8. White refers to Holleran's third novel, *The Beauty of Men* (New York: William Morrow, 1996).

very poor, Picano tells me he is still just hanging on by a thread, and most of us were in our late thirties before we had even a first small taste of success.

I'm certainly not complaining, since I'm grateful that I've been able to live by my pen, even if I have to flesh out my income with journalism assignments and teaching; I know how privileged I am. I'm sure all of us in the Violet Quill are grateful that we were able to make our mark; so many writers of our generation were struck down by AIDS before they could get a book published or find their voice. If you think of the great writers in history, we would remember almost none of them if they'd died before age forty, yet that has been the fate of so many gay writers of our times, of my generation and younger.

Which returns me to my theme of memory. The other day, I was at a party for Salman Rushdie, and there I was introduced to the parents of a student of mine at Brown who died two years ago from AIDS while he was in his twenties. His name was John Russell, and he left behind a marvelous play, *Stupid Kids*, that will finally be put on next year in New York. As everyone else at the party was gawking at Rushdie or calculating the risk they were running by being in the same room with him, the Russells and I were oblivious to our surroundings. We were weeping and hanging on to each other and smiling because we knew that John's work would have its moment in the sun, even if it was just the brief neon sun of a New York theatrical season.

Imagination and the Mockingbird

Keynote Address

February 23, 1996

Outside in the night, a full moon is shining, and in the moon glow, a mockingbird is singing the cadences of all the birdsong it has ever heard. It imitates the raucous jayjay of the blue jay, the locomotive slur of the redbird whistle, and a hundred other calls, day sounds that shock and entrance the ear as they echo through the silent summer night. Sometimes it mimics the nocturnal, the fugitive lament of the chuck-will's-widow.

The mockingbird creates a rhapsody but not for love or money. It has a song of its own only by learning and repeating the liquid buzz, the hoot, the twitter, the triplets, the trills, the quavers, the queh queh queh, and the pure fluted tones, ascending, descending, of many others.

Inside, I am kneeling at my open window, listening. Outside, beyond the mockingbird in the crepe myrtle tree, beyond the pasture desiccated by summer heat, beyond the line of cedar trees that mark the farthest dark boundary of my sight, a pack of dogs is howling at I don't know what, at I don't want to know what. Outside and inside, it is 1955 in the Deep South, and I am surrounded by the unknown, which I have been taught to fear.

I know only the road into town, the road to school, the road to church. All along the way, there are signs posted to remind me that there is a strange other, unimaginably different. Even a substance as common as water is labeled with words that divide it into us and them; white and Black; mind, body; good, evil.

Minnie Bruce Pratt. (*Photo credit: Photo by Robert Giard, copyright Estate of Robert Giard.*)

I am surrounded by other sounds, other voices in other rooms, that I cannot yet hear. But there are words that bridge the divide between me and the other, words that couple, bond, bind me to the other.

In Montgomery, there is the whisper of barely shod feet on dirt paths, Black folk walking to work in the bus boycott. At the Highlander Folk School in Tennessee, Rosa Parks and Beulah Johnson are telling the organizers they had got tired of being run over; they say, "Well, let's fight it out—if it means going to jail, then go to jail." And then one recites from a poem by Langston Hughes: "I'm comin' but my head ain't bended low."[1]

---

1. Documentation of this is available at the Civil Rights Movement Archive: "Mrs. Rosa Parks Reports on Montgomery, Ala., Bus Protest," Civil Rights

In New York, there is the swish of silk when Marian Anderson steps onto the stage of the Met for Verdi's *Masked Ball*, her voice sweeping into the future, behind her those forbidden to stand there, and Dunbar whispering, "We sing, but oh, the clay is vile / Beneath our feet, and long the mile; / But let the world dream otherwise, / We wear the mask."[2]

In Idaho, a gay man protests to the judge—"But I don't think I've committed any crime. As far as I'm concerned, it was a natural act to me"—who later remembers, "They kept us locked up [in solitary] for six months. For six months I went through every book in the library. . . . I was by myself in a cell maybe a yard wide and a yard deep."[3]

In Georgia, a sing of white and Black women gather at Lillian Smith's house up on the mountain; a stride piano gallops as they begin: "Lean-ing, lean-ing, safe and secure beyond all harm." Theirs is a confidence not broadcast over any network, while Governor Talmadge campaigns by attacking racially integrated TV programming because it will lead to "a complete abolition of segregation customs."[4]

In Washington, DC, Harry Hay's voice trembles as he practices with his attorney for an appearance before the House Un-American Activities Committee, repeating, "My civil right to defend the integrity of my convictions." But when the day comes, he resorts to the "real Gay consciousness" and "confuses them with all [his]

Movement Archive, accessed April 5, 2021, https://www.crmvet.org/disc/parks_mbb.pdf.

2. Marian Anderson was the first African American to sing with the Metropolitan Opera in 1955.

3. Jonathan Katz documents this case in *Gay American History* (New York: Thomas Y. Crowell, 1976; New York: Avon, 1977; New York: Penguin, 1992).

4. Smith keeps on fighting racism, keeps asking "How Am I to Be Heard?" in books and letters collected in Lillian Smith, *How Am I to Be Heard? Letter of Lillian Smith*, ed. Rose Gladney (Chapel Hill: University of North Carolina Press, 1996), written to people ranging from her lover Paula Snelling to Richard Wright, Pauli Murray, Eleanor Roosevelt, and many others.

gab" without admitting a thing. When he sees the committee member stand up and yell—"like the Commendatore in Don Giovanni, rising up out of the floor"—he defies their questions with "I'm not in the habit of confiding in stool pigeons or their buddies."[5]

And in Los Angeles, locked up in the postmaster general's files, confiscated by the authority of the Comstock Act, a short story condemned as "cheap pornography" murmurs silently about lesbian love, "Sappho Remembered."[6]

Outside and inside, it is 1955. I am surrounded by the voices of the others who are like me and not like me, but I have not heard them yet.

I kneel at the window and wish I were a mockingbird, who can turn its body into pure sound and then fly away.

* * *

Instead, I grow up and read Shelley, who says of another night-singing bird, "A poet is a nightingale, who sits in darkness and sings to cheer its own solitude with sweet sounds."[7] But I ask myself, "What if the singer, the poet, the writer, has been taught to fear the darkness? How do I sing in a language imbued with the most grotesque images of darkness, with a language in which solitude exists only in relation to a damned, damaged other?"

In the place I grew up, my sawmill county seat town in Alabama, the people who ran the economic sexual system, the racist state, were determined to damn mind, body, and imagination in every way.

There was always the danger that folks might decide to go back to raw data, to our sensual world and sensory experiences, to the

5. Katz, *Gay American History*, 108.
6. Lillian Faderman, *Odd Girls and Twilight Lovers* (New York: Columbia University Press, 1991), 146.
7. Percy Bysshe Shelley, *Essays, Letters from Abroad, Translations and Fragments* (London: Edward Moxon Dover Street, 1840), 14.

immediate history and shared memory of our lives. Without walls, we might begin to make our own comparisons, draw our own conclusions, act individually and collectively, write poems and stories about what was not allowed.

So judgments were erected as partitions between us. The authorities put up signs, everywhere. These were the public words, relentless, repetitive reminders to convince us of the inevitability of white racial superiority, of the impossibility of escaping the fact that some were bosses and others servants, of the immovability of a whole system of category and metaphor.

Of course, almost every southern child, white or Black, stopped at least once at water labeled "Black" or "white" and sneaked a sip. We said, "This is just like my water; what's the difference between us?"

But this was a hidden secret, making of a bond between us; this was an unspoken metaphor. Any public speech or action that crossed the oppositions of "race" was discouraged by the authorities, to say the least. To say the most, people often died when, with their lives, they sought to imagine and then act on a way out of the categories imposed on them.

Public transgression was violently punished, while those who made the laws did their best to control what Trotsky has called "the physical power of thought"—the way an account of the ideas and deeds arising from one struggle for freedom might fire the imagination of people in other circumstances.[8] The state of Alabama at one time even had a "literature ordinance" that made it unlawful to possess one or more pieces of "radical" literature, which was defined as antifascist or labor publications, and liberal magazines, like the *Nation* and the *New Republic*—a violent suppression of both words and people documented by Robin D. G. Kelley in his *Hammer and Hoe*.

---

8. Leon Trotsky, *Literature and Revolution* (New York: International Publishers, 1924), 104.

Anything might happen if we began to question the words *Black* and *white*, if we began to question what we'd been taught about the other. Anything might happen if we went underneath the words, back to our bodies, and asked them to speak—or if we listened to the other speaking of her and his and their life.

Anything might happen if we took those horrors and wonders and claimed them with words and metaphors that refused to abide in the opposition of white and Black or, for that matter, male and female, normal and queer.

Queerness was not marked officially with any sign. But anyone who crossed white and Black was assumed to be queer; any lover across guarded borders, any challenger to the necessity of rich and poor, anyone who did these things was called queer.

Art was queer, and so were artists. And so was the innate human ability to create—the ability from which language itself arises: The power to see correspondences between two things and make a word from that; the power to find similarities between dissimilars and create language for what is shared; the power to make metaphor, to be a poet, writer, artist; the gift of carrying life back and forth, back and forth, between two distinctly different others.

That gift was the queerest act of all.

*   *   *

In a sweet gum tree, in the warm fall noon, a young mockingbird just this summer out of its shell is murmuring to itself, almost under its breath, little broken phrases, whispers, fits and starts. It is practicing. It is trying to remember the songs it heard all summer; it is piecing them together to make its own song.

I sit in the languorous heat of my car and look across to the side door of the windowless printing plant. Any minute it will be quitting time, and my lover will be mine for the weekend. She'll walk across the gravel lot to sit with me and listen to the mockingbird; her fingers rough from chemicals will rasp against mine. The car will smell of ink and solvent and the spicy scent of the fallen gumballs, brown spiky pomanders.

We'll drive across town through the red brick canyon walls of the tobacco warehouses, through the sweet poison of the curing smell, to my little shotgun apartment, where a tobacco worker used to come home at the end of the day to stand at the sink and strip black tar from her hands. I'll stand at the sink and wonder how to get all of this into a poem.

Instead, I make a book, my first book. It's 1981, and I make it almost completely with my own hands, the way my grandmother hooked rugs, the way my mother sewed all my clothes. I learn to burn words on the flimsy metal printing plates, to trim the printed pages with a blade like a guillotine. I've learned these skills from other women: we belong to a collective that edits a lesbian magazine in the South, *Feminary*. After it evolved from a twopenny women's liberation mimeo into a newsletter, it had been given its name, from a passage in Monique Wittig's *Les Guérillères*, in which the women had small books called feminaries, made of pages with inscriptions and blank pages where the women wrote as they pleased.

Of this writing, several women said to a "great gathering of women," "There was a time when you were not a slave, remember that. . . . You say you have lost all recollection of it. . . . You say there are no words to describe this time, you say it does not exist. But remember. Make an effort to remember. Failing that, invent."[9]

When we expand this newsletter into a lesbian magazine for the South, we are the daughters of the great mass liberation movements of our century—the labor union battles of the 1930s, the Black civil rights and nationalist movements of the 1950s and 1960s, the anti-Vietnam War and women's liberation movements of the 1960s and 1970s. We are creating in a space that has been cleared for us by these struggles, a space onto which different memories, histories, imaginations can be written.

---

9. Monique Wittig, *Les Guérillères*, trans. David Levay (Boston: Beacon, 1985), 88–89.

We know that there was a time, almost within our living memory, when some of our grandmothers' mothers were slaves, and some were not. We ask ourselves, What does it mean to recover memory and history under these circumstances? Whose memory? Whose history? What do we truly know about the past, about our past? How much of that memory is to be trusted? How much of it is institutionalized lies? How much of what we think has been made up, stories imagined by the owners to control the owned? How much is still buried in our psyches or lost to us because we have been separated from others who know truths and have memories that are not ours? How much of what we cannot remember is suppressed knowledge, the knowledge that is buried/driven deep within us when oppression suddenly intervenes at the moment of perception?

To invent, to imagine, means that you have to trust your memory, where stores of images and tales lie, waiting to be picked up and used to make new knowledge: "This, which is new, is like that, which I already know . . ."

If we are to invent, we have to burn off the debris of history, like burning over the straw and stalks of an old field to let it lie fallow and ready for the green shoots of spring. We have to find the foundation stones of another history, the tumbled stones of the old house and its choked wellspring hidden under honeysuckle thickets beside the field.

If we mean to be writers, we have to laboriously reconstruct our memories and our imaginations.

For me, this meant learning about those from whom I had been separated. To be a writer in the fullest sense, I had to reeducate myself about the ones who had been named as most different from me.

I had to do antiracist organizing and read literary testimony—like Toni Morrison's novels of the 1970s—drawn from the mythic depth of African American lives. I had to read historical testimony—like the congressional proceedings to hear southern Black folk testify about being terrorized in the 1870s by the Ku Klux Klan.

I had to gain something more than a new vocabulary. I had to begin to hear the voices of the others who had surrounded me all along.

I had to become suffused with new understanding, knowledge flowing like spring water through me. Then I had to be able to trust my imagination to go down into my unconscious and converse there, by the water, with those voices.

* * *

But my imagination had been trained not just in the white folkways of terror but academically, rigorously, in the literary ways of colonialism and imperialism. I feared my imagination was still possessed by the past fathers, mill bosses, plantation owners.

My literary fathers stretched four hundred years back to Edmund Spenser and Sir Philip Sidney. Both were directly involved in the English colonial "planting" of Ireland—forever linking the word *plantation* to colonization. Both these poets were directly involved in and defended the land seizure and mass slaughter of Irish peasants fighting for their commons and livelihoods—Sidney as aide to his father, an English lord deputy of Ireland, and Spenser as secretary to an Irish governor-general.

I was trained to admire Spenser, who wrote the epic *Faerie Queen*, for his imagination, which was a "Vein of fabulous Invention . . . his Political Magick." And Sidney's *An Apologie for Poetry* was the first defense of imaginative literature I ever read. Sidney believed the European Christian poet could use God's gift of imagination to exercise an "erected wit," to rebuild a world in ruins from original sin.

How could I not be suspicious of this sense of the imagination, with its larger implication that people of color were barbaric, uncivilized, and half human? This definition of *imagination* was based on an imperialism that saw oppressed peoples as the Calibans of the world, to be "raised up" only by an imagination trained in the economics, literature, and art of the Western world.

When I was a young poet, I knew all the allegorical interpretations of *The Faerie Queen*—except the relation between its epic struggles and my own life. Now I know the epic poem is an example of how brilliantly—and servilely—the imagination can be used to reinforce structures of oppression.

Now I know the epic stories of the enslaved farmworkers of my own country, my own region: the cotton-chopper day workers of the southern Black Belt who struck the white plantation owners for better wages and a modicum of respect; the Black and white sharecropper farmers who waged bloody armed struggle with the owners in the 1930s; the history of how these battles fed the modern Black Panther movement as it arose in the 1960s and their connection to the urban rebellions, like Los Angeles, in the 1990s.

Now I know something of the queer life of the cities, the lives of the queer folk damned and doomed to hell by many who raised them and knew them. I know the grit of their rebellions—the drag queens, the real fairy queens, the Latinx and African American flamboyant fighters, the drag kings—who cleared with fists and stiletto heels another space: the new liberated space like a mirrored pool of light on the dance floor that I could come into and imagine a new life.

*   *   *

As I have recovered for myself the history of oppression, I understand more about the mechanisms of social control and its relation to literature and to the imagination.

We have all heard dehumanizing exclusion applied verbally to some groups on a regular basis in the form of a simple devastating disclaimer: people say of someone they believe to be fundamentally "different" from them, "Well, I can't imagine what it would be like to be —— (and here a blank is filled in), to be Black, Latinx, deaf, a lesbian who has her children taken away, a person living with AIDS, a trans person."

This is a commonplace unthinking language construction that places "the other" outside the bounds of humanity and human experience. This statement says there is no place shared by the two of you upon which to build a bridge of metaphor, likeness, simile—no way to construct a common bond.

As writers, because our imagination is a tool of our trade, used daily, perhaps we don't usually make such a crude excluding statement. But I stood at a plenary at the very first OutWrite conference, in San Francisco, and heard poet Essex Hemphill hissed at loudly from the audience because he asked, as an African American writer, that we simply consider what distortions around race might have limited white gay male Robert Mapplethorpe's vision as a photographer.

Among that group of writers, there were certainly some who refused to extend their imaginations to include the lives of Black people.

Now Robert and Essex are both dead. We are left with their memory, their history, their art, and this fact: if we attempt to contain or dismiss the questioning of "others" in our lives, whoever they are, they will still live on in our psyches and in our art, enormous, invisible, present. They will dwell within us, and we will shape our lives in relation to them without even knowing it.

Without conversing with those others, we will still imagine them and write them, and the form of our images and stories will unthinkingly carry forward the structures of oppression.

But we know this unconsciousness does not have to be: Essex asked us a question. We can try to answer him, and we can ask each other.

We long to move forward toward each other; we long for each other's voices. As we close the distance between us, our conversations grow more and more frequent, the Doppler effect of dialectic motion.

This dialectic is not about limitation of vision or language—but about expansion, about how to liberate imagination that has been held in thrall by oppression.

In this liberation, we refuse to appropriate the lives of others and use them as stand-ins for our fantasies. In this liberation, we walk, awake and self-conscious, through our own daily lives, present to all who travel there with us, alive and dead, asking ourselves what is our relation to them, for good or ill.

In Toni Morrison's words about literature, "The subject of the dream is the dreamer."[10] The daytime work of questioning comes back in moon glow as dream work.

My daily task now—my day work—as a writer, before I release my imagination to converse with the so-called other, is to prepare myself by knowing the hidden histories of economics, art, music—to know the dialectics of oppression and solidarity between me and the other.

Then I can ask myself the dream questions of the imagination. Then I can sit by a silent hidden pool waiting for the feathered brushstrokes of water stirred by the breath of an answer or stand near an oily rainwater puddle watching for new images boldly reflected as people move past me on the street.

*   *   *

In 1981, I make my first poetry book, a chapbook, with my boy children helping me hand collate and trim and staple. In the end, we hold the finished book in our hands, and on one page are the lines "The mockingbird singing / cantata in a score of voices / from the angled boughs." The voice of joy.

Later, I write a book about losing custody of these children because I am a lesbian. In one poem, a voice threatens me because I dare imagine the possibility of a life together with them: "Reality is flesh of your flesh taken. / What you want to last is fantasy, imagination."[11]

This damning voice is familiar. It is, in fact, the voice of the current demagogue, U.S. senator Jesse Helms, who the year I made

---

10. Toni Morrison, *Playing in the Dark* (Cambridge, MA: Harvard University Press, 1992), 17.

11. Pratt references her poetry collection *Crime against Nature*, which was the 1989 Lamont Poetry Selection from the Academy of American Poets.

that first poetry book introduced a "Human Life Bill" to regulate women's relation to sex, abortion, childbirth—to erect his imaginary purified nation on the silent field of our prone bodies.

Ten years later, Helms began investigating me, as well as other artists who are lesbians, gay men, and feminists—calling us pornographers, perverts of the imagination, underminers of morality — because we say it is possible to live another way than his.

The fear that gripped me during those attacks was familiar, out of childhood, a bone-deep memory of the sound of dogs howling across the silent fields, no way to venture out across a land marked off by unseen authorities, no human voice calling to me, only the mockingbird in song and terrible loneliness.

Helms's assault is just part of the larger "culture wars" of the 1990s, a concerted attempt to eliminate, or at least contain, any art and information that crosses over those all-too-familiar lines laid down between "us" and "them."

It is an assault in which all art is suspect as potentially queer, as the embodiment of dangerous connections between thought and feeling and action.

In this attack, overtly queer art, such as that of Audre Lorde or Holly Hughes, is spotlighted as having fulfilled that evil potential. This art, say the righteous men, should be trapped and crushed like the head of a snake under a boot.

All sorts of queer art get caught in this dragnet: segments of Marlon Riggs's exquisite film *Tongues Untied* get used by presidential candidate Pat Buchanan in a political ad to illustrate the so-called homosexual threat to the country. At a radio interview, I'm told that I cannot read the word *breast* that's in one of my poems because of federal regulations that forbid "indecent language" except during the midnight hours. No graphic drawings of sex are allowed in federally funded AIDS education brochures, even though it's clear they contribute to safer sex and therefore less death.

The right-wing attack is not merely censorship; its consequence is not only the loss of artistic words or images. As with all bashing, ultimately the cost is human lives.

Meanwhile, the demagogues, the politicians and preachers, raise millions of dollars by shouting about the "disgusting" details of homosexual art that spreads corruption. And the assault continues, only two weeks ago resurfacing as a Decency Act that attempts to ban sexual discussion on the internet, using in part the Comstock Act, originally passed in 1872 and in force into the 1950s, to keep gay, lesbian, and feminist literature from traveling through the mail.[12]

All art is queer as it brings together dissimilarities. Some queer art is tolerated if it simply reproduces the unequally hinged relationships of things, peoples, body, that the powers that be put together in oppressive ways.

But the art that draws together dissimilarities to show relationships of forbidden solidarity and forbidden love—that art can be dismissed as corrupt pornography or dangerous propaganda.

Art moves out of these condemned categories only through a political struggle that redefines the boundaries of what can be lived publicly, out in the world. This political struggle is what makes it possible for creative work about forbidden lives to be called "art."

Writing the poems that the demagogue condemned, writing as lesbian/mother/woman/poet, I connected selves that had been set in opposition to each other; I connected seemingly mutual contradictions.

I have had to free my art from the condemnation of my own mind, planted there by the demagogues. I have had to claim the gift of imagination I am giving to the world, even if many in that world don't seem to want it—this gift I have received from the lesbian/gay/bisexual/trans communities.

---

12. Peter H. Lewis, "Protest, Cyber-Space Style, for New Law," *New York Times*, February 8, 1996, sec. A, p. 16. The Telecom Reform Act of 1996 contains a provision referred to as the Communications Decency Act that extended to the internet prohibitions to talking about abortion and ostensible protections for children.

In the grip of violence and condemnation, despite loneliness and isolation, we gather ourselves up and fight back to find each other, to love and be loved. We affirm the human dignity of our pleasures; we bless our gift of crossing man-made boundaries of gender, sex, and sexuality.

And out of the massive struggle of our daily lives, we emerge with a unique and specific intelligence. Because we are bound together as sexual beings, because we have had to struggle through oppression just to touch another's hand, just to hesitantly voice one word or two about our sexual desire, we have developed, as a people, a brilliant self-consciousness about sexuality, about how people live out their variations of sex and gender.

We know these secrets; we are these secrets. We know all the queer details of everyone's life. And our gift to everyone is that we tell. This is the gift of a revolutionary queer imagination.

We refuse partition into us and them; we refuse the degradation of the body and its desires. And we give that gift of liberation to the world with our lives, our political struggle, and our art.

The pressure on us not to tell, not to live as ourselves, is intense—the pressure on us to be self-effacing, to deny our gift; the pressure to deny ourselves, to say, "We don't have a choice about what we do."

And it's true—we don't have a choice about how we love. But we do have a choice about how we live. The writing of our lives visibly, audibly, visually into the daily chronicle of this world does have an effect on the world.

We give others an imagined possibility: that there is a way, many ways, to walk through the invisible confining walls and find the others.

*　*　*

In Jersey City, the mockingbirds imitate car alarms and sparrows and starlings. They imitate the signal whistle the boys use to gather on the corner, the call whistle the girls use to bring their friends down from the fourth floor next to me.

Sometimes on spring mornings Leslie and I lean out the window and imitate the mockingbird mimicking the car alarm. Sometimes at night I lean out the window over the grit of the city street and say to myself that these are my people now: the bodega owner who is from Cairo married to a woman from Italy, the gay Filipino poet around the corner, the Puerto Rican schoolchildren whistling in the street, and my African American mail carrier who teases me about adding an extra cart for all my letters and manuscripts.

All of us struggling to live, with too much work to do and not enough money. How do I write of our future together, the connections between us all?

I read *Literature and Revolution*, and Trotsky says, "The nightingale of poetry . . . is heard only after the sun is set. The day is a time for action, but at twilight feeling and reason come to take account of what has been accomplished."[13] What happens when we as writers use our dream imagination to work on the actions of the day?

The mainstream approach to considering the interaction of artist and the world is conveyed in the headline of a recent *New York Times Book Review*, "Holding a Mirror Up to China": "The work of a . . . writer who refused politics for the sake of the purely human."[14]

This language reflects the view that a writer who approaches literature with a political perspective is a flawed human who somehow sullies and damages literature. The language also uses the common metaphor of writer as mirror holder, the approval of someone with no point of view whose art consists of passively reflecting every detail of the world.

There is some truth, partial truth, in these concepts, enough truth for Plato to fear poet writers for our imitative skills: like the mockingbird, we tend eventually to repeat everything we hear and

---

13. Trotsky, *Literature and Revolution*, 19.
14. The cover of the December 17, 1995, *New York Times Book Review* featured a review of Shen Congwen's *Imperfect Paradise*.

see. And Plato wanted writers who said not what was but rather what should be—that's why he threw us out of his city.

No one wants to be thrown out of their city. As queer writers, we feel tremendous pressure not to look at and repeat how our art interacts with the life of the world. For instance, one metaphor for the socially concerned artist is that you are someone who wields art like a hammer—an image that suggests, Who wants to be bludgeoned with art, when we have enough blows in our life already?

But we know our relation to our work is more dynamic than blunt. And we know we are not merely passive mimickers. We know that the interaction between our experiences, our memory, our unconscious, and our imagination is intricate.

And we know in the censoring capitalist state, the reality is that our work has been confiscated, that we have been fined or imprisoned for writing it, that we have been denied access to publication, and literally sometimes the printing companies have refused to reproduce what we have to say.

Some of us have lost our jobs or our lovers or our children because of what we have written. We have been on the defensive; we have had to protect our imagination against these assaults, against those who have an agenda of what should be, which does not include us or our work.

But we, those of us gathered here, are not the state. We are the evolving revolution. And the work we make is part of the world that will come to be.

CHERYL CLARKE

A House of Difference

Audre Lorde's Legacy to Lesbian and Gay Writers

AUDRE LORDE MEMORIAL LECTURE

FEBRUARY 24, 1996

driven. . . .
by lust for a working tomorrow.[1]

It is my honor to be speaking in a space that commemorates Audre
Lorde, one of the most brilliant poets of the twentieth century, one
among an illustrious sorority of contemporary Black women and
radical lesbian writers and thinkers who have changed literature
and the world, and one of the first feminists to insist that integration of identities is crucial to politics, culture, activism, and "feeling deeply." All of our selves (and some of *his* tools) are needed to
replace the "master's house" with houses of liberation. And writing
is one of the tools the so-called master tried to keep from us that
we have used tirelessly to sustain our revolution. So we need to be
writers at least as much as we ever did. We need our bookstores,
publishers, and (progressive) movements to keep us writing, for we
write and live in the dangerous imaginary that the world wants
our writing.

---

1. Audre Lorde, *The Collected Poems of Audre Lorde* (New York: W. W. Norton, 1997), 406.

Cheryl Clarke. (*Photo credit: © Lynda Koolish.*)

I welcome the chance to rediscover with you Lorde's exquisite language and her lifelong preoccupations with geographies—of relationships, of political moments and movements, of identities, of cities.[2] I will read from the poetry that is charted in sharp relief on *my* everyday as a fin de siècle Black lesbian poet.

We are familiar with the uses to which Lorde put writing: critique, instruction, exhortation, incitement, self-reflection. As the speaker sharply questions "Willie sweet little brother" in her stately elegy "On My Way Out I Passed Over You and the Verrazano Bridge,"

I am writing these words as a route map
an artifact for survival
a chronicle of buried treasure
a mourning. . . .

2. In the speech, Clarke references reviewing Lorde's *Cancer Journals* in *Conditions: Eight*, 1982, 148–154.

oh, Willie sweet little brother with the snap in your eyes
what walls are you covering now
with your visions of revolution. . . .

and have you learned to nourish your sisters at last
as well as to treasure them?[3]

The question was put to all of us—not just "Willie sweet little brother"—who think we have our minds set on freedom and won't be turned around and before we'll be slaves we'll be buried in our graves, who undervalue our contradictions, or who are immobilized by difference, or who refuse mutuality, or who are not mindful of our own contamination by the systems we seek to overthrow.

Certainly, we have been irrevocably changed by Lorde's essays: "The Great American Disease,"[4] "Sexism: An American Disease in Black Face,"[5] "Breast Cancer: A Black Lesbian Feminist Experience,"[6] "Uses of the Erotic," "Uses of Anger," "Poetry Is Not a Luxury,"[7] "Black Women Organizing across Differences,"[8] and so many transformative other essays. Like two of her contemporaries, Adrienne Rich and June Jordan, Lorde is loyal to poetry and to feminism. All three poets leave the chamber of reverie to foray into the arena of the essay. *The Cancer Journals, Sister Outsider, A Burst of Light* place Audre Lorde, as well as Jordan, in the tradition of essayists like Frances E. Harper, Ida B. Wells, Alice Dunbar Nelson, Mary Church Terrell—each of whom kept alive the dialogue on Black women's identity and duty, warned the race of its own pitfalls, and protested injustices

3. Audre Lorde, *Our Dead behind Us* (New York: W. W. Norton, 1986), 55.
4. See "The Black Sexism Debate," *Black Scholar* 10, no. 8/9 (May/June 1979): 17–20.
5. Audre Lorde, *Sister Outsider* (Trumansburg, NY: Crossing, 1984).
6. Audre Lorde, *The Cancer Journals* (Argyle, NY: Spinsters, 1980).
7. Lorde, *Sister Outsider*.
8. Audre Lorde, *A Burst of Light* (Ithaca, NY: Firebrand Books, 1988).

done to the race and to the women of that race. However, Lorde goes further and deeper, dissolving the visceral silence surrounding sexuality/intimacy between/among women, death, illness, giving them public voice.

Yet for twenty-five years, we lived also with a poet whose poetry bespeaks an inveterate traveler for whom no place or emotion is too far to go the distance. As lesbian poet and fiction writer Becky Birtha commented at an Audre Lorde memorial service in 1993 at the University of Pennsylvania, "Audre was *out* there—reading, meeting people, traveling." That so many people, including many young people, across differences and generations encountered Audre personally—had not only read her work and met her but also talked deeply with her, shared their work with her, partied intensely with her, had been encouraged by her, driven by her— always amazes me. She was *out* there. She considered herself a "travelling, cultural worker," going and reading her poetry, dropping "seeds" and then leaving—hoping they would spring into something, finding out they did, sometimes never finding out, having "faith and fun along the way."[9] In the poem "Touring," she offers a somewhat racier and overly determined conceit of the traveling cultural worker whose good intentions are mediated by endings and the temporal failure to make deep connections:

> Coming in and out of cities
> where I spend one or two days
> selling myself . . .
> I leave poems behind me. . . .
>
> Coming in and out of cities
> untouched by their magic
> I think without feeling
> this is what men do

---

9. See the conversation with Lorde in Claudia Tate, ed., *Black Women Writers at Work: Conversations* (New York: Continuum, 1983).

who try for some connection
and fail.[10]

What are we bequeathed—as lesbian, gay, bi, trans, Black, white, young, colored, old, men, women, queer, and multiply challenged writers—in the poetry of Audre Lorde, that "strong" reader of the world, that transgressive public intellectual? In this space devoted to our thoughts and feelings on Audre Lorde, is it appropriate—and perhaps, indeed, *urgent*—for us to recommit ourselves to her legacy, the study of her work, the example of her life, as we prepare to take our work and words into the twenty-first century?

How do we use Audre Lorde's poetry to live, act, think? How do we resist pedestalizing and canonizing Audre Lorde, resist immobilizing ourselves by false comparisons, resist *not* acting and *not* feeling? In "Diaspora," she gives us a compelling metaphor: "Afraid is a country with no exit visas."[11]

Lorde's poetry has never been as transparent as her prose, in which she faithfully enunciates her "Black lesbian feminist socialist mother of two" subjectivities.[12] Also, as in the sequence just read, she is more prone to enunciate and to analyze her diaspora identity, her Black Atlantic heritage, her Pan-Africanist consciousness. There is the legend that, after hearing Lorde read a poem in workshop, the late John O. Killens said, "Yeah, you're a poet. I don't know what you're saying, sweetheart, but you're a poet."[13] (Imagine calling Audre Lorde "sweetheart.") For many years, I was critical of what I called her "hermetic inaccessibility." The realm of the literal is not a place Lorde visits long. One can construct of her

---

10. Audre Lorde, *Black Unicorn* (New York: W. W. Norton, 1978), 36.

11. Lorde, *Our Dead behind Us*, 32.

12. Lorde, *Sister Outsider*, 114.

13. John O. Killens (1916–1987) was an American writer, a founder of the Harlem Writers Guild, and known for his contributions to the Black Arts Movement.

poetry narratives of inability, uncertainty, and possibility—always possibility:

> You cannot make love to concrete
> if you cannot pretend
> concrete needs your loving.[14]

Pain, alienation, travail hover always at the margins of Lorde's poems, vying for prominence with anger, hope, and rectitude/righteousness. The poems are most often effected in short, tight lines. Frequently, the line bounds the idea, image, insight: just as often, however, the thought is running or fragmented or disappearing and running up later in the same or another poem or book. There is hardly any punctuation, except the occasional, well-placed period. The "spatial pauses"[15] between words and lines, the imagined spaces after lines, the appositives are some of the more obvious stylistic practices that characterized her poetry from its earliest soundings. For one whose "So it is better to speak / remembering / we were never meant to survive" is so often quoted and lived by, the uses of silence are as powerful as repetition.[16] Lorde's prosodic efficiency is as evident in *The First Cities*,[17] her first book of poems, as it is in *The Marvelous Arithmetics of Distance*,[18] her last voyage, in which her lifelong themes, concerns, rhetorical brilliance are reprised. She refuses us the comfort and inevitability of the vamp, of the rhyming couplet, of the blues, the sonnet, the ballad, the spiritual, iambic pentameter—gives us instead some

---

14. See Audre Lorde, "Making Love to Concrete," in *The Marvelous Arithmetics of Distance* (New York: W. W. Norton, 1993), 5.
15. See Gloria T. Hull, "Living on the Line," in *Changing Our Own Words*, ed. Cheryl A. Wall (New Brunswick, NJ: Rutgers University Press, 1990), 150–172.
16. Audre Lorde, "A Litany for Survival," in *Collected Poems*, 255.
17. Audre Lorde, *The First Cities* (New York: Poets Press, 1966).
18. Lorde, *Marvelous Arithmetics*.

spare R&B refrain and some lost percussion solo. The angry, spare, and varied refrain—seven times in all—in the poem "Moving Out or the End of Cooperative Living" is an example:

> *I am so glad to be moving*
> away from this prison for black and white faces
> assaulting each other with our joint oppression
> competing for who pays the highest price for this privilege
> *I am so glad I am moving.*[19]

Audre Lorde found the first community for her voice in the late sixties with the New Black Poets (of the Black Arts Movement), whose mission was to liberate the Black mind from Western tutelage. Even then and before then, refusing to be silenced by the conflicts between Black men and Black women, she wrote woman-centered, mythic, and sorrowful poems of motherhood and childhood, poems of failed love relationships, of ambivalence and uncertainty. Lorde is unparalleled in her concern for children and young people, except by her sister poet Gwendolyn Brooks, whose poetics and poetic concerns diverge so sharply from Lorde's. In "Generation," published in 1968, the speaker elegizes innocence before the onset of experience:

> How the young attempt and are broken
> differs from age to age
> We were brown free girls
> . . . .
> and the wind had made us golden
> made us gay.[20]

---

19. Audre Lorde, "Moving Out or the End of Cooperative Living," in *Collected Poems*, 74 (italics mine).
20. Audre Lorde, "Generation," in *Collected Poems*, 17.

And again, the popular "For Each of You," a poem published four years later, in which the speaker exhorts the imagined Black community to take pride in its matrilineal and slave heritage. In a parenthetical phrase, the speaker also makes that imagined Black community accountable to children—not just those we parent:

> Speak proudly to your children
> where ever you may find them
> tell them
> you are the offspring of slaves
> and your mother was a princess
> in darkness.[21]

Audre Lorde leaves us a sexual legacy as blatant and as subtle as we ourselves want to be in our own "uses of the erotic." The poems never doubt the body or the body's desire, only the objects of its desire. How can we use the poems to teach us about sex? Sex energy is life energy. The love object/subject of desire is either ungendered or gendered female—enunciating possibilities other than but grounded in the specificity of love between women (perhaps I might say "among"): "When you love, you love. It only depends on how you do it, how committed you are, how many mistakes you make. . . . But I do believe that the love expressed between women is particular and powerful because we had to love ourselves in order to live; love has been our means of survival, and having been in love with both men and women, I want to resist the temptation to gloss over the differences. We all have the ability to feel deeply and to move upon our feelings and see where they lead us."[22]

Sex is spectacular, oracular, primal, and dangerous, especially for women, especially for lesbians. The poems are in the here and now, always prophesying the potential for rejection and destruction. Her metaphors are awesome as much for their exquisiteness

---

21. Audre Lorde, "For Each of You," in *Collected Poems*, 59.
22. In Tate, *Black Women Writers*, 155–156.

as for their earthy explicitness—as in this series of metaphorical
and literal images of digital penetration, cunnilingus, female genitals, body parts, secretions, and erogenous zones in the incompa-
rable "love poem." The speaker's voice is active (and rather butch):

> And I knew when I entered her I was
> high wind in her forest hollow
> fingers whispering sound
> honey flowed
> from the split cup
> impaled on a lance of tongues
> on the tips of her breasts on her navel
> and my breath
> howling into her entrances
> through lungs of pain.[23]

And even lesbians suspend their guardedness in the transcendent "woman":

> I dream of a place between your breasts
> to build my house like a haven
> where I plant crops in your body
> . . . .
> and your night comes down upon me
> like a nurturing rain.[24]

In "Sisters in Arms," from *Our Dead*, the mythic and real instability of the erotic is displayed, and sex and death coalesce shame-
lessly in the context of a dangerous and violent world (and a world
where light is still possible):

---

23. Audre Lorde, *Undersong* (New York: W. W. Norton, 1993), 141. *Undersong* was originally published in *New York Head Shop and Museum* (Detroit:
Broadside, 1976).
24. Audre Lorde, "Woman," in *Collected Poems*, 297.

I could not return with you to bury the body
reconstruct your nightly cardboards
against the seeping Transvaal cold
. . . . so I bought you a ticket to Durban
on my American Express
and we lay together
in the first light of a new season.[25]

"Smelling the Wind," from *The Marvelous Arithmetics of Distance*, is a compressed (love) lyric (and almost sonnet) that encapsulates the intentions of this posthumous volume and the intention with which Lorde lived her life as an artist, lesbian, and African in diaspora:

rushing headlong
into new silence
your face
dips on my horizon
the name
of a cherished dream
riding my anchor[26]

Gloria Hull argues in "Living on the Line," "Almost as soon as she achieves a place of connection, she becomes uneasy at the comfortableness (which is, to her, a signal that something critical is being glossed over) and proceeds to rub athwart the smooth grain to the roughness and the slant she needs to maintain her difference-defined, complexly constructed self."[27] I think surely Lorde leaves us this legacy of unease and of refusal to be consoled.

I'd also like to spend some time reflecting upon the deaths of Terri L. Jewell and Toni Cade Bambara—each of whom we lost in

---

25. Audre Lorde, "Sisters in Arms," in *Collected Poems*, 357.
26. Lorde, *Marvelous Arithmetics*, 3.
27. Hull, "Living on the Line."

1995. Poet and friend Miguel Algarin said to me recently, "1995 devastated our community."[28] I'd like for us to take a minute of silence for all those we have lost, especially in 1995.

Bambara was a name Toni Cade gave herself somewhere around 1970, after the publication of the groundbreaking anthology *The Black Woman*. In fact, it seems she named herself all her life. Born Miltona Mirken Cade in 1939, at age five, she is said to have announced to her mother that she had renamed herself "Toni"— not short for anything. And for me, who encountered her all too briefly at several crucial points in my life, the name "Toni" will always be held to the standard set by Toni Cade Bambara. "Any dude who wants to hang with me can take my name [Bambara]," I remember hearing her say sometime around 1972.

In the words of Ella Baker, another formidable Black woman leader, Toni Cade Bambara was a "facilitator," whereas Audre was more of a director. As Audre, she inspired a whole generation of people from all kinds of diasporas to do something, to take leadership, to get, as poet Nikki Finney said at Toni's memorial service, a "plan."

As a groping young writer, my experience of this teacher, mentor, and beautiful star, Toni Cade Bambara, validates Finney's reminiscence. Around 1970 or 1971, I attended a reading, from the soon-to-be-published *Gorilla, My Love*, Toni did when she was teaching at Livingston College (Rutgers University, 1969–1972). (Toni's article "On the Issue of Roles" in *The Black Woman* had already moved me to feminism.) I was so taken by her performative talents, her fabulous ear for Black urban East Coast language, her seriousness, and her sidesplitting humor that I went up to her to ask her how she did it. But of course, I couldn't appear so naïve and needy. So I asked a question about *The Black Woman* as a subterfuge. "How'd you pull it together, Toni?" I asked, in mock self-composure. "A group of us got together, decided we had something to write, and wrote it," she answered crisply, looking back at me for

---

28. Miguel Algarin died in November 2020 at age seventy-nine.

further input, sort of underneath her eyes. I fumbled and just finally blurted out, "How do you just . . . write?" She said genially, "I just sit down and write. It's the only way, Cheryl." After that quick and pressed advice, I got a plan. Many an artist, writer, scholar, intellectual, student, activist, and community *got* a plan because Toni Cade Bambara said, "The most effective way to do it, is to do it." A serious sister, race woman, and feminist, Toni Cade Bambara *practiced* freedom—and resistance—daily.

Almost ten years later, holding the first edition of Cherríe Moraga and Gloria Anzaldúa's *This Bridge Called My Back: Writings by Radical Women of Color*, I encountered Toni Cade Bambara again, at another crucial location, created primarily by lesbian of color feminists. And there she was writing the foreword to *Bridge*, urging us on to its promise, holding us—we "radical women of color" writers—accountable for fashioning "potent networks of all daughters of the ancient mother cultures . . . an awesome . . . mighty . . . glorious work."[29] How could we falter after this splendid exhortation?

Like Audre, Toni Cade Bambara was a seer, also a strong reader of the world, and one of our last best race women at a time when there is so much pressure and pretention to deconstruct race and gender without destabilizing racist-sexist structures. Toni Cade Bambara died at the age of fifty-six on December 9, 1995, in a hospice in Philadelphia after a two-year struggle with cancer. Friend and mentor Toni Morrison committed herself to gathering all of Bambara's published and unpublished work and seeing that it never goes out of print in her lifetime.[30] Read Audre Lorde's 1972 poem "Dear Toni Instead of a Letter of Congratulations upon Your Book and Your Daughter Whom You Say You Are Raising to

---

29. Toni Cade Bambara, foreword to *This Bridge Called My Back* (Watertown, MA: Persephone, 1981), vi.

30. The book became *Deep Sightings and Rescue Missions: Fictions, Essays, and Conversations* (New York: Pantheon, 1996). Morrison wrote the introduction.

Be a Correct Little Sister" for a stunning portrait of Toni Cade
Bambara and a rich testament to the passions of both writers:

> I see your square delicate jawbone
> . . . as well as the ease
> with which you deal with your pretensions.
> I dig your going and becoming
> the lessons you teach your daughter
> our history
> for I am your sister corrected and
> already raised up
> our daughters will explore in the old countries
> as curious visitors to our season
> using their own myths to keep themselves sharp.[31]

A lot of people will miss Toni Cade Bambara a lot. She and Audre
are definitely two people who made a difference in how the world
turned. But I guess will have to just keep on trucking, as it were.

Singer Phyllis Hyman, actress Rosalind Cash, painter Michael
Kendall, New York City entrepreneur Dellon Wilson, poet Essex
Hemphill, costume designer Judy Dearing each died in 1995—and
are losses to our communities. I was ill prepared for the shock of
Terri L. Jewell's suicide in November in East Lansing, Michigan. I
was not prepared for the power of her absence. I recall the last five
lines of "The Uxoricide," the first poem by Terri L. Jewell I edited
and the first poem I ever edited period. How nearly prophetic
those lines seem now:

> He threw a net over her and waited
>   for her to look up at him
>   before shooting
>   her
>   in the head.[32]

---

31. Audre Lorde, "Dear Toni," in *Collected Poems*, 93.
32. Terri L. Jewell, "The Uxoricide," *Conditions: Eleven/Twelve*, 1985, 136.

In *Succulent Heretic* (1994), Terri L. Jewell's only collection of poetry, she changed and trimmed the last three lines of the above-cited stanza to

> before shooting her
> coolly
> between her
> lovely
> still eyes.[33]

Revision seemed always a possibility for Terri, though living had become much too burdensome. From 1985 to 1990, the *Conditions* editorial collective published poems by Terri L. Jewell in each of its issues, except the *Conditions: 16* (1988). And as a member of the collective, I corresponded with Terri regularly about her poetry. I admired her work then and I still do. Since my first reading of her poetry in 1985, I felt humbled by the grace of her language, its startling insights, the horror hugging the contours of her voice—the humor and sarcasm as well. I understand from a close friend she has paintings, writings, as well as two or three anthologies she was completing. Should we not, like Toni Morrison, commit ourselves to gathering and preserving Terri's work? Who among us will do for Jewell what Morrison claims she will do for Bambara?

On my way up and down the New Jersey Turnpike in the weeks (well, actually, the day, maybe the hour) preceding this necessary conference—OutWrite—I have tried to figure a conclusion: some hortatory remarks of my own. Read one of my poems? Write a new poem for this important occasion? Read from one of Audre's? Thunder the poem "Sacrifice" at you, which warns us that even with all our righteous precautions, "pleasure will betray us."[34] Perhaps I can read from "Oshun's Table," a simple lyric in which lovely food is a temporary bond for the unstable:

---

33. Terri L. Jewell, *Succulent Heretic* ([Lansing, MI?]: Opal Tortuga, 1994), 44.
34. From Lorde, *Undersong*, 172–173.

A short hard rain
and the moon, came up
before we lay down together
we toasted each other . . .
handsome
untrustworthy
and brave.[35]

Perhaps from "Blackstudies," her enraged admonition to those
Africans in diaspora, who hold too fast to notions of "real blackness," yet we can read all of us in the subtext, all of us who are
duped by the sacred cow identity, are dogmatic, doctrinaire, and
fixed in our politics and visions:

Now all the words in my legend come garbled
except anguish [and]
strangle me in a nightmare of leaders
at crowded meetings to study our problems
I move awkward and ladylike
. . . I worry on nationalist holidays.[36]

Or:

It is better to speak
remembering we were never meant to survive.[37]

Or:

I have been woman
for a long time
beware my smile

---

35. From Lorde, *Marvelous Arithmetics*, 37.
36. From Lorde, *Undersong*, 178.
37. Lorde, "A Litany for Survival," in *Black Unicorn*, 32.

I am treacherous with old magic . . .
I am
woman
and not white.[38]

Or:

I do not believe our wants
have made all our lies
holy.[39]

Or:

But I who am bound by my mirror
as well as my bed
see causes in colour
as well as sex

and sit here wondering
which me will survive
all these liberations.[40]

Or:

I cannot recall the words of my first poem
but I remember a promise
I made my pen
never to leave it

---

38. Audre Lorde, "A Woman Speaks," in *Chosen Poems* (New York: Columbia University Press, 1982), 5.

39. Audre Lorde, "Between Ourselves," in *Making Face, Making Soul*, ed. Gloria Anzaldúa (San Francisco: Aunt Lute, 1980), 113.

40. Audre Lorde, "Who Said It Was Simple," in *From a Land Where Other People Live* (Detroit: Broadside, 1973), 39.

lying
in somebody else's blood.[41]

I wish to give no advice about what in Audre Lorde's life and legacy we must emulate and carry forward—only that we must do something. I find my own answer in the poem with which I began, "On My Way Out I Passed Over You and the Verrazano Bridge":

And I dream of our coming together
encircled   driven
not only by love
but by lust for a working tomorrow
and the flights of this journey
mapless   uncertain
and necessary as water.[42]

("I owe a great deal to Gloria Hull's magnificent essay 'Living on the Line,' one of the only works of criticism to plumb the layers of Lorde's poetry," I said foregoing in 1995, and in 2021, I still mean it.)

---

41. Audre Lorde, "To the Poet Who Happens to Be Black and the Black Poet Who Happens to Be a Woman," in *Our Dead behind Us*, 7.
42. In Lorde, *Our Dead behind Us*, 57.

Keeping Our Queer Souls

KEYNOTE ADDRESS

FEBRUARY 20, 1998

The question I have been most frequently asked in my thirteen years at Firebrand and five years at Crossing Press about my publishing life is, "Do you really want to be a writer?" And aside from the sort of professionally correct and actually true response—which is that I think it would not be a good idea to be a publisher who was also a writer, trying to make decisions and be useful to other people's writing—I don't want to be a writer. It is a much too solitary endeavor for somebody who could say yes to talking in front of a thousand people with twenty-four hours' notice. I enjoy the opportunity to talk, and Kate Clinton offered very generously this afternoon at lunch to provide me with some routines if I needed them.[1] So if I stumble a lot in the middle and Kate is in the room, she could just pipe up with what she thought was an appropriate line at the moment.

What I really want to be rather than a writer is the thing that I struggled the hardest in my own personal life to find the time to be, and that is more of a reader. My idea of absolute pleasure, and I have said this to several people privately who share with me the notion that it's not so farfetched, is to have a rather large amount of time—now, for me, anything more than a week seems a really

---

1. Kate Clinton is a comedian and self-described femorist (humorist + feminist). She emceed a variety of lesbian, gay, and feminist events during the 1980s, 1990s, and the first and second decades of the twenty-first century.

large amount of time—to have a large amount of time in my favorite vacation place, which for me is at the ocean. And there is a decent amount of sunshine, and I have the right sunscreen, and my partner is with me, and we are getting along very well, and I have packed a bag of books, and in the bag of books are not manuscripts that I have to read. They are not galleys on which I am doing the final edit. They are books that are the wish list of books. Nobody but me cares whether I have read them. Most people won't even ask me about those books. Now, I would like to hope that in this room there are lots of people who feel that even if that is not the thing they wish to do with every available vacation time that happens, there is some part of their lives that yearns for that sense of being alone with, engaged in, and absolutely caught up by those printed words that somebody else, probably unknown to you, has written.

This is my love affair as a reader. I'm a person who comes from the tribe that is sometimes known as the people of the book. It was a different book, one that I didn't read very much, but I was taught as a child that some of the most significant things in the world were encompassed between the covers of a volume, and one of the pleasures that I remember as a kid was getting my first library card— big deal, very grown-up, got to sign my own name. They let me go by myself. I grew up in New York City, so it was a great way to walk the blocks to the place that otherwise I wasn't allowed to go.

Reading was also one of my first acts of civil disobedience. I used to take a flashlight to bed with me and read under the covers after I was supposed to be asleep. I liked the worlds that books opened up to me. I still like the world that books open up to me. It is for each of us, as writers or people who function in the publishing world, an absolutely special kind of relationship that does not exist in any other form than the written word. You are alone with it. You are comfortable in however you define that space, that physical space you do not and should not in many instances communicate with anybody about what you're reading. Your life, your psyche, your emotional life, your pleasurable life—all get opened up because somebody has somehow magically encompassed in the language that we have learned to speak together, words that make sense and make meaning bigger.

There are many reasons for all of us to be here at OutWrite. There's networking, also known as cruising, but it really does exist as networking as well. There are skills to be gained. Many of the workshops are a very specific focus so that folks can learn how to do something or more about doing something that they didn't know when they started out. There's a community that we say that we're a part of, which is a community that is tied to, on the one hand, being queer and, on the other hand, being concerned with the writing, the thinking that is expressed in the writing, the activism that is behind the intent of doing the writing, that ties us all together.

Now, what does it mean to be a publisher? I don't know if I'm the first publisher to give a keynote, but I'm certainly one of the few, and publishers are generally, and maybe even especially in leftist progressive circles, thought of as being those kinds of businesspeople who are separated off from the creative process that the artists do. Publishers just have all of that money-related stuff that they have to deal with, and artists get to deal with the meat of the issue, the words on the page.

As a publisher, I have many pragmatic functions. I am at the place that is the intersection between what the writer does and what gets opened up to the world. There's a certain amount of power in that, which I think I have struggled with over the years to learn how to (1) not deny that I have it and (2) use, at least most times, wisely. As a publisher, I feel myself to be a part of a movement that helps put those words, those ideas that come from the community in which I too live and read, out into the world for a larger audience.

Cecilia Tan has called that the commerce of writing.[2] Writing, if it is intended for publication, does not exist in a vacuum. Nobody

---

2. Cecilia Tan is a writer and editor. She was cochair of the program at OutWrite 98.

needs a justification to write. That is a solitary act, and anybody is entitled, if you will, to do that without guidance from other people, without interference from anybody else, without suggestions from anybody else, without any modification of tone, shape, size, language. As I've said on a number of occasions when I've been at writing workshops talking about the pragmatics of publishing, the choice to write is between the writer and their own heart and intellect. The choice to be published is a different decision than the choice to write. If you choose to be published, if that is one of the goals that you have as a writer, then you enter into a larger world where you no longer are able to completely control every word on the page or in the computer.

You can't control what people think about what you've written, whether they misunderstand your intent, whether they attribute motivations to it that you never dreamed of, whether they have a grudge against you and it comes out in the reviews that are done, whether people think it's the definitive book on the subject and it gets adopted for classroom use. You can't control that. You can *influence* some of that, but you can't control it. Art made public becomes public property as far as the uses to which it is put. Publishers, when we function both effectively and with good intent, try to give a book the best life it can have out there and therefore are always, I think, partners in the process of making words real on the page and then multiply them outside of one's journal or laptop computer, putting them out into the marketplace.

That commercial world is not static. The rules that govern it, the economic and political forces in which the writing gets launched into the world change. We are living in a time now in 1998 that is markedly different from the publishing world that existed, let us say, five years ago. I actually would say that, if I had to put a month on the demarcation when it became noticeable to publishers that the world had changed, it would be July 1996. Two years ago, this July, it was noticeable. Publishers large and small were accustomed to receiving 25–30 percent returns, even of books that had already been sold, right back into their warehouses; many of those books were damaged and therefore not saleable. Many of those books had already been counted on the ledger sheets and royalties paid to the authors. Bookstores have up to two years to return books. No other industry in this country allows that, but conventional returns practice for booksellers is up to two years. Publishers had learned how to factor these returns percentages into their business models. Only blockbusters, where volume sales made the difference, were above the fray. Profit on each item is very marginal. You must do volume in order to make money.

In July 1996, returns shot up to 50 to 65 percent across the board. University presses, small presses, trade houses weren't any different. How various institutions deal with that reality depends on how much money they have. Obviously the less capitalized you are, the less money you have to absorb unusual and unexpected expenses. That's the easiest way of saying it, right? If you have a small bank account and you have an emergency repair to your car, you are in better shape than if you have no bank account and your car does the same bad thing. You are even better off if you have a big bank account and you can buy a new car. It's the same principle. It's just different issues.

So the publishing world has changed, and the publishing world has changed for many different reasons that people much smarter than I am economically have written about. They've written about it in the *Nation*. They've written about it in the *New York Times*. They've written about it in the *Wall Street Journal*. They've written about it in the *Lambda Book Report*. They've written about it in *Feminist Bookstore News*. They have written about it in a variety of places that intelligent readers can get their hands on, especially intelligent readers who are also writers.

Most writers don't want to know about it. I sent a package of materials from all of these different places to my authors with their royalty statements. It wasn't about *Firebrand*; it was about life. Right? I said, "If you want to talk to me about this, just give me a call, and I'll see what I can do to explain it better." But they didn't call. They're not publishers; they're writers. They don't want to know about it because it is very upsetting. When you're struggling as a writer, and nobody is supporting you financially, and there isn't a lot of money in writing, then to be told it's only going to get worse . . .

It's like Starbucks moves into your neighborhood and you are a small cappuccino maker. You no longer can do very well with your small cappuccino stand. In Ithaca, my story goes like this: we don't have a Home Depot—I don't know why; the demographics aren't right—that means that when I want to buy a cup hook to hang a potholder in the kitchen, I go to my local hardware store and I say, "I think this one is the right size." I take out my ruler and I buy one cup hook for thirty-three cents, and it is whatever size I need. There are twelve different sizes to choose from in cup hooks at my local hardware store. If Home Depot were there, it would only be one package of twelve in mixed sizes.

There are lots of good things that chain stores do. They do not allow for diversification and individual judgment. In an independent bookstore, each shop has one buyer. When Barnes & Noble buys, there is one buyer who buys for the entire country. This is not to single out and make bad guys. I'm not saying, "OK, fine. No one should walk into Barnes." I'm saying the industry has changed because the corporate structure of the industry has made the rules different. We are dealing with different rules that we don't control. I do not control them. I do not pretend to control them. In addition, more and more of trade publishing is owned by Hollywood-like entertainment organizations. Many of them *are* Hollywood entertainment organizations.

The thinking today in the book businesses is we're going to get a blockbuster. We're going to make our money on the blockbuster. Everything else is unimportant. In many ways, including in the lesbian and gay community, we have been affected by it. There are books that have gotten advances that nobody in their right business mind—business mind meaning dollar-for-dollar business mind—should have assumed would sell the number of copies that would have had to be sold to earn back those advances.

That's not to say the authors aren't wonderful people. That is not to say it's not good that some queer people have money in their pocket. That is not to say that either the agents and/or the editors who sold those books for large amounts of money or who bought those books for large amounts of money are bad people. Like all of us, we get caught up in a system that says the rules are changing. We want to survive. We're going to stay on the carousel, and maybe we'll be the one that gets to grab the big one.

But in a homophobic world, where they do not like us to begin with, these practices are destroying the ability to sell gay and lesbian books in the trade world. I know of one agent who has said, "I'm not coming to this conference because I cannot tell people that I won't take them on without even reading their material because I know that I can no longer sell the stuff that three years ago I was selling. So I just won't come to the conference."

That is what's happening. It's not about blaming people; it's about understanding the context. Plus, there are lots of folks who in their discretionary two hours of free time a day are on the World Wide Web. So there were people who were readers, who would die without reading, who say, "I think it's more interesting and more fun and easier to be on the web, and therefore I'm not reading anymore." Book sales are reflecting that. You can talk to anyone who's your favorite bookseller, gay and lesbian bookstore, women's bookstore, independent bookstore, and you can ask. You can look at the figures in *Publishers Weekly* and see the total number of books being sold and book sales are flat. I'm not saying that certain books don't sell a huge number of copies. They're not the ones that we're writing; they just are not.

Now, the other piece of this is status. I don't think there are many people in the industry who would argue this. They might disagree with the implications, but they're not going to argue with the fact. My own personal opinions about our queer world are as follows: I don't think we have any historical perspective as a community on how we got here and who we are. We have a great sentimentality about Stonewall and the great divide before, and the great divide after, and the marches in Washington. We don't have a sense of what it really took to make us a visible community, nor are we discussing what it will take to keep us a viable community.

We no longer have to worry about the gayness, the queerness of musicians because we have kd and Melissa—of people on television because we have Ellen. And as Urvashi pointed out in her article without mentioning Ellen's name, the show may or not be a good show.[3] It may be great that teenagers can turn on the television and see in prime time, in spite of the warnings and all of this stuff, see that there is a lesbian who barely, occasionally touches her partner's shoulder or hand, right? Because we know girls just don't do it, right? And she defines herself as not political and says she doesn't want to be, and she's entitled not to be. And we are fools if we make her our speaker.

Sarah Schulman has a terrific piece in the current *Harvard Gay & Lesbian Review* on commodification.[4] Queerness is product. There are certain things I don't think that we can do anything about because capitalism is our ocean. It's not about Marxism is good, capitalism is bad, let's all become Marxists. That's not what I'm saying. I'm talking about the nature of the ocean that we're swimming in. We are becoming a product. And we have to look, act, dress, be certain ways in order for it to be a definable product, and then it's sold back to us. Gay and lesbian bookstores make an enormous amount of money over nonintellectual property, sidelines. It helps keep them alive. So the more bumper stickers that we see making us happier as we drive down the road because we always

3. During the 1990s, Urvashi Vaid was a leader in the LGBTQ movement. She wrote a regular column for the *Advocate* during this period, in which she discusses Ellen DeGeneres and others mentioned, but Bereano likely references Vaid, "Thoughts on the Movement's Style," *Gay Community News* 23, no. 2/3 (Fall/Winter 1997/1998): 8–11.

4. Sarah Schulman, "The Making of a Market Niche," *Harvard Gay & Lesbian Review* 5, no. 1 (Winter 1998): 17–20. The *Harvard Gay & Lesbian Review* is now known as the *Gay & Lesbian Review / Worldwide*.

knew that we were 10 percent of the population, now we can say, "You *see*; we're 10 percent of the population because there are rainbows every place," right? The less money is spent on books, which are the things that under the best of circumstances make us think about ourselves in the world.

Don't fault the bookstores. They have to stay alive. It's not the bookstores' fault. Fault, however, we as a community, and I don't mean the people only in this room but ourselves as a queer nation. What is it about that the college student who you know has been out since she's been twelve years old, since she thought about her sexuality in some clear way to herself, realized she was a lesbian, understood that she could plug into lesbian groups around, thought there is no problem with homophobia at all, and was fortunate enough to have parents who did not throw her out of the house and who said, "Fine, we love you. Maybe you'll outgrow it. Fine. We love you." And then when confronted—and this is a real story that my partner encountered while teaching at a college in Ithaca—when she, who had gone to the same camp as her siblings for six years, eight years, forever, they had gone to the same summer camp, so the directors knew the family, they knew the kids, they knew everybody, when it came time for her to be a counselor, they said, "We don't think it's a good idea because it's not a good idea to have an out lesbian counselor." Now that's very terrible, right? What is even more terrible is she had not a clue what to do about it. Should she make a fuss because, after all, her parents have been so supportive, and they know these people, and she's been there forever, and she's got younger brothers and sisters at the camp. Should she write an article with somebody exposing the hypocrisy of the liberal virtues of the camp directors? Should she just not do anything? Absolutely at a loss because she thought that she was growing up in a world where since gay was visible, gay was OK. Visibility does not equal a serious engagement in the public life of our bigger world. It just does not.

So many of us here came out of a movement, out of several movements. I could not be queer without a movement. I am not somebody who knew ever since I was sixteen years old and tried to figure out how to make a life. I came out when I was thirty-eight years old. I wouldn't have even known that it was a possibility for me were there not a visible feminist and lesbian movement. Many of us would not have known. Many of us, if we honestly look at our lives, can point to those political movements—Black activism, feminism, the queer movement—can point to those movements and understand how we have been able to make our lives. We, each of us bigger and richer, fuller, larger, more complex than we would have been able to be had those movements not existed. Movements that we helped make and movements where we joined that other people had already done a lot of work in. It is not a given. It is not a given, and history will show us over and over and over again, if we take the time to look, that if we do not nurture those movements, if we do not see ourselves in a movement, if we do not do the things that help keep movements alive, which is more than having only a conference once a year, if we do not, we will not be. Not individually in our lives. But we will not be as some kind of peoplehood that sees our possibilities ever expanding.

Last year, the Lambda Literary Awards added "transgender" as a category. It was previously unthought of. Most of us could not, myself included, have imagined when the Lambda Literary Awards started, not only that there would be gay and lesbian book awards, but that there would be a transgender category. That happens because we exist in a world that grows, not in a world where we fight like hell to just have what we have and not change it at all.

How do we keep our queer souls? How? How do we do this at a time when technology changes, economic pressures change? It's only the tip of the iceberg, you know? How do we do that? I have a lot of discussions with people about it. I don't pretend to have the answers. What I do know is that we must pay attention to the struggle of other oppressed groups. We must look to see what keeps other people alive. We must learn from that and take what we need. We must make common cause with people who are more on our side than less on our side—even if they are not just like us.

And I would argue that a very big piece of this, not the only piece, is culture, not politics. Culture is part of politics, is the writing that we do—the writing that we do in all of its many, many forms. I concentrated on the book because that's what I live with the most, but that's not, I understand, the only form that culture takes. I would like to close with a quote that was said at lunch today by Mark Doty: "Our job is to write so that the differences, the individual stories of our lives don't get homogenized in the mix-master of the dominant culture."

Making a Fresh Start

The Challenge of Queer Writers

KEYNOTE ADDRESS

FEBRUARY 20, 1998

I grew up in conservative, white, suburban Philadelphia, an only child adopted by deeply conservative, middle-class parents. My father was an FBI agent during the McCarthy witch hunts; my mother's family was Jewish, though she and her mother had converted to Christianity during Hitler's rise, and this fact was kept hidden from as many people as possible, including me.[1] Dim little me at the age of, what, ten (?) at last wonders aloud, "How come so many of Mom's relatives are Jewish?" Part of my torpor in coming to this realization may have been that both my parents made anti-Semitic remarks; they routinely employed the N-word, homosexuals (if mentioned at all, and only then in whispers of shock and disgust) were fairies, Nixon was a god, Communists were always the enemy. My schoolteachers were almost all cut from similar cloth. If it were actually possible to "recruit" children into one's own sexual orientation and belief system, I would now be a God-fearing, heterosexual Republican. I'm not.

---

1. *Gay Community News* (vol. 23, no. 4: 4–13) published this speech in its entirety; it is edited for inclusion in this volume.

Craig Lucas. (*Photo credit: Photo by Robert Giard, copyright Estate of Robert Giard.*)

The first stirrings of wanting to create something, make art, were concurrent with my earliest sexual imaginings. What is it about putting a crayon to paper, donning a costume and improvising a play, a dance, acting out with puppets or dolls? Listen to kids jabbering to one another, they are all little novelists and screenwriters, retelling and refashioning everything into art. I can remember with the intense pain of a new and unrequited love this overwhelming need to make something, but what? How?

I wanted to write musicals, paint paintings; I wanted to fly like Mary Martin as Peter Pan before the eyes of the world and sing about . . . about . . . what?[2] What could I tell them that was safe to say and yet worth crowing about?

2. Actress Mary Martin helmed the role of Peter in the 1954 Broadway production of *Peter Pan*, as well as the NBC telecasts of the musical in the late 1950s and early 1960s. According to historians Lillian Faderman and Stuart Timmons in the book *Gay L.A.: A History of Sexual Outlaws, Power Politics,*

I wrote puppet plays about witches and kings and severely endangered children and performed them for money at children's birthday parties and on local TV (my first taste of capitalism!), very much encouraged by my parents. I hand this to them— earning me enough to keep myself in show albums and a subscription to the *New Yorker*, where I encountered for the first time stories by Cheever and Salinger and the poems of Anne Sexton. Sophistication! Adultery! Miserable suburbanites with their martinis and swimming pools, their existential angst, their Zen Buddhism. I was in pig heaven.

Books and plays were my teachers, my best parents, doing the job nobody else wanted. When I found a hardback copy of *Who's Afraid of Virginia Woolf?* at a local library—I couldn't have been more than twelve—here were adults drinking and hurting one another in the name of love, something I had certainly seen but never heard discussed: it wasn't on TV. Plays by Thornton Wilder and Williams and soon novels by Isherwood, Vidal, helped pave the way out of that here-and-now, and on to some other then-and-there—this one right here-and-now. That road also included the novels of, yes, Gordon Merrick and John Rechy and the poems of Ed Field, all of which I squirreled home in my book bag from dime-store racks, library shelves, promising a potentially liberating but also scary and furtive existence; my first attempted suicide was only a month after the movie of *The Boys in the Band* played in our local movie theater. I'd loved it, seen it three or four times. The subterranean message, hidden (at least from me at the time) beneath this frantic joy up on the screen, was "There is no way out of this self-hatred, this hopeless alcoholism and abuse; even if you find others like yourself, you will all destroy one another with hollow laughter and joyless sex."

---

and Lipstick Lesbians, Martin was also rumored to have had lesbian relationships while married to her second husband, Richard Halliday, also rumored to have been a homosexual.

I took an overdose of barbiturates with a generous swill of alcohol, was hospitalized, and saw my first psychiatrist; it was almost too easy to convince him, in one session no less, that it was all a misunderstanding; he didn't want to discuss my sexuality any more than I did. And off he sent me to college, where within a day or two I learned that Anne Sexton was on the faculty. I wrote my first poem (I think I just wanted to meet someone famous, frankly), and I submitted it and was accepted into her writing workshop, where I produced coded, hopelessly clotted poems that she gingerly suggested might contain homosexual themes; I was outraged. How dare she?

Thank you, Anne, for giving me that first go-ahead. Thank you, too, for the vast world of poems you broke open and spilled at my feet—Roethke, Plath, Rich, Williams, Merwin, Bishop, Merrill.

Plays, however, were my primary oxygen then and still are. I prefer them to movies and TV; plays and their authors can afford to be iconoclastic; plays are cheaper to produce; twenty-five people sitting in a room on folding chairs, you've got a show. Queer characters marched up and down the Broadway, Off-Broadway, and Off-Off-Broadway stages long before movies and TV even figured out we existed. Oscar Wilde, Genet, Brecht, Shaw, Ionesco, Beckett—and suddenly in my undergraduate years there were John Guare, Jack Gelber, Rochelle Owens, Michael Smith, Megan Terry, Lanford Wilson, Terrence McNally, Rosalyn Drexter, Jean Claude van Italie, Caryl Churchill—these people tore into bourgeois conventions with a vengeance. And a lot of them, well, they seemed to be queer.

I showed almost no one the coded fantastical one acts I was writing then in case they might glimpse me peeking out between the shower of words and borrowed mannerisms from Gertrude Stein.

I also joined the Worker's League, a tiny Trotskyist party, where I was informed that homosexuality was the last vestige of bourgeois capitalism, a decadent phase that would wither away along with the church once the working class assumed power. Queer men were simply refusing to grow up; lesbians were not discussed,

ever. This all fit nicely into my parents' scheme. Both the Right
and the Left seemed to agree: homo was bad, so I didn't have to
come out—shouldn't, in fact. But I could still sneak around and
suck a few cocks and try getting fucked—ouch, no thanks—and I
couldn't for the life of me figure out why I was having such a hard
time writing. My plays all stalled; I abandoned them midway, just
as I had been abandoned at birth by my biological mother. Maybe
I just didn't have any talent.

After college, I moved to New York with my girlfriend, whose
parents were conveniently both Stalinists, and they agreed homosexuality was a sickness, a refusal to be a responsible adult.

People seem to forget that sexual liberation politics did not
spring full born from the brilliance of the Left—I'm glad the
Nation and the *New York Times* have belatedly come around, sort
of—but liberation politics came, at least in my experience, from
feminism: Boston's Bread and Roses were the first folks I heard
speak of gay liberation, and they saw it as being linked to the
struggles of women.[3]

Filled with dread because I probably didn't *want* my struggles
linked to those of women, god no, I tried writing a novel about
Icarus and Daedalus—no one could spot me as a fag in some
souped-up myth about a flying boy and his dad, trapped together
in a tower (could they?), but again, my words knotted up and
choked me. And my girlfriend dumped me—thank you, Robin.

---

3. Bread and Roses defined itself as a "Revolutionary Autonomous Women's
Liberation Organization," founded in 1969 in the Boston area. The name of
the group derived from women's leftist and activist movements of the early
twentieth century. In 2014, Tess Ewing delivered an informative speech,
"Bread and Roses," on the history of the formation at the conference "A Revolutionary Moment: Women's Liberation in the Late 1960s and Early 1970s,"
organized by the Women, Gender, and Sexuality Studies Program at Boston
University, available here: Tess Ewing, "Bread and Roses" (paper presentation, "A Revolutionary Moment: Women's Liberation in the Late 1960s and
Early 1970s," Boston University, March 27–29, 2014), https://www.bu.edu/
wgs/files/2013/10/Ewing-Bread-and-Roses.pdf.

And miraculously—really, because I'd never studied singing—I got hired to sing in the chorus of an out-of-town musical that came to Broadway and ran for years.

So all right, coming out as a gay man backstage in the chorus of a Broadway musical is not perhaps an act of unparalleled heroism. But I did it and came out to my parents, told them how happy I was (they were not) and how it wasn't their fault and wasn't something that required blame anyway. I would thrive; I wouldn't grow old and be alone and miserable, an outcast; and I returned to New York and tried to kill myself with so many barbiturates washed back with vodka I was in a coma for four and a half days.

Despite *Ellen*, despite *Angels in America*, despite *In and Out*, gay teens are still four times more likely to commit suicide than straights.

The psychologist I had to see before they would agree to release me from the hospital said that I was in big trouble. She said that being a homosexual was not an illness, didn't need to be changed, but that I was suffering from another disease altogether. She didn't use this word, but what she described was homophobia—the world's and my own. I would have to work very hard and dig—go places I was terrified to go. She said that I had in fact been abused and that my anger needed to be turned outward toward real, appropriate enemies.

Thank you, Connie Weinstock.

Without the subsidy of three long-running Broadway musicals, I would never have been able to afford therapy, and I often wonder how it is more people don't perish for the lack of appropriate healing.

It should be no wonder now to any of you that I began suddenly to be able to finish my plays—not without struggle, not without real agony, in fact—but for the first time, I had a theme, a self to express, utilize, fight against, a me from which to imagine. I had moorings.

I want everyone now to imagine themselves as they were as little children—at eight, six, ten, I don't care how old you want to picture yourself—but I want you to place yourself up here beside me, envisioning yourself as you were at that age, in the clothes you were dressed in, as you see yourself in those photos you still have, and I want you to say out loud to your child's self (you can tell I've had a lot of therapy, right?), "Craig," your own name goes first, "Kate, Urvashi, Michael, Patrick, Sarah," you're to say, "It is all right to . . ." and here you are to insert the name of a sexual act you enjoy and that you were not encouraged to engage in during your adolescence. "Craig," go on, do it, say it, "Craig—it is all right to suck cock. . . . It is all right to lick pussy. . . . It is all right . . . to put that inside there where you know you want it. . . . It is all all right."

Good.

I've been accused by at least one queer theorist of being a "closeted gay writer" for creating straight characters in some of my plays, thus trying to appease and pander to straight audiences. I want to say for once and for all that imagination is the stuff of art. I take for myself the right to write whatever I want—white, Black, male, female, straight, lesbian, young, old. I don't care what anybody says: people your art with anyone and everyone you choose. The old adage about writing what you know, if taken too literally, is little more than the death of art itself. To every critic who tells you what you should be writing, remember, it's very valuable to be able to say "Fuck you, go and write your own play."

I don't know; I find this helpful.

Norman René, the man who read my first play and produced and directed it, is dead: two years ago, from AIDS. He directed all my plays and screenplays until he was too sick to work, and I learned from him a great deal about the craft of playwriting, which is not merely narrative skills but most essentially the careful study of people, how they behave under many circumstances, and how their stories are best told through behavior, an honest examination of actions and motives, one's own and the characters'. He maintained that people go to the movies or plays, read books, watch TV to learn how to live their lives better—that art was, among other things, a map for living. It could be another century, another world; the characters could do all the wrong things, but still we would be sorting through the tale for signposts, for understanding, for connections, growth.

Thank you, Norman.

The people who say that good art is not political and never politically useful, that it changes nothing, and that its value lies only in its aesthetic perfection—may themselves be great voices; I've heard this idea put forth by, among others, Auden, Nabokov, Elizabeth Bishop, Salman Rushdie, and I don't devalue the art any of them have made. But they are wrong. Their thinking is too narrow. Art helps. As one develops keener appreciation for subtler works of expression, a higher sensitivity to the complexity in great works, one also hears the voices struggling: between the inside and the out, between society and the individual, oppressor and oppressed. It's all a question of perspective, and from where I stand, *King Lear* and *Medea* and *Death of a Salesman*, *Angels in America*, *Rat Bohemia*, *Almost History*, *Two Serious Ladies*, *Giovanni's Room*, *O Pioneers!*, *The Diary of Virginia Woolf*, and on and on are all capable of saving lives. You say they can't? I say, "Prove it."

Of all the dangers now to art, to the writing and teaching of history, and to ourselves as individuals, I think the most pernicious is the marketplace. And I know most of us don't have the luxury of saying no to work. That, obviously, is how they get us. I do know I've done my best work when nobody was paying me or when the money came without strings attached, in the form of a grant or a commission from a not-for-profit theater or from public broadcasting. And that's another difference between theater and movies: playwrights, like novelists, own the copyright to their work; write a movie or a TV script, and your words are no longer your own; they literally own it—in perpetuity throughout the universe.

It may seem a simple observation, but people who are not working for profit are far more apt to tell the truth about profit-based systems.

No movie studio would make *Longtime Companion*; it was paid for by Public Broadcasting with money from, among others, the National Endowment for the Arts. We were answerable to no one but ourselves. I wrote about a world I knew: upper-middle-class white gay men in New York. Everything in that script reflects something I have seen in the world. Still, it gives me pause to realize the vision we depicted may have been used to further the lie that gay men live in privilege and are across the board more well off than straights.

Political correctness may threaten artists from one side, but it pales next to the blind vitriol and venomous uses of reactionary political agendas from the other, and that is another kind of political correctness, one the pundits never mention.

The movies I have written for studios have all been compromises. Most of them don't get made, and whenever I squeeze in a little bit of myself, that's the part they hate the most.

So I'm going to go on writing for the theater, as much as I can, on my own time, the same way I wrote at night and on weekends when I was a secretary in a publishing firm after my chorus work dried up. The wonderful surgeon I fell in love with and lived with and loved for eleven years has died of AIDS; I no longer have a lover who is also my benefactor—thank you, Dr. Tim. And Public Broadcasting is no longer making movies under the aegis of American Playhouse—thank you, Lindsay Law—and so I am going to have to subsidize the work I want to do, and that is more than all right. There are many, many worse things than working two jobs. Or three. Or four.

What sustains me in all this is my belief that there is something better than what the corporations are pitching. I don't believe that we will always live under "free-market" capitalism; democracy demands increasing rights for all. It is progressive; it doesn't stay the same. Once only white landowners could vote, and slowly others have been admitted into the process. The Bible was used to justify slavery, it was used to justify the persecution of Jews, and now the Evangelicals have turned Christ's unwavering insistence upon giving to the poor into a wholesale endorsement of personal greed.

Until we have an economic and social system that feeds all the people, affords them all access to health care and education and art, and does not require or permit these vast discrepancies between rich and poor, I simply have to assume, and insist, that we can do better, and my personal struggle to write well, survive in this climate, and still be true to my queer soul is but one part of a larger struggle.

Finding a true voice as an individual enables expression. But the enemies of equality have learned to pit us against each other. What we do with our hard-won freedom to speak for ourselves will determine whether any of us succeed. At the risk of once again being accused of being un-American, I will leave you with my truth as I make a new fresh start:

Our individual voices will not save us. We are in the battle for our lives.

Join hands.

A Menopausal Gentleman

An Excerpt

Closing Performance

February 22, 1998

(Instrumental music for a song in the style of "My Way" comes on.)[1]

Just pick the piece you want
and when I pull myself back together again
with the morning light,
I'll think of you.
I'll think of you and who you want me to be.

(Peggy moves into the audience, speaking the song as a poem. When the spoken song ends, the chords of the music continue under her monologue, which she continues to address to the audience.)

I know now I didn't eat enough tofu.
You're supposed to start really young.

---

1. The full script is in *A Menopausal Gentleman: The Solo Performances of Peggy Shaw* (Ann Arbor: University of Michigan Press, 2011). The selection here begins on page 84 in the book and continues through page 88. At Out-Write 98, Shaw performed the full show *A Menopausal Gentleman*. Shaw performed the piece not in a theatre but in a hotel ballroom, without any theatrical lighting. This selection from the middle of the show begins with Shaw riffing in her lesbian way to Paul Anka's "My Way."

Peggy Shaw (*Photo credit: Courtesy of the Bromfield Street Educational Foundation records at the Northeastern University Library's Archives and Special Collections.*)

You should start right away.
In Japan they don't even have a word for hot flashes.
I don't know if I can live the rest of my life like this.
Everything is catching up to me.
That feeling I had in 1977 that I never dealt with in Amsterdam.
I have gotten to the end of my blood.
Where has it all gone to?
What excuse do I have for my moods or tears
or not being able to fall asleep
now that I can't count on my blood anymore for an excuse?

(Peggy leaves the audience and returns to the stage.)

They say women have a certain amount of eggs
to use up in a lifetime. I DID IT!
My companions of forty years (the blood) have left me.
Like the boarded up Polish store on Ninth Street
that used to have fresh eggs on Thursdays.

The good old days.
When I had eggs!
I'm a grandmother gentleman now,
and have a three-year-old grand-companion-son.
I think we get along so well
'cause we're both going through a lot of the same things:
we're experimenting with saying no.
He understands me.
We go for long walks together on the edge.
I took him one Sunday to the Museum of Natural History.
As good a place as any to start teaching him
not to believe everything he reads—
as if they can tell that a rock is three million years old.
They make it all up!
I couldn't read the inscriptions to him in good conscience,
so I made up my own stories
about how the dinosaurs exist now,
only on a separate plane,
and if you drink too much alcohol
or take bad drugs
the electric shield around your body breaks down
and that's when you can see how close the dinosaurs are to us.
Then I let him run really far and fast
'cause that is the best thing about the museum of Natural History,
he can break into a run on a shiny marble floor.
I figure that's enough to learn for one day.
As he was leaving
I also told him not to try to make an oil painting in Florence,
or a play in London
'cause they're full of them already.

Maybe parents stay too long with their children.
Maybe you're not supposed to spend so many years together.
It's like being in love.
They say it takes as long to get over someone
as how long you were with them.

Like grieving,
not understanding why the sun still comes up anymore.
Then one morning
you wake up
and realize you haven't thought about that person
and you've already had your coffee.

I remember when I hadn't thought of my mother for a whole day.
It made me so sad.
When I realized it,
I wept and wept
and was scared that I was capable of forgetting that.

(Fake Barry White mood music in background, words spoken in the style of Barry White.)

I ran out of luster in my hair a few years ago.
The sun is merciless when you're in your fifties.
You do love me in the daylight, don't you?
In the amber light? In the night light
My mother told me there's nothing in the dark
that's not in the light.
I can hear you breathing but I can't see you.
What did you say?
There's a word for me.
Apart from the one that springs to your lips.
I have a short memory.
You're not the first one disappointed
that I don't act the way I look.

(Music ends.)

It's okay that someone who loves you doesn't necessarily feed you organic food or keep you off antibiotics. Just that you know you're loved, so that when you're walking on a snow-covered hill with the moon lighting up the night like daylight and the shadows are

purple grey and there's no one around for miles, that you feel loved,
and you know that someone kissed the moon before it got to you.

night flashes
hot night
sweaty clothes
insanity
insomnia
in the dark
menopause
the menopause blues
calcium, calcium, *calcium is big.*

My head bone connected to my neck bone
My neck bone connected to my shoulder bone
My shoulder bone connected to my back bone
My back bone connected to my hip bone
My hip bone connected to my thigh bone
My thigh bone connected to my knee bone
My knee bone connected to my ankle bone
My ankle bone connected to my foot bone
Now hear the words of the lord
Dem bones dem bones dem   dry bones
Dem bones dem bones dem   dry bones
Dem bones dem bones dem   dry bones
Now hear the words of the Lord.

(A light that looks both spooky and celestial shines down on Peggy
from directly above, which signals her move into the next musical
number, a wild, scary lip sync to a song in the style of Screamin' Jay
Hawkins's "I Put a Spell on You." Peggy does a macabre dance that
makes it seem like the song is controlling her body. When it ends,
her suit jacket is on backward, making it look as though her arms
are sticking out the back of her coat.)

Voices from OutWrite

While organizing the speeches in this book, we talked with a variety of people who attended OutWrite or worked as volunteers on the conference. Their voices inspired us as we compiled the speeches into this book and are a vital part of the history of the conference. This final chapter brings these other voices into the conversation about OutWrite, capturing the energy of this decade of queer writing conferences in multiple, cacophonous reflections.

*　*　*

I was a founder and editor of *OUT/LOOK: National Lesbian & Gay Quarterly* back then and helped organize the first OutWrite conference in San Francisco. As art director and editorial board member, as well as author of two articles, my identity straddled art and writing in an emergent, giddy kind of way. My experience of the publishing world was entirely through *OUT/LOOK*, and *OUT/LOOK* meshed perfectly with my history of grassroots organizing. The one memory that is indelible and enduring is the absolute ecstatic rush of the beginning convocation in the grand ballroom of the Cathedral Hill Hotel on a Saturday morning March 3, 1990.

We were nervous about attendance. Would people show up? Would they think a writers' conference was important? Our grandest hope was to fill the auditorium with maybe five hundred attendees, a modest aspiration in retrospect. On that day, feeling at once bleary eyed from lack of sleep and alert with a kind of hyperfocus, I sat about midway from the stage waiting as people poured in. It wasn't long before groupings were searching for seats, climbing over those of us near the aisles. Next, people filled the aisles, sat in front of the stage, stood in the back, trickled into every possible nook and cranny. Only later did I learn there were over 1,200 people in that auditorium—people I knew, ones I recognized, total strangers, and almost all some kind of queer.

My clearest memories include poet Judy Grahn saying in her keynote address, "If there's any gay or lesbian writer who hasn't done any (political) organizing, then he or she has gotten a free ride." I remember being moved by Allen Ginsberg's words, moved that he thought what we were doing was important. I still have faint glimmers of other speakers, most addressing the pain of discrimination within the publishing world and some speaking to the pain of racism and sexism within the queer world. Essex Hemphill, gay Black poet from Philadelphia, spoke vulnerably about the pain and frustration he experienced in a racist gay male community. It was illuminating; his words brought many of us to tears as he said "I deal with tolerance by night, intolerance in the morning." When Hemphill's voice choked and paused with emotion, a woman broke the silence with "We're with you!" Lesbians of color in my circles spoke out often about racism within the lesbian movement, but it was a rare moment for me to hear a Black gay man break such a profound silence.

Throughout the conference, there was disagreement: the kinds of arguments that came up mirrored our everyday struggles back then—how to be more inclusive of those who are underrepresented, how to prioritize aesthetic and political concerns, how much and what kind of sex do we talk and write about. At OutWrite, efforts at inclusiveness were most obviously successful with regard to gender. The overall number of women and men were amazingly matched, panelists and audience alike. Judy Grahn spoke of a writers' conference twenty years before where three hundred men and ten frustrated women met—all but one of them white. She put in historical context how women battled to be heard but later left to build a separatist lesbian base, one that allowed lesbians to hash out their own issues of identity, power, and culture. It is interesting and significant that no panel topics at OutWrite were categorized by gender, though lesbian concerns were articulated often by men and women alike. Instead, the weekend was sandwiched between an all-lesbian reading Friday night and an all-men's reading Monday night—both attended by mixed crowds.

My most palpable memory is of a great big complex tangle of emotion, one shared and felt within a crowd of 1,200, tears of joy and astonishment in which strangers felt familiar. It was kind of like having a public love affair; people cried and laughed and touched a lot, more like a march or a parade than a conference. This was a rare situation, in the context of that first decade of AIDS, when our tears were not just from pain but also from joy—and both were vividly present in that hall.

> E. G. Crichton is an interdisciplinary artist, writer,
> and teacher who lives in San Francisco.

*   *   *

The OutWrite conference was born in a community culture that no longer exists, the offspring of the first national lesbian and gay quarterly, *OUT/LOOK* magazine, that took as its mission to spark conversations across gender, genre, culture, and ideology. The writers, editors, and artists who shaped the journal and the conference gathered the widest range to date of writers and artists of the lesbian and gay movement during a brief time period where their many and significant conflicts and differences could cohabitate and sometimes cross-pollinate in the same small rooms.[1]

> Lisa Kahaleole Hall is the program director of
> Indigenous Studies at the University of Victoria.

*   *   *

---

1. Lisa Kahaleole Hall also wrote about the OutWrite conference experience in "Chock Full of Irony," *OUT/LOOK*, Fall 1991, no. 14, pp. 17, 24–27.

What I remember about OutWrite 90: Meetings upstairs in the tiny A Different Light bookstore office on Castro Street, thanks to Richard Labonté, who hosted us there. Walking over with Dorothy Allison from our apartments in the Mission District (she lived on Oakwood; I was on Nineteenth Street). Watching Kevin Killian drink a can of Tab at every meeting. (Kevin died in 2019.) Hanging out afterward, laughing with Bo Huston, who had something wickedly sarcastic to say about everyone. (Bo passed away in 1993.) Organizing with Dorothy the Impact Benefit Reading to fund travel. Chrystos, Jewelle Gomez, Marilyn Hacker, Cherríe Moraga, Eileen Myles, Minnie Bruce Pratt, Sarah Schulman, Kitty Tsui read to a packed house at the Victoria Theatre on Sixteenth Street. Meeting Sarah Pettit, New York–based editor of *OutWeek* magazine. Inviting Essex Hemphill from Philadelphia to speak at the plenary session, and realizing we could be friends forever. (Essex passed away in 1995.)

What I remember about OutWrite 91: Bringing on Rex Ray to design the conference logo and program because for a few decades he designed everything I was involved with. (Rex passed away in 2015.) Inviting Sapphire from New York City to read at the second annual Impact Benefit Reading—with Paula Gunn Allen, Cheryl Clarke, Judy Grahn and the Electric Poets, Holly Hughes, Ana Maria Simo—and watching everyone blown away by Sapphire's work. Bringing David Wojnarowicz to speak on the AIDS panel, and finding time to talk about our plans for his next book. (David passed away in 1992.) Meeting Gil Cuadros from Los Angeles, who spoke at that same panel as David, whose *City of God* I would publish at City Lights in 1994. (Gil passed away in 1996.) Falling in love with Sarah Pettit. (Sarah passed away in 2003.) Realizing that from one year of OutWrite in 1990 to the second OutWrite in 1991, there were too many people who had died to list them on an "In Memoriam" page in the program. Instead, we offered a page to the memory "of the many people our literary communities have lost."

Amy Scholder is a producer of *Disclosure*,
a Netflix Original documentary feature film.

*   *   *

I attended the first two incarnations of OutWrite, under the sponsorship of *OUT/LOOK* magazine, in San Francisco with an eye to write about them for the *Guide*, a (mostly) gay male magazine in which I reviewed books and movies since the mid-1980s. I had worked in, written for, the LGBTQ press since the early 1970s, when I moved to Boston and joined the Fag Rag Collective in 1971—publishing the paper as well as Good Gay Poets books and broadsides as well as titles for Fag Rag Books. In 1975, I started contributing—sometimes weekly—to *Gay Community News* (*GCN*) as well as other gay publications.

By 1990, I was fully entrenched in the queer literary world. Even with all of that, the first OutWrite was a revelation. All those writers, readers, editors, publishers in one place talking, cruising, laughing, and just hanging out was, well, emotionally staggering. Not just because it happened—but because, in some way, it was like my teenage dream of queer life come true: an endless potential of books and sex—the exotics of the intellect.

When Jeffrey Escoffier suggested that *OUT/LOOK* move OutWrite east for a year, he asked *GCN* to be the local sponsor. It stayed there, under *GCN* sponsorship for the next eight years. I was on the programming committee for the first year and then became the coordinator of the committee for the rest of the conference's life as it remained in Boston.

Any brief reflection feels inadequate. Those conferences were dizzying, all-consuming, exhilarating, exhausting, and a near-perfect manifestation of an ideal of community that I have ever experienced. The generous, ample collective spirit and energy that was already embedded in *GCN* was the most essential component in making the conference work. *GCN*'s progressive political vision—in a world in which LGBTQ media was increasingly more mainstream—ensured that OutWrite continued to be as expansive as its original vision and the community it represented.

Of course, we drew on the incredible—and growing each year—numbers of queer novelists, poets, memoirists, journalists who published. Some were marquee names, others newly published; some from mainstream presses, others from small presses. After one year, we began expanding—filmmakers, playwrights, rural poetry collectives, photographers, visual artists, songwriters, cartoonists. After two years, we started a series of panels for young queer people that they programmed and ran. The permutations of creativity were endless and the possibilities joyfully explosive. The aim was the breakdown of boundaries between panelists and their listeners, between creators and their audience.

All of this occurred not in the shadow of AIDS but in the eye of the epidemic. I remember the calling out of names at each opening plenary when we invited audience members to shout of names of the dead to be remembered. But this was the easy—celebratory—part of what AIDS meant. More difficult were the phone calls with writers who said they were too sick to come to the conference in a few months or that they were feeling OK now but feared they'd be too sick by March to attend. Harder still were the last-minute, often the day before, phone calls from friends or lovers of writers who said they were too sick or had just died. Even more painful were the notes from friends of random registrants—whose names were only known to us on checks or registration forms—who said they had died and would not be there. This starkly and frighteningly brought home the reality that what made OutWrite great, what made it vital especially in those dark times, was not the writers who spoke but the enormous community that made their work possible, that gave it life by accepting it into their lives, minds, and hearts.

> Michael Bronski is professor of the practice in
> media and activism at Harvard University.

*   *   *

We are family. No words have rung truer than when we gathered at an OutWrite conference. Together we laughed, cried, and danced.

We were activists who were in love with the written word. As a matter of fact, when Judy Grahn was delivering her keynote address, she said, "If you are a gay and lesbian writer and you are not an activist, you're getting a free ride!" Thunderous applause followed.

It was 1992 in Boston when I first presented the OUTSPOKEN Literary Series. I created the series so I could bring forth voices that needed to be heard. I wanted to help new and established writers reach a broader audience. OutWrite was the perfect place to do just that. The series went on to host hundreds of writers nationwide at many different venues.

OutWrite will always be a bittersweet memory for me. As I remember those who were there, some are still here with us and many are not. We still call their names.

Michele Karlsberg runs a publicity and marketing agency.

* * *

OUT/LOOK is committed to providing a bridge between worlds which have often been quite separate. We need a national "town meeting" in which we can hear a wide range of voices engaged in serious (but not always solemn) dialogue about the issues that touch our lives as lesbians, gay men, and bisexual people. We hope *OUT/LOOK* will be that forum.[2]

When *OUT/LOOK*'s statement of purpose was published, my phone rang off the hook. Did you see bisexuals are included? Word spread fast. Such was the state of bisexual visibility in 1988: every mention was celebrated.

The rise of a national bisexual movement in the late 1980s and early 1990s challenged the national lesbian and gay leadership and the movement's status quo. The strategy was based in the exclusive either/or assumptions of heterosexism. The growing

---

2. "Welcome," *OUT/LOOK National Gay & Lesbian Quarterly* 1, no. 1 (Spring 1988): 4.

numbers of out and vocal activists speaking to the complexity and truth of bisexual lives exposed the movement's dependence on the faulty monosexual framework that denied the middle ground represented by bisexuals and by transgender activists who were also mobilizing. Recognition of bisexual and transgender people within the lesbian and gay movement at that time was at best token talk but no walk.

Fast-forward a bit.

In 1991, Loraine Hutchins and I coedited the groundbreaking feminist anthology *Bi Any Other Name*. Our book was one of five nominated for a Lambda Literary Award in the lesbian anthology category. There was no bisexual category until 2006. I was working at National Gay Rights Advocates in the Castro at the time— serving on the Gay and Lesbian Advisory Committee to the San Francisco Human Rights Commission—and was honored to be invited to submit a letter of interest to join the *OUT/LOOK* editorial board.

OutWrite 91 was an awe-inspiring experience. You could feel history in the making. Bisexuals were there in great numbers; many traveled across the country to participate as bisexuals on numerous panels. Many had secured publishers and were working on soon-to-be-published books. I'd organized a well-attended and lively workshop, "Bisexual Visibility in Print: Coming of Age in the Gay 90s." The description read, "The invisibility of the queer-identified bisexual experience within the lesbian and gay media is legendary within the bisexual movement. Not only is there a heterosexual assumption to contend with, but within the monosexual framework there is also the homosexual assumption that must be challenged."

With that description, how could I have been surprised by the total lack of a bisexual mention in all three conference articles published in *OUT/LOOK*? I did find an odd reference to bisexual participation in my colleague Karl Bruce Knapper's article "Albee Stirs up OUT/Write" that appeared in the *Bay Area Reporter*; he wrote, "Organizers strived to achieve cultural and racial diversity of authors and topics, offering panels on Chicano/a, Native American, Mexican, Jewish, and Latin American writing, as well as that of sexual minorities and bisexuals."[3] Hey, as curious as this placement was, it was something.

Playwright Edward Albee presented a provocative closing keynote that elicited boos from the audience. I scribbled many notes as I did with all those who spoke. I was left with one Albee quote that was especially meaningful to me: "The responsibility [of the writer] is to try to persuade the people who pay attention to him (her) to become different people, to change, to hold a mirror up to all society and say look, this is who you are, this is how you are behaving. Why don't you stop it."

A year after I submitted my letter of interest to join the *OUT/LOOK* editorial board, I was told I was too single focused.

Stop it.

After a decade focused on her family, Lani Ka'ahumanu is once again working on her activist memoir *My Grassroots Are Showing*. Her goal is to have it published before she turns eighty in 2023.

* * *

The energy at the first OutWrite conferences in San Francisco in the 1990s was overwhelming—in a good way, an excellent way. I remember thinking, "So many writers, so many queers, and so many heroes." I've never forgotten Judy Grahn's words in her keynote speech. She said, and this may be a paraphrase after all this time, "You can't be a writer without being an activist."

One year I gave a ride to writer Robert Friedman and another fellow from the radical faerie men's land just north of where I lived in Oregon. And that was a culture clash for me. At the conference, there were so many men. Lesbians were coming out of an era where excluding men was the whole point. John Rechy, groundbreaking

---

3. Karl Bruce Knapper, "Albee Stirs Up OUT/Write," *Bay Area Reporter*, March 7, 1991, 30, 48.

author of the erotic novel *City of Night*, spoke. Allen Ginsberg spoke. Edward Albee was booed when he objected to the very concept of gay literature.

This was possibly the most diverse gathering in which I'd ever participated—Native Americans and European Americans, disabled and Jewish writers, African American and Chicano/Chicana writers, writers with HIV, Japanese American writers, and old, gay, and very young writers.

It was empowering, I wrote at the time—that's what OutWrite was about, empowering our authors, poets, playwrights, publishers, editors. I wrote that I could not imagine the wattage of empowerment created by 1,200, 1,800 queer writers. Then I wrote, yes, I can, because this is what I want to do by writing, pass on the power I got from Radclyffe Hall, Jane Rule, Isabel Miller, Judy Grahn, which snowballed as I wrote, gathered its own momentum personally and collectively until those days of OutWrite.

> Lee Lynch is the author of numerous novels,
> most recently *Accidental Desperados* (2021).

*   *   *

I attended OutWrite 90: the first national lesbian and gay writers conference in San Francisco in March 1990. I had had one of my first nationally published pieces in *OUT/LOOK* 2, a year or so earlier. It was the start of my writing about gay men's spiritualities as a way of escaping and transcending traditional—and antihomosexual—religion, and I felt part of the *OUT/LOOK* family. The conference was obviously the next step. I had a science fiction novel coming out later that year I was hoping to promote. I was a gay bookseller in those days; my partner Kip Dollar and I were running Liberty Books, the lesbian and gay community bookstore in Austin, Texas. We'd attended a couple of American Bookseller Association (ABA) conventions and participated in meetings with other booksellers and publishers working to expand

gay genre publishing. Our little corner of the huge literary industry was thriving at the time.

Perhaps I remember my impression that, as writers, most of us
didn't understand the business of what we were involved in. Having been running a gay/lesbian bookstore in a college town for a
couple of years, I'd seen how important books are to people's
understanding of themselves and their sexualities. The bookstores
were real gay community centers where knowledge and wisdom,
news and local gossip could be found. And I'd also seen how
driven the industry is by the rules of commerce. We writers may
have been inspired by our muse and by our desire to save the world.
The people who were publishing our books were driven by that
proverbial "bottom line." The book business is about discount
rates, numbers of units, freight costs, return rules.

I'd met John Preston at an ABA in 1987, and we'd started a cor-
respondence. I palled around with him during OutWrite and got to
feel part of the in-group—John Preston, after all, a founder of the
Advocate and prolific writer. AIDS was, of course, a specter that
hung over the conference. And Preston was dealing with that in his
own life. We weren't just talking about our writing process. We
were talking about saving our culture and saving our lives.

As a gay psychotherapist, a gay writer, and now a gay bookseller,
I was very committed to that culture that recognized how
different—dare I say "special"—we were as gay men and lesbians
discovering for ourselves and revealing to the world a different
kind of experience of sexuality and embodiment.

Toby Johnson is the author of *Gay Spirituality:*
Gay Identity and the Transformation of Human Consciousness.

*   *   *

I cannot remember how it came to pass that I had the privilege of coordinating OutWrite with the extraordinary Michael
Bronski, who seemed to know every queer writer, publisher, and
editor in the United States—wait, the universe! True, I knew a

few more lesbians in that world than he did, but the breadth and width of Michael's knowledge, wisdom, and vision were incredible, and I learned so much from him. What I mostly remember about coordinating that conference was what came before—phone calls with writers whose work I admired but had not yet met, reconnecting with writers and friends I had not spoken to in many years, organizing panels and conversations with all of these folks and then some. OutWrite also afforded me the opportunity to travel back to Massachusetts from Minneapolis and stay with my girlfriend at the time and our two wonderful friends, the poet Janet Aalfs and her partner (not yet wife; we didn't have those yet), Janis Totty, and to show off my organizing skills to my parents, who drove in from Worcester to take us all out to dinner.

I attended several OutWrites before I helped make this one happen, and so they blur sometimes in my head—I remember I missed Dorothy Allison's 1992 keynote because I was in Chinatown having dinner that night with a very distressed old friend, but I did hear Allan Gurganus read from *The Oldest Living Confederate Widow Tells All* that same year. I remember reading there myself in an afternoon with Kate Bornstein among others, but what year was that? In my coordinating year, I remember meeting radical publisher and producer Amy Scholder for the first time, hanging out with my Minneapolis pal Barrie Jean Borich, watching the in and out action at the men's room door the night of the big final party. But the most liberating moment for me of any of those OutWrites was watching playwright and performer Luis Alfaro roller-skate his way around the OutWrite stage. He was wearing a black slip, and he was screaming beautifully. My creative life has not ever been the same.

Judith Katz is the author of *The Escape Artist* and *Running Fiercely toward a High Thin Sound*.

* * *

To recall OutWrite is necessarily to recall writers who later died of AIDS. David Feinberg and Paul Monette, Marlon Riggs and Essex Hemphill come immediately to mind, as well as several aspiring San Francisco writers who did not live long enough to realize their dreams. "I admire you for sticking with it," Greg Bex told me at that first conference; six months later, he was dead. Six months after that, I was sitting in Eureka Theater with two hundred other people watching the world premiere of *Angels in America*, and it says something important about that moment in literary history that at least half of those in the audience expected to be dead within a few years, and most probably were.

AIDS was not the only topic of those first OutWrite conferences, of course, but its demands gave every word and gesture a surreal intensity. At that particular moment in San Francisco, everything was life-or-death, with writers and activists aware and proud that we were setting the pace for the nation and the world. In 1990, San Francisco was still the place to be, still the only place in the world LGBT persons could claim as home.

No full accounting can be made of the impact of those absences—the awards not received, the books not published, the ideas not given birth, the revolution not achieved. And yet thirty years later, you, my reader, are the greatest reward for those years of activism and agony and death. LGBT literature would never have achieved its place in the mainstream—and memoir would never have moved from the margins to the mainstream—except for the dead whose flesh and bones, passion and words, acknowledged or (more often) not, are the foundation on which all contemporary LGBT writers rest our feet and our words. OutWrite was a catalyst, one of the principal places to meet and greet, to share ideas and stories, to organize, and above all to teach and learn the power and importance of literature to bear witness.

Fenton Johnson is the author of *At the Center of All Beauty: Solitude and the Creative Life.*

* * *

I attended two OutWrite gatherings, in 1992 and 1993. I know
many will speak of the excitement of being with so many other
queer writers, some already trailing clouds of literary glory, but
it is the memory of two men that most captures what my time in
attendance meant. Both writers, both dying of AIDS: John Preston and Melvin Dixon. John and I had worked over the year trying
to finish up our manuscript for *Sister and Brother*, and this was
a rare chance to be in each other's presence, for me to be on his
home turf of Boston streets. He was surrounded by admirers, but
we found time to sit on a Common's bench and just hold each
other. "Two pornographers," he laughed into my ear. All those
hotel rooms filled with dazzling writers, but I remember most this
and my coming upon Melvin Dixon, the poet, the novelist, sitting
alone in a grand empty room, looking, it seemed to me, through
walls. Writers can be isolated beings even at grand gatherings.
OutWrite gave us a chance to say hello and goodbye. In his wonderful book *Change of Territory* (1983), in the poem "Fingering the
Jagged Grains," Melvin Dixon wrote, "What did I do? You lived,
you lived! / And the jagged grains so black and blue / open like lips
about to sing."[4]

Joan Nestle is the author of *A Restricted
Country* and *A Fragile Union*.

* * *

When I first went to OutWrite, the only writers' community I had
experienced was the small group in my MFA program and I wasn't
out, so hardly anyone knew who I really was. By the time I got to
OutWrite, I wasn't just out; I was out in my writing, which broke
new ground for weaving together serious Jewish and gay themes,

---

4. Melvin Dixon, "Fingering the Jagged Grains," in *Change of Territory*
(Lexington: University of Kentucky Press, 1983), 52.

along with exploring the legacy of the Holocaust on the second generation. Jewishness wasn't peripheral in my fiction, a doily on a side table. It was central.

I had been publishing those stories in the 1980s and had the good fortune to work with Michael Denneny at St. Martin's Press on my Lambda Literary Award–winning first collection *Dancing on Tisha B'Av*, which was published in 1990. I'd met gay writers and editors I admired, like Edmund White, George Stambolian, and Christopher Bram. But none of that prepared me for OutWrite.

It was called a conference, but OutWrite was much more than that. It was a festival, a celebration, a street fair, an extravaganza, and I was thrilled to be there, to be with my people. Everywhere I turned, I ran into writers whose books I had either read or wanted to read: Joe Keenan, Nisa Donnelly, Jewelle Gomez, Melvin Dixon, Dorothy Allison, Richard McCann, Michael Nava, and many more.

Looking back, my experiences at OutWrite remind me of the first time I attended a queer Jewish conference. At Friday night's Welcoming Shabbat services in Toronto, when I looked around, I experienced wholeness. As services began, the man standing in front of me dramatically flung one side of his large tallis over his shoulder as if it were a fur stole. I laughed and did the same. It felt great. And so did listening to the hermeneutical analysis by the woman rabbi of the Torah passage where the Hebrews had no more water after Miriam died.

OutWrite was like that: flashes of comedy and moments of insight following each other in a cascade. It was an inspiring way to start the 1990s when I had no idea I would eventually end up publishing twenty-seven books in a dozen different genres, have my work translated into fifteen languages, become a regular book reviewer and even get my own radio show, be sent on international book tours, see my work widely anthologized, find my fiction analyzed by academics in print and at conferences, sell my literary papers to a major university, and have students read my fiction and essays in classrooms. Maybe that last thing is what I'll have put on my tombstone down the road: He Became Homework.

Lev Raphael is the author of twenty-seven
books, from memoir to mystery.

* * *

OutWrite, for me, was a crossroads between two worlds—a coming-of-age experience and perhaps a loss of innocence. I attended the San Francisco conference while in my first, and greatly beloved, editorial position at the "old" Dutton—still an independent company when I joined but in the process of being absorbed by a larger corporate entity, Penguin (now Penguin Random House). It was a job in which I had been able to support and bring forward authors like Dorothy Allison, Jan Carr, Andrea Dworkin, Sarah Schulman—later, Jenifer Levin, Jacqueline Woodson, and others—and begin to make good on my personal commitment to diversify the mainstream publishing field to include lesbian and feminist voices and writers of color. I remember feeling freed up to speak truthfully about the experience (including its struggles) and was also aware of crosscurrents in the community—the tensions between smaller presses and the area of the culture I represented—that some called selling out. Then and later, in Boston, I argued that mainstream publishers were a viable avenue for supporting such a diversity of voices. OutWrite was part of that—an expression of our fierce, vivid, colorful defiance and hope as a community, a seedbed of creative ideas, an arena for conflict and the airing of truths (including trauma and grief), and a source of support and encouragement. The publishing industry was responding, showing signs of opening up and cultivating audiences in new ways—although not, as it turned out, quickly enough. We did not yet understand the larger changes soon to engulf us—those brought on by Amazon (which was then still a rumor), a defensive environment of further mergers in the mainstream trade press, and a posture in publishing that narrowed toward sales performance and platform as the measure of viability and inclusion. I remember having to exit my last OutWrite conference for a work situation unfolding in New York, missing out on the parties after the panels. I remember the heart-tearing sadness of leaving the warmth of that community to make sure I kept my job—reassuring myself that it was not, in fact, a bellwether of changes yet to come. But OutWrite was an expression of the life force and an enduring one. Seeds planted then incubated for a generation, through interim forms and efforts to grow in challenging conditions. We needed it and now need its memory.

> Carole DeSanti was executive editor at Viking/Penguin,
> a division of Penguin Random House, until 2018;
> she is now the Elizabeth Drew Professor of English
> Language and Literature at Smith College.

* * *

I remember OutWrite as being something that I did not want to miss, and anytime that I did miss it, I was very sad. It was one of the few times that I was able to be around creatives from the LGBT community, and we could be as quirky and as silly or as deeply intellectual as we wanted to be without having to worry about what somebody else was going to say.

In the early days of it, I was pretty critical because there weren't that many people of color who were there. That did change over time, and there were a few times when, as the numbers got bigger and better, we came together as communities of color to share some of what we were doing and to have deeper discussions, but it was still very frustrating in the early days of it because even some folks who I thought ought to be there were not there.

I remember talking in the early days about all of these assumptions; it really wasn't just Edward Albee, because something similar happened at Creating Change, the conference of the National Gay and Lesbian Task Force. There is the self-referencing in the LGBT community, in terms of what white men, particularly white middle-class men, have done. There has been a big distortion of how we, the movement, got started. It was all the work of working-class folks of all colors that created a lot of the different events that allowed it to become acceptable for these people who had money to come together and be more out at events like OutWrite.

Publishing is not as diverse as it could be in terms of LGBTQ people of color. There is still a lot of pigeonholing. For instance, in terms of writings by Jewish lesbians or gay men are almost all white. There's not been enough support for the publishing houses that have been willing to put out the very academic as well as the funny and silly work that we do. If there's any downside of there being more departments that actually study gender and LGBTQ history, it is that it has become too academic and not people oriented.

There were a lot of people who I think deserve more credit than they get—all of my brothers who died of AIDS, including Essex Hemphill and Melvin Dixon, and all of my sisters who died of cancer. I think of Paula Gunn Allen. She was among the first; she was involved in the movement and had her own audience, and it was expanded by her involvement. Carla Trujillo is somebody who doesn't get as much attention as she should. Gloria Anzaldúa and her work, her mixing of the personal with the political, still have a very big philosophical impact. Her book *Borderlands / La Frontera* brought a new voice to American-based philosophy. That in and of itself is something that may not have happened without OutWrite.

> Sabrina Sojourner is a shaliakh tzibur and community
> chaplain in the Washington, DC, area.

* * *

Attending OutWrite and later co-programming OutWrite was an exhilarating, important experience for me, both as a gay man and as a gay writer. While I was on the one hand giddily verklempt to be meeting so many authors whose works I had read and loved, rather than feeling starstruck or out of place, the conference felt like coming home, of being welcomed into this vast, amorphous queer literary community. Because it was a national conference, it was something larger than all of us individually but to which we all belonged—whether famous or aspiring, young or old.

So it was an honor to be asked to co-program OutWrite, together with Cecilia Tan—even if it was also a challenge, since we had only three months to put together programming for over two hundred participants on sixty-five plus events in different thematic tracks. Cecilia and I knew we wanted to mix things up as much as possible. We nixed outright any panel that didn't integrally have at least one person of color on it and likewise any single-gendered panels. We also did away with the genre segregation that often occurs at these kinds of events, by having the queer mystery panel or the queer sci-fi panel. Instead, we scattered those queer genre writers across the programming, so you might have a queer mystery writer talking about "Writing the Second Novel" alongside litfic authors (and readers) who would normally have "ignored" the genre programming. We wanted to get people out of their comfort zones and talking to one another, and we think it resulted in interesting literary cross-pollination (and hopefully chipped away at a lot of snobbery on both sides) that enriched all parties.

Professionally, the conference resulted in many wonderful connections and collaborations and friendships—including some quite directly referencing OutWrite, including begging Tony Kushner for his lasagna recipe for my AIDS-benefit cookbook *Food for Life* (Cleis) after hearing his OutWrite keynote address ("On Pretentiousness"), in which he talks about lasagna as his paradigm for writing a play.

Personally, the conference involved a lot of self-exploration as well, resulting in multiple intense relationships (sexual, intellectual) over the years. In particular, I still recall the powerful flirtation, as a young femme gay cis-man, with a butch dyke writer (who also wrote gay porn under a male byline). I found it confusing how

attracted I was to her butch energy and hooked up with a nice
kinky Jewish boy, a young thirtysomething daddy, ten years older
than myself. We mirrored each other: ethnicity, upbringing, neu-
roses. He might have been me a decade from now. She, too, found
a partner for the evening, a soft-looking woman with close-cropped
hair, about her age but Caucasian. Difference at play for her; nar-
cissism for me. We chatted, the four of us—two boys on one
couch, two girls on the other. She asked me questions: intimate,
male questions. What does an erection feel like? Can you ejaculate
without orgasm? Can you orgasm without ejaculation? We were
flirting, she and I, and we both knew it. Certainly, I was flirting,
too, with the boy I was with—flirting after the fact, since we'd
each already decided to spend the night together and had been on
our way to his room when she distracted me. We got a lot of nosy
questions out of the way, he and I, before we went up to his room
and had sex. We told each other what we liked, what we wanted,
even though none of this was overtly for each other. It was all
directed at her, answers to her questions. In some ways, I was reaf-
firming my identity as a gay boy to her—and to myself. I was prov-
ing my masculinity, in the locker room bravado of sexual conquest.
She merely smiled and waited.

Lawrence Schimel is a poet and
translator based in Madrid, Spain.

*   *   *

Attending OutWrite conferences in Boston as a gay man in my
twenties from Flint, Michigan, made me feel less isolated, less
endangered. OutWrite gave me a sense of belonging in the early
1990s that I rarely felt in my blue-collar hometown, where queer
folk had to hide themselves, where bookish gay boys didn't fit in,
where everyone at the bar smoked and making out with a guy
tasted like tonguing an ashtray.

The personal impact was immediate from the moment I heard
Dorothy Allison give the Friday night plenary for OutWrite 92,

urging painful truth telling—as if she was talking directly to me. The next day, I witnessed Jim Kepner, Joan Nestle, and Brenda Marston on a panel on Archives, tapping my penchant for documenting. At another session on humor and AIDS, I remember Larry Kramer raging from the audience that writing with humor "makes things all right and AIDS isn't all right."

All three times I attended OutWrite, I stayed at the AYH Hostel, then out by Fenway. I remember waking up the Sunday morning of OutWrite 92 to find famed porn star and publisher Scott O'Hara mischievously grinning down at me. He had slept in the bunk above mine. Scott and I went for dinner that evening at Durgin-Park, the ancient Yankee eatery near the Faneuil Hall Marketplace. Even in such a middlebrow tourist trap, someone recognized him, testament to queer erotic reach too often overlooked.

I joked afterward that OutWrite exposed me to people and ideas and appendages I would otherwise never have encountered. More so, OutWrite provided some vital inspiration in my young adulthood that spurred me on into life as a writer and archivist and historian. OutWrite showed me that even as a queer kid from Flint, I could dare to aspire. I could dare to reach.

Tim Retzloff is a historian based in East Lansing, Michigan.

*   *   *

I attended the first OutWrite conference in San Francisco in 1990 and the later one in Boston. I still have vivid memories of seeing famous writers for the first time, some of them from a distance when they were at the podium, some of them up close at a party in someone's apartment in San Francisco. Sarah Schulman gave a fierce and moving response to the question, Why should lesbians be activists in the AIDS movement when the epidemic affected mostly gay men? Allen Ginsberg was disheveled, but his aura was unmistakable; John Rechy was perfectly turned out and unapproachable in his white Lacoste shirt; the demure Ann Bannon was

strikingly neat. If I don't have stories to relate about my encounters with those writers, and the many others who were there, it's
because my interactions with them were limited to bedazzled fan
worship from afar.

I am still more interested in queer literature than in any other
kind of literature. I teach my favorite books, but some of them are
out of print. There is a canon of queer lit, but it is increasingly
unknown; my students have never heard of the writers I admire.
And yet their best books and poems speak to our situation today:
the queer canon may belong to its time, but it is not dated. It
deserves a large audience, and perhaps more to the point, queer
folks need the great literature they already possess.

David Halperin is the author of *How to Be Gay*.

* * *

to imagine or look not just with the right and the left eyes but also
beyond with Other visions, we also need to look into the past.
across *Olmeca* space-time, i relax my mind to remember those far-
away times and places that allowed for the freedom of rainbow
encuentros and treatises and (wo)myn-i-festos—gatherings where
we celebrate creativity in the face of contemporary too-white
houses being burned and replenished with our light and love at
the ends of, yes, our own multiplicity of rainbows.

the first days of March 1991, i was in the trenches of postproduc-
tion editing rooms splicing *The Olmeca Rap* (1991, 5mins). it would
premiere at the San Francisco Kabuki! remember the feeling of
being rushed in and out of OutWrite 91, i acknowledged the privilege of sharing with so many fabulous and vital gente from different walks of the earth. to be a (w)Riter means and feels like so
much—an honor, a therapy, a duty, a curse, a love of mine, a first
language, *flor y canto*, poesia. i come from several generations of
Latina/o/x/Xx writers. and then, hello, to be able to add the world y
cultura of "queer" to the mix—"it feels just right," said the bear.
but don't believe she goes through the world without a care.

as we come around the micro and macro bends of the gigantic inner galactic 2020, i give thanx for being able to reflect on an-Other huge super radical time and space, the coming together of many queer folk, *artista activistas*, and literary two-spirited convening *en san pancho, califas*, in that fresh new decade of the previous century and millennium. lots of high energy in the skies then and now, as well as in this anthology, and during that wonderful OutWrite 91 *encuentro* at the Windham Hotel on Van Ness, behind the San Francisco City Hall. at that time, i had recently returned from nearly a year *en europa* in search of our pre-colombian *arte*-facts that had been "in safekeeping" with—well, you know the history. i shared this story of my travels as a dark-skinned low-income short and fluffy bear among the land of the giants. getting to the conference i recall riding some fancy escalators to get to the entrance. those butterflies since youth began to revisit my stomach. upon entering the grand hotel, i hurried to my seat at the panel "Queer Chicana and Chicano Writers."

Carla Trujillo was our moderator. we make an educational video decades later when she was the director for diversity and equity at UC Berkeley and I was a visiting lecturer in Ethnic Studies at Cal. Moraga, my cuzin was there, as were Ronnie Burk and dear Rodrigo Reyes. i shared with the audience about my travels, obsession with the Olmecs, and that i recently completed a video, *The Olmeca Rap: Mujeria Part I* (1990). i told the folk that i was fascinated by this *indigena cultura* that preceded the Maya who built a multitude of *piramides*. i had animated that little rap video and because these ancient monolithic stone heads had no bodies, nor genitalia. being the *mujerista lesbiana* that i am, i believed there was at least a fifty-fifty chance that these ten ton stone heads were probably female. females are the majority population of the planet—so there was really a 51 percent chance that these heads could've been female! i remember the entire room broke out into a loud laughter. this made me feel comfortable, accepted, and a part of this important *encuentro*.

during OutWrite 91, *Olmeca Rap* was just completed. all these years later, we just recently completed *ME and Mr. MAURI: Turning Poison into Medicine* (2020), a documentary about six close friends of my family who died of SIDA/AIDS. Rodrigo Reyes, who i had the honor of sitting with on our "Queer Chicana and Chicano Writers" panel, is one of these friends portrayed. and i am forever indebted to their memory, life, and love. as i (w)Rite these words, i see a future, as a cancer, pandemic, post-dystopic-not-my-president situation changes. thanxxxx to the goddesses for LARGE favors. the future is NOW, *c/s y qué! Sí se puede.*

> Dr. Osa T. Hidalgo de la Riva is a filmmaker,
> public scholar, and writer.

* * *

I attended an OutWrite conference in Boston. I remember it clearly because I met lesbian and gay writers who would become some of my closest friends. I felt that I belonged, even though I was asked to turn in my gay card, since I might have been the only gay man who didn't fuck anyone that weekend.

I had just signed my first novel with a publisher. A friend jokingly suggested that I would now be a celebrity at OutWrite. I told him that I would always be a celebutante, part celebrity and part debutant. He made me a small pin that said "celebutante" that I proudly wore on my jacket at the conference. I was introduced to a small gathering of writers. A writer asked about the pin. I began to explain, but she interrupted. She knew what it meant. She wanted to know why I added an *e* at the end, since debutant did not have one. I knew then that I was among my people: bitches who would correct your grammar.

> RABIH ALAMEDDINE is the author of
> *The Wrong End of the Telescope.*

Acknowledgments

Julie writes,

Melika M. Fitzhugh, introduced to me by the wonderful Jenny Factor in Boston, made multiple treks to the Northeastern University Archive to photograph material for this book; thank you, Melika, for your extraordinary work and patience in the earliest days of this project. Nora Della Fera, a Sinister Wisdom intern, helped with transcriptions. Kelly Wooten, one of my go-to archivists, was helpful early in the genesis of the research and a vital thought partner. Molly Brown, Reference and Outreach Archivist at Northeastern University, assisted us on repeated occasions; her work made this book possible, especially in the time of COVID-19. Tim Retzloff, mad collaborator and dear friend for now over thirty years (eep!), was present in the early genesis of the idea and the early research. Conversations with Tim made this project richer and more meaningful, and his detailed feedback on the introduction helped us think more carefully about a number of important ideas. Michael Bronski was exceedingly generous on every front in thinking about this project and inspiring us to make it the best it could be. David Groff assisted with contacts for permissions and congenially supported the project in every way he could. Lynda Koolish and Jonathan Silin were generous, as always, granting permissions to use their photographs; I am grateful to both of them for their support of my work over many years. Thank you to Kim Guinta for saying yes and to the excellent editors, publishers, marketers, and publicists at Rutgers University Press—consummate professionals all and vital collaborators. Thank you to my writing companions—canines Tiberius, Samantha, and Sadie and feline Vita—and always heartfelt thanks and appreciation to my most beloved Kim.

One of my greatest regrets is that I did not attend OutWrite during the 1990s. I was aware of the conference and its vital work but never organized myself to attend. I am grateful to all of the organizers for making that space in the world. This project was a gleam in my eye when I was doing dissertation research, and I am enormously grateful to Elena for saying yes.

Elena writes,

Like the conferences themselves, this project could not have come together without the efforts and support of so many people, organizations, archives, and inspirations. I would like to give tremendous thanks and recognition to E. G. Crichton for inviting me to participate in the project OUT/LOOK and the Birth of the Queer, which first led me to OutWrite; to the GLBT Historical Society / GLBT History Museum in San Francisco, which has provided, time and again, inspiration and dedication to queer history; to the wonderful editors and marketing team and everyone at Rutgers University Press for all of their hard work on this project; to every single contributor to this collection; to all of my friends and family but especially my sweet girlfriend, Sarah Kershaw, my perma-collaborator Leila Weefur, and my (former) work wife and forever friend Emily A. Kuhlmann; to the sweetest and most curious creature I have ever had the pleasure of being violently awoken by at 4 a.m., my cat, Walnut; and of course, to my comrade and coeditor who has provided so much for this project, not least of which friendship and enthusiasm, Julie R. Enszer.

Notes on Contributors

Luis Alfaro is a multidisciplined artist, director, curator, producer, educator, and community organizer. A Chicano born and raised in the Pico-Union district of downtown Los Angeles, Alfaro is the recipient of a John D. and Catherine T. MacArthur Foundation fellowship, popularly known as a "genius grant." Alfaro spent over two decades in the Los Angeles poetry community and toured North and Latin America as a performance artist for over ten years. He is currently a member of the artist collective at Center Theatre Group. His solo performance work has been seen throughout the United States, England, and Mexico. He has an Emmy-nominated short film, *Chicanismo*, and an award-winning recording, *down town*, on SST / New Alliance Records. Currently, Alfaro is an associate professor of dramatic writing at the USC School of Dramatic Arts.

Dorothy Allison is the author of the novels *Bastard Out of Carolina* and *Cavedweller*, the short story collection *Trash*, essay collections *Skin* and *Two or Three Things I Know for Sure*, and the poetry collection *The Women Who Hate Me*. She is an award-winning editor for *Quest*, *Conditions*, and *OUT/LOOK*—early feminist and lesbian and gay journals. Her work has won many awards. For more information, visit DorothyAllison.com.

NANCY K. BEREANO is the former editor and publisher of the groundbreaking, award-winning lesbian and feminist press Firebrand Books. During its fifteen-year existence (1985–2000), Firebrand published many significant authors, including Dorothy Allison, Alison Bechdel, Cheryl Clarke, Leslie Feinberg, Jewelle Gomez, Judith Katz, Audre Lorde, and Minnie Bruce Pratt.

PAT CALIFIA changed his name to PATRICK CALIFIA when he decided to transition to a male gender identity. He is an author, pornographer, and cultural critic. Among his most noted books are *Coming to Power*, *Macho Sluts*, *Melting Point*, *No Mercy*, and *Speaking Sex to Power*. His writing and activism have revolutionized queer sex.

CHERYL CLARKE is still a Black lesbian feminist poet. She is author of the collections *Narratives: Poems in the Tradition of Black Women* (1982), *Living as a Lesbian* (1986), *Humid Pitch* (1989), *Experimental Love* (1993), and *By My Precise Haircut* (2016). Clarke's iconic essays are included in *This Bridge Called My Back: Writings by Radical Women of Color* (Anzaldúa and Moraga, eds., 1981, 1983, 2000, 2015) and *Home Girls: A Black Feminist Anthology* (Smith, ed., 1984, 2000). Clarke retired from Rutgers University in 2013 after forty-one years of service. With Barbara J. Balliet, her partner, she co-owns Blenheim Hill Books in Hobart, New York, the Book Village of the Catskills, and co-organizes the annual Hobart Festival of Women Writers.

CHRYSTOS is a Menominee poet and activist. She is the author of several collections of poetry, including *Red Rollercoaster* (2003), *Fire Power* (1995), *In Her I Am* (1993), *Dream On* (1991), and *Not Vanishing* (1988). With Tristan Taormino, she coedited the anthology *Best Lesbian Erotica 1999*. Her work has been featured in the anthologies *This Bridge Called My Back: Writings by Radical Women of Color* (1981), *Living the Spirit: A Gay American Indian Anthology*

(1988), and *When the Light of the World Was Subdued, Our Songs Came Through*, edited by Joy Harjo (2020).

SAMUEL R. DELANY is the author of over a dozen science fiction and fantasy tales; numerous volumes of essays and criticism, including *Times Square Red, Times Square Blue*; a seminal nonfiction book of twin essays exploring the rapid gentrification of New York City's Times Square district and the cultural shifts within the city's queer, sexual, and minority communities; and the autobiography *The Motion of Light in Water*. Delaney's work is lauded with prizes and recognitions, including the Nebula Award for Best Novel for *The Einstein Intersection* in 1968 and a Hugo Award for his autobiography. He lives in Philadelphia with his partner, Dennis Rickett.

MELVIN DIXON (1950–1992) authored two poetry collections, *Change of Territory* (1983) and the posthumous *Love's Instruments* (1995). Dixon was also the author of the novels *Vanishing Rooms* (1991) and *Trouble the Water* (Fiction Collective 2, 1989) and the translated work *The Collected Poems of Leopold Senghor* (1990). He received a BA from Wesleyan University in 1971 and a PhD from Brown University in 1975. Dixon taught English literature at Wesleyan University from 1976 to 1980, when he joined the English faculty at Queens College. He received a fellowship from the National Endowment for the Arts in 1984. Dixon died of complications from AIDS in Stamford, Connecticut, on October 26, 1992.

JULIE R. ENSZER, PhD, is a scholar and a poet. Her book manuscript *A Fine Bind* is a history of lesbian-feminist presses from 1969 until 2009. Her scholarly work has appeared or is forthcoming in *Southern Cultures, Journal of Lesbian Studies, American Periodicals, WSQ*, and *Frontiers*. She is the author of four poetry collections, *Avowed* (2016), *Lilith's Demons* (2015), *Sisterhood* (2013), and *Handmade Love* (2010). She is editor of *The Complete Works of Pat Parker*

(2016), which won the 2017 Lambda Literary Award for Lesbian Poetry; *Sister Love: The Letters of Audre Lorde and Pat Parker 1974–1989* (2018); and *Milk and Honey: A Celebration of Jewish Lesbian Poetry* (2011), which was a finalist for the 2012 Lambda Literary Award in Lesbian Poetry. She has her MFA and PhD from the University of Maryland. Enszer edits and publishes *Sinister Wisdom*, a multicultural lesbian literary and art journal, and is a regular book reviewer for the *The Rumpus* and *Calyx*. Read more of her work at www.JulieREnszer.com.

ALLEN GINSBERG (1926–1997) was an American poet and writer. Ginsberg was part of the San Francisco Poetry Renaissance, which included Kenneth Rexroth, Lawrence Ferlinghetti, Gary Snyder, Michael McClure, Robert Duncan, and others. Lawrence Ferlinghetti published *Howl and Other Poems* in 1956. For that, Ferlinghetti was charged with publishing an obscene book, garnering enormous publicity for the book and Ginsberg. In the 1960s, Ginsberg was a spiritual leader to the hippie and yippie movements. In 1974, he helped found the Jack Kerouac School of Disembodied Poetics at the Naropa Institute in Boulder, Colorado. Ginsberg published extensively with independent presses; in addition to poetry, he published prose and made many sound recordings.

JEWELLE GOMEZ (Cape Verdean / Wampanoag / Ioway) was on the founding boards of the Astraea Lesbian Foundation and the Gay and Lesbian Alliance against Defamation. She is the author of eight books, including the double Lambda Award–winning novel *The Gilda Stories*, which was recently optioned by Cheryl Dunye for a miniseries. Her plays about James Baldwin and about Alberta Hunter have been produced in San Francisco and New York City. Her fiction, essays, and poetry have appeared in numerous anthologies, including *Dark Matter: A Century of Speculative Fiction from the African Diaspora*, *The World Treasury of Love Stories*, and *Red Indian Road West: Native American Poetry from California*. Follow her @VampyreVamp.

JANICE GOULD was of mixed European and Concow (koyangk'auwi) descent and grew up in Berkeley, California. She was a graduate of the University of California at Berkeley, where she received degrees in linguistics and English, and earned her PhD from the University of New Mexico in English. Gould's books of poetry include *Beneath My Heart* (1990), *Earthquake Weather* (1996), *Alphabet* (an art book / chapbook, 1990), *Doubters and Dreamers* (2011), *The Force of Gratitude* (2017), and *Seed* (2019). Gould coedited *Speak to Me Words: Essays on American Indian Poetry* (2003) and edited *A Generous Spirit: Selected Work by Beth Brant*. After earning an MLIS from the University of Arizona, she was awarded an internship at the Smithsonian's NMAI and received certification in museum studies. Gould was an associate professor in the women's and ethnic studies program at the University of Colorado, Colorado Springs, where she developed and administered the undergraduate certificate in Native American and Indigenous studies. She died in June 2019 of pancreatic cancer.

JUDY GRAHN is an internationally recognized poet, writer, and social theorist. She is the author of fourteen books, including the groundbreaking *Another Mother Tongue, Blood, Bread, and Roses: How Menstruation Created the World*, and most recently, *Eruptions of Inanna* and *Touching Creatures Touching Spirit*. Her website is www.commonalityinstitute.com.

SUSAN GRIFFIN is an essayist, poet, and playwright. She is the author of more than twenty-one books, notably *Woman and Nature: The Roaring Inside Her* (1978), *Rape: The Power of Consciousness* (1979), *Pornography and Silence: Culture's Revenge against Nature* (1981), *The Book of the Courtesans* (2001), and *A Chorus of Stones: The Private Life of War* (1993), which was a finalist for the Pulitzer Prize. More information is available at susangriffin.com.

ELENA GROSS (she/they) is the curatorial manager of Exhibitions and Emerging Artists Program at the Museum of the African

Diaspora and an independent writer and culture critic living in
Oakland, California. She received an MA in visual and critical
studies from the California College of the Arts in 2016 and her BA
in art history and women, gender, and sexuality studies from St.
Mary's College of Maryland in 2012. She specializes in representa-
tions of identity in fine art, photography, and popular media.
Elena was formerly the creator and cohost of the arts and visual
culture podcast *what are you looking at?*, published by *Art Practical*.
Her research has been centered on conceptual and material
abstractions of the body in the work of Black modern and contemporary artists. She has presented her writing and research at institutions and conferences across the United States, including Nook
Gallery, Southern Exposure, KADIST, Harvard College, YBCA,
California College of the Arts, and the GLBT History Museum.
In 2018, she collaborated with the artist Leila Weefur on the publication *Between Beauty and Horror*. Her most recent writing can be
found in the publication *This Is Not a Gun*.

ALLAN GURGANUS's first published story "Minor Heroism"
appeared in the *New Yorker* when he was twenty-six. In 1974, this
tale offered the first gay character that magazine had ever presented. In 1989, Gurganus published the novel *Oldest Living Confederate Widow Tells All*. This first book spent eight months on the
New York Times bestseller list. Gurganus's other works include
*White People, Plays Well with Others, Local Souls, The Uncollected
Stories*, and *The Practical Heart: Four Novellas*, which won a
Lambda Literary Award.

ESSEX HEMPHILL was a poet, editor, and activist. Hemphill is
the author of *Ceremonies: Prose and Poetry* (1992), which won the
National Library Association's Gay, Lesbian, and Bisexual New
Author Award, and two chapbooks: *Earth Life* (1985) and *Condi-
tions* (1986). He also edited *Brother to Brother: New Writings by
Black Gay Men* (1991, 2007). His work has appeared in the

anthologies *In the Life* (1986), *Gay and Lesbian Poetry in Our Time* (1986), and *Life Sentences: Writers, Artists and AIDS* (1993), as well as several newspapers and journals. His work was also featured in the documentaries *Tongues Untied* and *Looking for Langston*. In 1994, he died from complications related to AIDS.

Born in New York City and raised in Lake Charles, Louisiana, TONY KUSHNER is best known for his two-part epic *Angels in America: A Gay Fantasia on National Themes*. His other plays include *A Bright Room Called Day*, *Slavs!*, *Hydrotaphia*, and *Homebody/Kabul*, as well as a musical, *Caroline, or Change*, and an opera, *A Blizzard on Marblehead Neck*, both with composer Jeanine Tesori. Kushner has won multiple prizes for his work, including a Pulitzer Prize for Drama, an Emmy Award, two Tony Awards, and a PEN / Laura Pels Award. He lives in Manhattan with his husband, Mark Harris.

CRAIG LUCAS wrote the plays *Blue Window*, *Reckless*, *Prelude to a Kiss*, *The Dying Gaul*, *Small Tragedy*, *Prayer for My Enemy*, *The Singing Forest*, *Ode to Joy*, and *I Was Most Alive with You*, among others. His screenplays include *Longtime Companion*, *The Secret Lives of Dentists*, and *The Dying Gaul* (which he also directed). His musical libretti include *An American in Paris*, *The Light in the Piazza*, *Amélie*, *Orpheus in Love*, and the opera *Two Boys*. He received the Lambda Literary Award, the Excellence in Literature Award from the American Academy of Arts and Sciences, the Hermitage Greenfield Prize, the Sundance Audience Award, the New York Film Critics Award for Best Screenplay, three Obie Awards, and three Tony nominations and has been a Pulitzer finalist. His newest play will premiere at Arena Stage and the Huntington Theater in Boston under his direction; he has written a new musical with composer/ lyricist Adam Guettel as well as a musical based on his play *Prelude to a Kiss*, with music by Dan Messe, lyrics by Sean Hartley and Dan Messe, scheduled to premiere at South Coast Repertory.

MINNIE BRUCE PRATT is the author of nine books of poetry, creative nonfiction, and political theory, including *Crime against Nature*, *The Dirt She Ate*, *S/HE*, *Inside the Money Machine*, and most recently, *Magnified*. Originally from Alabama, she is a managing editor of *Workers World / Mundo Obrero* newspaper.

JOHN PRESTON published forty-two books, including *Franny, the Queen of Provincetown* (1995) and the anthologies *A Member of the Family* (1992) and *Hometown* (1991). He was a pioneer in the early gay rights movement, cofounding Gay House, Inc., in Minneapolis—the nation's first gay community center—and editing the *Advocate*, the national gay magazine. He died of complications related to AIDS in April 1994.

MARIANA ROMO-CARMONA, Nuyorquina, born in Chile, has taught creative writing, Spanish, and comparative literature for many years, including at CUNY Colleges and the Goddard College MFA. She has a PhD in Latin American, Iberian, and Latinx culture, and she currently teaches in the Latin American and Latinx Studies Program at City College, CUNY. She is the author of *Living at Night*, *Speaking like an Immigrant*, *Sobrevivir y otros complejos*, and *Conversaciones*. A longtime activist on the Latinx and queer fronts, she was an editor with Kitchen Table Press and *Conditions Feminist Journal*. She coedited *Cuentos: Stories by Latinas* and cofounded *COLORLife! Magazine* and Escritorial Press.

KATE RUSHIN (MFA, Brown University, BA Oberlin College) is the author of *The Black Back-Ups*, Lambda Literary Award finalist, and "The Bridge Poem," which was selected for inclusion in *African American Poetry: 250 Years of Struggle and Song* (Kevin Young, ed.). She has received fellowships from the Fine Arts Work Center in Provincetown, the Artists Foundation, Bread Loaf Writers' Conference, Brown University, and the Cave Canem Foundation. Kate Rushin was named Distinguished Visiting Poet in Residence for 2021–2022, Department of English, Connecticut College, New

London, Connecticut. Rushin notes about her work in the book, "While I stand by the experiences and deep emotions these poems intend to convey, I no longer use violence as metaphor or hyperbole in my poems."

SARAH SCHULMAN is a novelist, playwright, screenwriter, nonfiction writer, AIDS historian, journalist, and active participant citizen. Schulman is cofounder of MIX: NY LGBT Experimental Film and Video Festival, codirector of the ACT UP Oral History Project (www.actuporalhistory.org), and U.S. coordinator of the first LGBT delegation to Palestine. She is the author of ten novels, including *The Cosmopolitans* (2016), *The Mere Future* (2010), and *People in Trouble* (1990). She is the author of five nonfiction books, most recently *Let the Record Show: A Political History of ACT UP* (2021).

PEGGY SHAW is a performer, writer, producer, and teacher of writing and performance. She is a 2019 Guggenheim Fellow, a 2016 USA Artist Fellow, and was the 2014 recipient of the Doris Duke Artist Award. Shaw cofounded Split Britches and WOW Café in New York City with Lois Weaver. Shaw has received five NYFA Fellowships and three OBIE Awards. She was the recipient of the 1995 Anderson Foundation Stonewall Award, the Foundation for Contemporary Performance Theatre Performer of the Year Award in 2005, the 2012 Edwin Booth CUNY Award for her "significant impact on theatre and performance in New York," and an honorary doctorate of letters from Queen Mary University of London in 2017.

LINDA VILLAROSA is a journalist, author, editor, novelist, and educator. She is a contributing writer for the *New York Times Magazine*, covering race, inequality, and health. She has won awards from the American Medical Writers' Association, the Arthur Ashe Institute, Lincoln University, the New York Association of Black Journalists, the National Women's Political Caucus, the National

Lesbian and Gay Journalists' Association, and the Callen-Lorde Community Health Center. She is the author of, most recently, *Under the Skin: Race, Inequality, and the Health of a Nation*. Her other books include *Body and Soul: The Black Women's Guide to Physical Health and Emotional Well-Being* and the novel *Passing for Black*, released in 2008 and a finalist for a Lambda Literary Award. She teaches journalism and Black studies at the City College of New York.

EDMUND WHITE is the author of thirteen novels, including *A Saint from Texas* and *Forgetting Elena*; a handful of autobiographical works, including *A Boy's Own Story*, *The Beautiful Room Is Empty*, and *The Farewell Symphony*; and biographies of Jean Genet, Marcel Proust, and Arthur Rimbaud. In addition, he wrote the travel memoir *States of Desire* and coauthored *The Joy of Gay Sex* in 1977. He is one of the last living members of the New York gay literary group the Violet Quill and writes unabashedly about gay male identity and same-sex relations. In 1982, White cofounded (along with Nathan Fain, Larry Kramer, Larry Mass, Paul Popham, and Paul Rapoport) the Gay Men's Health Crisis, the world's first provider of HIV/AIDS care and advocacy. In 2019, the National Book Foundation presented White with the Medal for Distinguished Contribution to American Letters.

Permissions

Index

Page references in italics refer to photographs.